# Goodbye iSlave

THE GEOPOLITICS OF INFORMATION

Edited by Dan Schiller, Pradip Thomas, and Yuezhi Zhao

*A list of books in the series appears at the end of this book.*

# Goodbye iSlave

## A Manifesto for Digital Abolition

JACK LINCHUAN QIU

UNIVERSITY OF ILLINOIS PRESS

Urbana, Chicago, and Springfield

Library of Congress Cataloging-in-Publication Data
Names: Qiu, Jack Linchuan, 1973– author.
Title: Goodbye iSlave : a manifesto for digital
    abolition / Jack Linchuan Qiu.
Description: Urbana : University of Illinois Press,
    2016. | Series: Geopolitics of information |
    Includes bibliographical references and index.
Identifiers: LCCN 2016017207 (print) | LCCN
    2016028653 (ebook) | ISBN 9780252040627
    (hardback) | ISBN 9780252082122 (paper) |
    ISBN 9780252099069 (ebook)
Subjects: LCSH: Information technology—Social
    aspects—China. | Information technology—
    Moral and ethical aspects—China. | Internet
    industry—Employees—China. | Slavery. |
    BISAC: BUSINESS & ECONOMICS / Industries /
    Media & Communications Industries. | SOCIAL
    SCIENCE / Media Studies.
Classification: LCC HN740.Z9 I56795 2016 (print) |
    LCC HN740.Z9 (ebook) | DDC 303.48/330951—
    dc23
LC record available at https://lccn.loc.gov/
    2016017207

# Contents

# Acknowledgments

This small book benefits from the encouragement and constructive critique from many people who have been so generous in supporting my intellectual inquiries and interventions. While taking full responsibility for this text, I have to thank the editors of The Geopolitics of Information book series: Dan Schiller, Yuezhi Zhao, and Pradip Thomas; as well as Daniel Nasset, acquisitions editor at the University of Illinois Press. Dan Schiller introduced me to some of the most foundational readings in the history of slavery and provided truly helpful feedback in every major developmental phase of the manuscript. Yuezhi Zhao supported and emboldened my ideas when I was hesitant about constructing my argument.

I am indebted to the anonymous reviewers during both the internal and external rounds of review, who provoked me with sharp but well-reasoned criticism. Richard Maxwell and Jenny Chan shared detailed comments on my working draft, from the subtitle to empirical evidence to writing style. Conversations with PUN Ngai, GUO Yuhua, SHEN Yuan, BU Wei, Joseph Bosco, JI Deqiang, Toby Miller, Scott Lash, Marina Svensson, Adam Arvidsson, Jeroen de Kloet, Jose van Dijck, Graeme Turner, and Ralph Litzinger were most helpful. Christian Fuchs, Gordon

Matthew, Rutvica Andrijasevic, WANG Hongzhe, Aswan Punathambekar, and Michael Curtin suggested key references that are essential to my thinking about the issues at stake.

Working ideas behind this book were presented at various academic and public events at the University of Amsterdam, University of Lund, Tsinghua University, Hong Kong History Museum (organized by Hong Kong Anthropology Association), University of Tartu (organized by the Sixth COST Conference on Dynamics of Virtual Work), the "Communication and Global Power Shifts" joint summer school at Simon Fraser University, the "Locating Television" symposium at University of Queensland, annual conference of International Association for Media and Communication Research (IAMCR) in Dublin, annual conference of the Association of Internet Researchers (AoIR) in Daegu, International Communication Association (ICA) regional conference in Brisbane, the Seventh Global Studies Conference in Shanghai, LaborTech conference at Stanford University, and the Groundbreaking Saloon (破土沙龍) in Beijing.

Thanks to GUO Yuhua and colleagues attending the "labor sociology forum" at Tsinghua University, my article titled "Farewell iSlave: Foxconn, Digital Capitalism, and Networked Labor Resistance" appeared in the Chinese-language journal *Society* (社會 34, no. 4: 119–37) in 2014, which spurred discussions among readers who sent me useful comments via social media and in person.

The School of Journalism and Communication and the Universities Services Center for China Studies at the Chinese University of Hong Kong provided institutional support for this book, which also received funding from Hong Kong's General Research Fund project "Working-Class Public Spheres: Media and Activism since the Foxconn Suicide Express" (project 14612715).

I am grateful to my research assistants Joy Lin and Sophie Sun for their careful work, and to Weiwei Zhang for her assistance.

Most important, I have been inspired by the enduring acts of resistance among the enslaved throughout history and by countless generations of abolitionists promoting our common humanity—in the past and at present. These include most prominently the international network of activists and artists who were behind the "iSlave" campaign of

2010: SACOM (Students and Scholars Against Corporate Misbehavior), GoodElectronics, Bread for All, the Berne Declaration, Feinheit, and Greenpeace Switzerland.

I dedicate this manifesto to future generations of abolitionists with the confidence that, one day, you will live in a world that is, at the very last, slave-free.

# Goodbye iSlave

# 1

# Departure

## A Changing World

The world is changing, not without its patterns, toward a future of great uncertainties. Writing from Hong Kong, China, I see how this city of seven million people has changed, almost overnight, from the world's leading free-wheeling economy to a hotbed of activism. Two months ago, going through a downtown crowd, I could hear the stereotypical Hong Kong question: "Where's the money?" Today, on the forty-fifth day of the Umbrella Movement, I sit next to students and citizens who turned into Occupiers, who have blocked the city's main traffic arteries by establishing barricades, camping on highways, and demanding: "I want true democracy!"[1]

From "Where's my money?" to "Where's my democracy?" the change cannot be more swift and surprising. Since the British turned Hong Kong into a trading post in the mid-1800s, the city has been known as a paradise of laissez-faire capitalism. For twenty-one consecutive years since 1995, the Heritage Foundation, partnering with *Wall Street Journal*, has ranked Hong Kong as the world's "freest economy."[2]

But walking through the main occupied site at the heart of Hong Kong Island, I am greeted by a huge banner: "Welcome to the Hong Kong Commune." A couple of blocks from it, a gigantic yellow balloon displays an incredible message in mid-air: "SUPPORT from the Advertising Industry." Beneath the balloon are hundreds of Occupy tents and thousands of pro-democracy artworks: installation art made from umbrellas battered in police crackdown, chalk drawings of flowers marking where teargas canisters landed a few weeks ago, and the Lennon Wall—a staircase of stunning beauty, made of countless colorful Post-It notes, each recording a word of encouragement and solidarity. A few artists use a website to collect Twitter posts from around the world and then project them one by one above the Lennon Wall.[3] One reads: "From Gaza to Hong Kong, we stand by you. Stay strong!"

On the other side of the Victorian Harbor, Mongkok, at the very heart of Kowloon Peninsula, is known as the most working-class of the occupied sites. Here, as in Zuccotti Park, Tahrir Square, or Gezi Park, appeals for liberty and equality are palpable and interwoven. Among the calls for freedom, references are often made to slavery: "Retreat, you and your children become slaves for ever!" reads one poster in the middle of Nathan Road, urging protestors to persist. "Wearing the shackle of 'non-violence,' you and I remain slaves!" roars another, demanding more militant counterattack. At an evening gathering of a couple hundred citizens, a speaker of the People Power political party agitated, "You think the authorities and the tycoons respect you? You think they listen to you?" He continued, as members of the audience shook their heads, "No, they see you as slaves!"

It is, of course, not just Hong Kong. With rising inequalities around the world since the 2008 financial meltdown, there has been a notable surge almost everywhere in recounting, rethinking, and re-appropriating slavery, its historical origins, forms, and contemporary variation, as renewed critique against deep-seated crises that confront humanity today. In popular culture, Quentin Tarantino's *Django Unchained* and Steve McQueen's *Twelve Years a Slave* both made a splash at the Academy Awards and in box offices worldwide.[4] In journalism, leading news organizations launched major campaigns such as the CNN Freedom Project, helping to end human trafficking or "modern-day slavery."[5] In politics, the Caribbean Community (Caricom) continued demanding official reparations from Britain, France, and the Netherlands for their role in slave trade centuries ago.[6] From Chicago to Oklahoma, reparations activists are at work against racist plunder not only historically but at present, including during the subprime crisis.[7] From Louisiana to Illinois, major university presses published at least four dozen new books between 2010 and 2014 on such topics as socioeconomic analysis of the transatlantic slave trade, slave resistance through music and dance, legal studies on slavery, and abolition movements from antiquity to today.

## Questions of Abolition

The specter of slavery is haunting the world—even in the present era of digital media technologies. All the powers of mass surveillance and the pundits of Silicon Valley have entered into an unholy alliance to conceal this specter. It is high time to reveal and confront it openly, in the time-honored spirit of antislavery that needs a new incarnation—digital abolition.

This small book presents a treatise of digital abolition against exploitation and injustice—against slavery, broadly defined. So far, there have been few attempts to connect studies of slavery with research on digital media, on the social, economic, cultural, and political formations based on the internet and the smartphone. The liberating and alienating consequences of digital technologies have spurred much debate. In this book, I take the conceptual connection between slavery and digital media as a point of departure to reflect on a few questions that are vital to today's world:

- Are digital media making the world a better place, and the human race a freer species?
- Why are there so many accusations of enslavement, despite the widespread use of electronic gadgets, in far-flung continents and from the depths of cyberspace?
- Why have these, rather than other, patterns of digital media industry emerged? Are alternative developments possible?
- How do digital media contribute to the continuation of and deterioration within twenty-first-century slavery?
- How do they facilitate social movements against enslavement—along the picket line and inside the data mine?

There are many ways to approach these questions. Often, pundits focus on the variables of change: in technological diffusion or economic growth, in the content of messages or its media effect, in people's perceptions and desires to be shaped by advertising and advocacy campaigns.

This book, however, starts from something more stable and humble, from a simple realization: no human being, in the past or in the twenty-first century, likes to be enslaved. Although people have many malleable *wants*—material or cultural desires that go in and out of vogue over time—we are constantly defined by fundamental human *needs* indispensable to our collective humanity.[8] These *needs*—safety and freedom, for instance—are constants not only in our subjective understanding of who we are; they have to be matched also by objective input from agriculture and industrial production—for instance, food, water, clothing, and increasingly from the digital-media industries. Otherwise, not only will we starve and fall sick, but our basic human dignity will be endangered, for example, if there is a severe shortage of bread or if the mobile-phone network is down.

The shared human ideal of freedom is probably better expressed in the negative: our *wants* for wealth and power vary, but everyone *needs* to escape from poverty, from insecurity, from constraint. Although people probably disagree on what it means to be a full human being, no one likes to be ignored or looked down upon. We all need to be free and, on that basis, we may agree that being a human means, at the very least, not being a slave.

Today, we may hold this abolitionist thesis as self-evident, that all humans need to be free. There was, however, no such consensus one-and-a-half centuries ago when the American Civil War broke out, when Hong Kong was a main entrepôt for the trade of coolies, when odd arguments were popular among the elite and the enslaved alike—that slavery was more than an efficient economic system, that it was also humane and fair—for the less intelligent and more vulnerable, for those who had to depend on their masters to take care of them.[9]

The definition of slavery is diverse and volatile. This is a thorny issue I shall return to over and again. But the basic idea is fairly straightforward: human beings should be free. This is true individually: no one would want to be sold as "chattel." Ditto collectively: we don't want our fellow human beings to be enslaved, either. Otherwise, if slavery is not eradicated on this planet, even if individually some of us enjoy freedom, dignity, and prosperity, as a species we remain semi-humans to a degree.

This is why, for so many centuries, the abolitionist struggle against slavery underlies so many collective endeavors—from British antislavery societies to the American civil rights movement, from European and Arab women's rights agitators to aboriginal land rights demonstrators in Africa, Australia, and Canada, from the black Jacobins in Haiti to the Occupiers in Hong Kong—pursuing emancipation for the oppressed, for ourselves and for others, in a better world, more civilized and more slave-free.

•   •   •

Welcome to a brave New World of profit making, propelled by high technology, guarded by enterprising authority, carried forward by millions of unfortunate fellows being deprived of their souls. These millions of bodies—with massive labor power—gather in factories to produce coveted commodities. They face punishment if they disobey. If they cannot take it anymore and attempt "to go away"—a euphemism for suicide—they have to penetrate the physical barrier of a tall fence or "anti-jumping net" in order to free themselves from this hopeless world.

The factories need these workers because their products are not ordinary goods. Rather, they are addictive substances—be they sugar or gadgetry or ephemeral content—which the Old World craves in huge supply, to be shipped to the other side of the planet for consumption by people with lighter skin, many of whom also lead shattered lives. These consumers depend on the importation of addictive commodities in order to be "productive," measured by productivity standards set by the new capitalist system. They keep feeding on it without ever needing to know about the harsh reality of the factories, oceans away.

The world turns and turns. So does the vicious cycle of coercion and exploitation, trade and addiction, culminating in unprecedented levels of profit maximization. The system seems to be "natural" and "perfect" despite, or precisely due to, its cruelty and animosity. It expands and expands, until rebel forces of activism one day emerge from the laborers, sneak into the factories, embed themselves in the new frontiers of accumulation, report to the world what they hear and see, and begin to agitate.

An abolition movement takes shape under new conditions of global geopolitics. Also empowered by new tools of communication, it starts to convince consumers that this New World is not heaven but hell, that a better world is desirable and possible, and that everyone can and should be part of this struggle for progressive change. The system is disrupted. Although it keeps working for some time, the endgame has already begun because, in addition to abolitionist mobilization and consumer awareness, the workers themselves have started to wield new and old weapons of grassroots networking, to express themselves and form solidarity, to initiate their own campaigns and redefine what it means to be a human being.

. . .

What system is this? The answer, as this small book will delve into, may be a little surprising. On one hand, there is slavery that began in the early sixteenth century but stabilized in the seventeenth century, known as the Atlantic system of "triangular trade," built on the most advanced seafaring technologies of the time, connecting Africa and Europe with the New World of the Americas.

On the other hand, there is the contemporary system of "twenty-first-century slavery" or "iSlavery," made possible by the latest digital technologies of our time. Expanding from the bowels of the earth to the New World of cyberspace, iSlavery sustains a planetary network whose central nexus is the Apple-Foxconn alliance—or Appconn—the "master," so to speak, who owns, manipulates, and exploits untold numbers of iSlaves. Almost all brands and contract manufacturers of the digital media sector have their share in sustaining this highly problematic world system I call Appconn.[10]

Between the two systems that occur in history and today, there are, of course, tremendous differences. But besides the obvious divergence, I shall identify and interrogate the profound parallels in between. As such, this book will shed light on the basic human conditions of the world today and the directions of global transformation in the future, illuminated by lessons from the past.

This is, however, not a history book. I make no claim to expertise as a historian, although I ask for no forbearance, either, and welcome critique from all readers. The purpose of historical comparison is to stimulate more acute sensitivity when we face contemporary problems of information technology in an era of global connectivity marked, more crucially, by spatial and historical disconnect. So many people have become so accustomed to the cocoons of social media and the associated modes of individual consumption that they don't venture beyond their usual comfort zones to ponder questions of serious intellectual and moral challenge. Hence, this little book is designed as a time machine that will take readers back and forth, between the seventeenth century and the twenty-first, between the Atlantic and the Pacific, between labor abuse and networked activism, at Appconn and beyond.

Much of this book is devoted to Foxconn, the world's largest electronics manufacturer, arguably also the world's most notorious factory because in 2010 it experienced a major scandal of at least seventeen incidents of worker suicides;[11] because it assembles most i-products for Apple, from iPad and iPhone to iMac and MacBook; because the bulk of its workforce (more than 1.4 million employees) are located in China, "the workshop of the world" at the beginning of the twenty-first century.[12]

It is erroneous, though, to read this volume as another charge against the evils of a particular corporation (or two of them) or as another round of China bashing. The ailment of a Chinese factory, let me emphasize, is a symptom of global pandemic, for which Appconn is but one concentrated embodiment. Foxconn also manufactures for HP, Dell, Nokia, Microsoft, Sony, Cisco, Nintendo, Intel, Motorola, Samsung, Panasonic, Toshiba, Canon, Lenovo, Amazon, Google, Xiaomi, and the list goes on. Some of these brands have their own assembly lines, yet they face similar problems: employee suicide, child labor, and vocational disease at Samsung are a few examples.[13]

My critique, therefore, targets the global IT industry as a whole instead of particular corporations or governments, even though Appconn and China are arguably the most emblematic of the global conditions. The new hegemon of Appconn not only follows the established model of "Wintelism"[14] but also pushes it to a new level of transnational production, relocating jobs from the United States and the rest of the world to selected locations in China. Some investors, managers, geeks, and others possessing "transnational corporate masculinity"[15] may see the rise of Appconn as an inevitable and natural process of technological evolution. But, as I shall contend in the following chapters, this is not true. The process is artificial, unsustainable, and a rather recent development.

Hence, to proceed with the argument for digital abolition, I have to first depart from the adamant assumptions about the technological sublime,[16] about digital media being inherently beautiful and emancipating. I have to ask: Does "progress" in digital media really bring more civility and dignity? More democracy and less poverty? More egalitarian space of common prosperity? More development opportunity and less exploitation? More freedom and less oppression?

Probably not. Technology does not guarantee progress. It is, instead, often abused to cause regress. What really matters is the people, especially those who suffer the most from the new capitalist systems, such as the black Jacobins of the 1790s[17] and Foxconn workers of the 2010s[18]—where they are, how they think and connect, what they do, using new and old technological tools as well, to pursue liberty, equality, and a better world without enslavement.

## iSlavery

What, then, is slavery? Throughout history, slavery has been defined in myriad ways. The task of finding a general agreement about the term is formidable, if not impossible. Fortunately, there is a recent consensus among legal scholars, historians, and NGO professionals on the subject that can serve as a solid starting point: the 2012 Bellagio-Harvard Guidelines on the Legal Parameters of Slavery (hereinafter, the Guidelines).[19] Building on the 1926 Slavery Convention, the most important document of international law on slavery in the twentieth century, the Guidelines define slavery under circumstances of the contemporary world as substantive "institutions and practices" that exercise over a person "the powers attaching to the right of ownership."[20] Such powers

> should be understood as constituting control over a person in such a way as to significantly deprive that person of his or her individual liberty, with the intent of exploitation through the use, management,

profit, transfer or disposal of that person. Usually this exercise will be supported by and obtained through means such as violent force, deception and/or coercion.[21]

Applying such a definition, this book develops the idea of iSlavery, figuratively and literally. A planetary system of domination, exploitation, and alienation, iSlavery is epitomized by the material and immaterial structures of capital accumulation through such electronic products as the iPhone and iPad, resulting in a gigantic structure: Appconn.

Slavery is, on the one hand, a metaphorical idea that highlights the previously invisible connections between the Atlantic system of "human cargo" trade four centuries ago and the problematic global digital industry today. This may sound like an overstretch to some readers, although in 2000 during the dot-com crash, commentators were already criticizing the New Economy because it was turning employees at internet firms into "Net Slaves."[22] The iSlavery thesis is, hence, not entirely new. As a cultural critique, it has existed for more than a decade and a half. This volume merely extends the criticism in a new and broader comparative light with additional empirical observations, including new and old condemnation of Apple's breaking its social responsibility promises,[23] as well as my fieldtrips investigating labor issues at Foxconn.

Meanwhile, iSlavery is more than an evocative metaphor; this book will draw on historical evidence from many decades of scholarship on the enslavement of Africans, African Americans, and abolition movements worldwide. Rich and thought provoking, this body of prior research provides rare comparative referents for a productive assessment of labor conditions within Appconn.

Much has been written, in Chinese and English, about the case of Foxconn, its "military management,"[24] its terrible working conditions, why these circumstances exist, as well as to what degree Apple is or is not responsible.[25] Building on previous studies, this book is primarily a work of synthesis, although it is also built on my fieldwork, participant observation, interview, news analysis, and multimedia action research since 2010. Besides describing what is going on in this or that factory, at this or that moment, a novel approach of this treatise is to situate Appconn in a world system whose epicenter is shifting—toward the transpacific U.S.-China duo of "Chimerica"[26] or toward a new clash of geopolitics.

Our transhistorical analysis, from seventeenth-century slavery to twenty-first-century iSlavery, raises inevitable questions: How does iSlavery happen, especially in the IT sector? How is it similar to the old system of slavery four centuries ago? Why does the world's largest electronics manufacturer—Foxconn—turn out to be a Taiwanese company profiting from the labor power of mainland Chinese workers? What's new about this IT-based industrial capitalism if examined from a historical standpoint?

More than a problematizing device, the parallel between old and new forms of slavery also draws attention to dimensions of collective resistance, from the achievements and lessons of abolition movements in the past to the rise of network labor through digitally networked action, or "DNA,"[27] to abolish iSlavery today.

Network labor is the organized formation of worker solidarity in this digital era.[28] Its social basis is the rapidly expanding rank of "the information have-less"[29] such as Chinese migrant workers with low socioeconomic status but who are now using mobile phones. When digitally equipped lower classes join hands in grassroots cultural expression and bottom-up political mobilization, staging collective and connective actions as a result of their networking, they become parts of a new class-formation process toward network labor. This is not a process determined by technological diffusion, although the spread of inexpensive working-class ICTs (information and communication technologies) does bring new opportunities of resistance as well as repression, calling for more systematic reflection.

The term "iSlave" originated from a campaign that arose after fifteen tragedies of Foxconn workers committing suicide in the first five months of 2010.[30] It was among the most notable campaigns against corporate social irresponsibility in the global IT supply chain. What can be learned from campaigns like this? How does it compare to abolition movements centuries ago? Does it harbor a new kind of labor activism?

• • •

This is the main idea of this book: even in the twenty-first century, we are still haunted by the specter of slavery, morphing from physical place to cyberspace. Confronting such an inconvenient truth and analyzing it in larger historical contexts will enhance our collective humanity. In so doing, fresh insights will emerge to shed light on the contemporary structures of capitalism, especially patterns in the digital-media industries, by developing new ways of critically understanding exploitation, suppression, and alienation, as they occur in Appconn. This allows also for better appreciation of workers' resistance and digitally networked labor activism, in China and beyond, through historical comparison with slave resistance and abolition movements.

How and why do all these happen: the continuation of slavery in blatant or deceptive modes of exploitation, the rise of Appconn, and the outbursts of labor resistance? Why does it make sense to use slavery as a strong framework of critique? Why is this among the most pressing problems of this digital era? While more detailed arguments will be laid out, this book is ultimately a provocation in order for all human beings to confront and engage in these fundamental questions, both conceptually and in action, when we think and make decisions, large or small, about digital technologies, not only how to consume them but more crucially how to use them for progressive social change.

Our first point of departure is a general position that the system of slavery persists, albeit in different shapes, because its root problem remains deeply embedded in "the modern capitalist world system."[31] It is this system that sprouts myriad forms of enslavement whereby the lives of many are forcibly sacrificed for the rich minority to accumulate even more. It is within this system that, geopolitically, the established core-periphery relations are being restructured, giving rise to such exemplary cases as Appconn. Also within this system, China's new digital media industry is likely to become a new frontier of resistance, "a tempest zone," as Samir Amin would call it.[32]

## Industrial and Informational Geopolitics

These clichés have been repeated too often and for too long—we live in a "postindustrial society"; our economy is becoming "weightless" and "friction-free"; our world is being "flattened" by computers, airplanes, and freighters. This may be true for those who choose to focus exclusively on content, on the virtual and ether, while ignoring the vast and growing body of electronic equipment we have to use to access and sustain whatever cyberspace contains. After all, smartphones and computers have to be industrially manufactured. In this sense, their manufacture and delivery system today requires valuable inputs—land, energy, labor, raw materials—in ways not too different from the British textile industry in the 1800s: the provision of key resources hinges on geopolitical patterns at regional and global levels, which spawns new dynamisms of power, supply, and consumption.

According to statistics from the United Nations, the overall trend for the world economy since Daniel Bell coined the term "postindustrial society" forty years ago is, in fact, continued industrialization rather than deindustrialization. Over the four decades between 1970 and 2011, global total manufacturing output has not decreased. On the contrary, it has more than tripled, from $2.56 to $8.92 trillion, measured in constant 2005 U.S. dollars. One reason for this continued global industrialization is precisely the spread of digital technologies.

Despite the talk about deindustrialization, digital media have not taken the world away from industrialism. Quite the opposite: they have intensified the penetration and heightened the role of a particular kind of manufactured industrial product—electronic gadgets—in our everyday work and life, which would have been impossible without newer, bigger, more efficient, and more ruthless factories like Foxconn.

Forty years ago, an ordinary family in an ordinary non-Western country had several people but probably only one electronic device—most likely a radio. In 2013 average mobile-phone penetration in the developing world reached 89 percent. Laptop and desktop computers, digital camera and game consoles, stereos, printers, digital TV—now it is common to find, in urban slums, rural villages, even some of the most impoverished communities on this planet, individuals each having multiple gadgets, the latest of which is probably a mobile phone.

When television invaded our living rooms and desktop computers our offices, they spurred much controversy. But when that iPad mini becomes almost a constant part of your backpack, when every time I reach into my pocket, I expect to grab a smartphone—these much more invasive technologies seem to have caused little more than quotidian interests, probably because they are too personal and pedestrian, probably because we are all becoming too individualized, too lazy, too servile, to engage in serious public discussions about them.

Gadgets come and go. Many people tend to forget, however, that these gizmos have to be produced materially. To make these tangible products, there has to be a global system to assemble, polish, pack, and transport them before they can be used to receive, generate, and circulate content, and to facilitate social networking. Digitization has, in this sense, made the world more industrial and more dependent on the geopolitics of industrialism, not less. Humanity taken as a whole, including the majority of our fellow human beings in the developing world, has become deeply entangled in a planetary industrial system operating by and through digital media.

This is Appconn, a world system of gadgets—complete with all the apps, games, and social media—that has engulfed us. Some may see it as a new opportunity for emancipation, others a reincarnation of enslavement, still others the "normal" progression of technological advancement, the much-anticipated continuation of Enlightenment entering its digital age. Despite the disagreements, it is essential to bear in mind that Appconn is not only around us, not only out there, but also infiltrating almost every corner of our social world, every mundane hour of our life, awake or asleep.

Where does this global system come from? This is how Christian Fuchs outlines "the international division of digital labour (IDDL)": first, raw materials such as aluminum, coltan, and plastics have to be extracted and processed into predesigned shapes and functionality. They then need to be traded, assembled, cleaned up, packaged, and delivered to warehouses before they are sold, personalized, and consumed. This is a global process of material culture and political economy that "involves various forms of labour, exploitation and modes of production that are organized in different parts of the world" including "agricultural, industrial and informational forms of labour."[33] Finally, in a couple of years, most gadgets are discarded to become e-waste, some recycled for the extraction of raw materials, others piled up as garbage mountains to pollute Planet Earth.

All this is about the materiality of gadgets. All the material manipulation requires labor, organized through old-style industrial geopolitics, albeit with some new traits, some of which fall under the rubric of "Chinese characteristics."

．．．

The Industrial Revolution took many forms. Be it British or American, Soviet or Japanese, the dramatic increase in productivity has led to miraculous growth, horrible pollution, as well as upheaval in world politics, with the rise and fall of great powers. Likewise, this ongoing Industrial Revolution occurring around us in the twenty-first century, centered on digital media, is marked by fundamental power shifts in global geopolitics.

This is not the first time that leaps and bounds in industrial productivity are intertwined with advancement in information technology to create social, cultural, and political ripples the world over. The digital "revolution" is but the latest embodiment of this grand historical pattern when IT breakthroughs contribute to and are conditioned by radical transformation in the industrial systems of machinery, commerce, consumption, and of the capitalist world-system itself. Since the 1840s, telecommunications systems have played a key role in shaping the trajectories of global geopolitics, from the earliest telegraph network serving as the backbone of the British "electronic empire"[34] to the spread of telephone and television accompanied by American supremacy.

Industrial and informational technologies have long gone hand in hand, being sometimes indistinguishable from one another. Take, for example, a slave ship crossing the Atlantic from West Africa to the Caribbean in the 1600s. It was full of advanced technologies at the time: woodcraft, metalwork, textiles, weaponry, magnetic compass. Although the goal of voyage was to transport people and goods from one place to another, the seafaring vehicle also delivered messages and forged cultures, while forcing others into oblivion via the exchange of information as well as communicable diseases, among not only Europeans but also Africans and Native Americans. This coupling of transportation and communication was the norm of business, of missionaries, of slave uprisings, of expeditions, and of geopolitics—until the much more recent separation between the two after telegraphy, also known as "the Victorian Internet."[35]

Yet the great transformation nowadays is also distinct, in that it is driven by "two poles of market growth," by which Dan Schiller refers, on one hand, to the prominence of the digital industries and, on the other, to the centrality of China, the most significant of the emerging economies.[36] With the globalization of commerce, the ascent of China is, of course, much more than a national phenomenon. The so-called "Chinese economic miracle" would have been impossible without European and Japanese technologies, Southeast Asian investments, Middle East oil and African minerals, Australian coal and Russian timber, and, above all, American consumption.

Since China joined the WTO in 2001, its ruling class has reaped tremendous economic benefits through job creation—often at the cost of other job markets—and trade surplus, transforming the country into the "workshop of the world," a title the United Kingdom and the United States previously held. For some, this title suggests power and glory. For others, it means incredible pollution, income disparity, and atrocious working conditions. If the dominant industry for the British version of the "world's workshop" was textiles, and the American version automobiles, then for China it is undoubtedly electronics. From iPads and Kindles to mobile phones, from laptop computers to cameras and stereos, most of these electronic products are made in China, the global manufacturing powerhouse of digital media gadgets.

There is, as in the past, remarkable social and environmental cost, distributed unevenly among the rich and the poor, producing seismic ripples regionally and globally. Chinese workers and farmers, their families and communities, have borne the brunt of the upheaval brought by this Industrial Revolution of the twenty-first century. Meanwhile, Taiwanese and Hong Kong factory owners, cadres and tycoons in Mainland China, and overseas Chinese entrepreneurs have moved toward the center of the exclusive club of the transnational capitalist class.

By the end of 2014, China had become the No.1 trading partner for more than 130 countries across the world. Besides the country's massive export-oriented manufacturing sector, it has also grown into a leading consumer of luxury goods and a major investor exporting capital to every world region, supporting the ruling elite there, becoming a target of xenophobic sentiments as well as a role model of modernization, for example, in Latin America and Africa. Under such circumstances, it should come as little surprise that China hopes to shape international institutions, to control trade routes, and, in so doing, to reshape geopolitics.

The tremendous impact is felt not only in the Asia-Pacific region but also across Africa, Europe, and the Americas. The result can well be a new global trade infrastructure under the auspices of China, marked by the fifty-billion-dollar Grand Canal in Nicaragua, the thirteen-thousand-kilometer (8,078-mile) trans-Eurasian railroad—the New Silk Road—connecting China's eastern seaboard all the way with Madrid. It is also manifest in the Asian Infrastructure Investment Bank (AIIB), a Beijing-initiated financial platform, which at its inauguration on June 29, 2015, included China, India, Russia, Australia, and fifty-three Asian, European (including Germany and the United Kingdom), and Middle Eastern (from Iran to Israel) countries. Almost all major economies of the world joined, except the United States and Japan.

Will China replace the United States as the "top dog" of global geopolitics? Or perhaps the two Great Powers have developed so much shared interest, as the neology "Chimerica" indicates, that it makes sense to consider a new kind of geopolitical symbiosis? What does the geopolitical transformation mean for neoliberal "accumulation by dispossession," for debt-financed "post-industrial" stagnation in the First World, for a de-industrializing Third World plagued by unemployment, and for other peripheral regions of the capitalist world-system—in other words, the Global South—facing hunger and armed conflicts?

As will be discussed, one way of appraising the Chinese model—how and why it occurs, what its implications are—is to examine it through a framework of critical geopolitics, a global geopolitics of digital media, of the content, applications, and social functions the gadgets are shaped to carry, and of their intended and unintended consequences. This framework has its novelty because it does not focus on war and military confrontation among nation-states. Instead, it attaches more significance to nonstate actors, to multinational corporations, nongovernmental organizations (NGOs), and local states. As such, patterns of industrial and informational development, of violence, coercion, and deception, of subaltern geopolitics as well, will be identified and discussed, including the unsettling yet persistent pattern that, to this day, we still live in the shadow of slavery.

## Book Structure

Consisting of six chapters, this small volume is a call to action through a critique of iSlavery and Appconn, including key issues of labor and technology, domination and resistance, activism and social transformation. It presents a heuristic argument for digital abolition that entails provocative reflections on the geopolitics of information, in China and the world, in history and now.

Chapter 2, "Patterns of Slavery," examines existing scholarship for the purpose of developing a relatively coherent conceptual framework. I shall first discuss thematic findings from generations of historians seeking to make sense of slavery: How and why did it happen? What are its main characteristics? Is it still going on today—and with what consequences? The most central issue, which is as thorny as it is intriguing, has to do with the definition of slavery. I will start by tackling this problem tangentially and from multiple historical perspectives. Then, the second part of the chapter will confront and dissect it based on the 2012 Bellagio-Harvard Guidelines on the Legal Parameters of Slavery.[37] This will provide some good yardsticks to assess the situation in Appconn and the digital media industry at large. As it will turn out, the main patterns from historical and legal scholarships are quite compatible despite their inevitable differences.

Is there enough evidence to support such a strong accusation of slavery? Chapter 3, "Manufacturing iSlave," briefly introduces the two primary modes of iSlavery, which engender manufacturing iSlaves and manufactured iSlaves, respectively. The bulk of this chapter is devoted to labor issues in Foxconn, the world's most notorious sweatshop, in partnership with Apple and a long list of IT gadget brands. Here I shall contend that the corporate practices are comparable, sometimes very similar indeed, to critical moments of seventeenth-century slavery, from the militarized "factories" to the Middle Passage to suicide-prevention nets. The chapter discusses lived experiences of workers, including testimonies from a work-injury case (Zhang Tingzhen) and a former employee

(Tian Yu) who tried to take her life during the 2010 Foxconn Suicide Express.

Chapter 4 deals with the "manufactured iSlave," beginning with a Chinese teenager who sold his kidney to buy an iPhone and an iPad. It compares fanatic consumption of digital media with voluntary servitude, organ trafficking, and the consumption of slave-produced sugar that led to what Sidney Mintz terms "desocialized eating."[38] This will be followed by a broader discussion on digital labor in its various immaterial and individualized forms—more disguised as well—of exploitation that amount to enslavement, especially for those who have developed addiction to Appconn gadgets and services. iSlaves are also manufactured along the temporal dimension as they lose control over their time while chasing the latest trend in digital media. Overall, the outlook of manufacturing and manufactured iSlaves is rather bleak. Can it be otherwise?

Yes, it can. This is the answer from chapter 5, "Molding and Resisting Appconn," which explains the rise of Appconn, with special attention to its pitfalls. Besides the usual factors of global capital and national policymaking, emphasis will be attached to local state in China, which constitutes arguably a more important force than the will of Beijing. Most of this chapter zooms in on grassroots resistance and efforts of abolition. I shall offer a bird's-eye view of WGC (worker-generated content) through a typology of workers' activism and collective action. Then the analysis will focus on the actual scenarios of workers using social media on the picket line while at the same time defending themselves against iSlavery through digitally networked action (DNA). Several instances of the modern abolition movement will be highlighted, including global solidarity action against "Poisonous Apple"; Fairphone, a social enterprise designed to address labor as well as environmental problems in the smartphone production system; and the Phone Story, an educational phone game that promises to deliver quality entertainment while exposing the underbelly of the digital-gadgets industry. Together, these endeavors short-circuit Appconn's efforts in labor discipline and deceptive marketing while showing possibilities of another, better world.

Finally, chapter 6 concludes with reflections on our past, present, and future. Three circular models will be discussed as a way to summarize the structural similarities between iSlavery and the seventeenth-century system of triangular trade, while proposing a tentative model of collective action toward an alternative future, a model in which gadgets serve people and promote global justice. The ultimate question is: What shall we embrace, after bidding farewell to iSlave, after the capitalist world system has enslaved the human species for so long?

# 2

# Patterns of Slavery

What is slavery? An adequate answer to this question is fundamental to developing a critique of iSlavery and forming subsequent actions of abolition. Since ancient times, there have been thousands of books and countless articles that describe, analyze, condemn, or justify slavery. This chapter condenses this enormous body of literature into a few basic patterns, including the origins and modes of slavery, its social consequences and possibilities for emancipation, its legal definitions and global implications, and its relevance to contemporary issues of digital labor and exploitation in the twenty-first century.

Schematic as it has to be, the summary is a modest attempt to construct two interconnected arguments: One, more than a rhetorical device, slavery encompasses a substantive set of human experiences—of suffering and resistance, of perseverance, creativity, and hope—that has given rise to analyses of unusual gravity, penetrating antiquity and modernity, individual agony and regime specificity. Two, based on the wealth of slavery studies, one may construct a consistent conceptual framework for the understanding of labor and geopolitics from preindustrial world systems to present-day digital capitalism, not as separate phenomena but as an ongoing historical process, a continuous struggle between humanity and barbarism, freedom and bondage.

## Themes of History

Slavery has been around since time immemorial. War captives, inmates, chattel, concubines, eunuchs, coolies, serfs, servants, gang labor, indentured workers, "comfort women," child soldiers—each of these terms has its distinct meaning, shaped under particular circumstances. How do they have something to do with each other? How does that commonality have any bearing on the present when it comes to labor conditions in the digital industry, in Foxconn and Apple, in the Appconn symbiosis and today's world system of gadgets?

Some may not be aware, but even in the twenty-first century, slavery persists in its classic forms: women trafficked into the sex industry, children sold to resolve family debt, prisoners forced to work with no pay.[1] Despite the diffusion of personal computer, mobile phone, and the Internet, despite commercials about perpetual connectivity and seamless "global village," the ancient trade of slaves has shown remarkable resilience, refusing to disappear.

This should not come as a surprise, though, if one is familiar with the history of slavery. The institutions of enslavement had survived campaign after campaign, age after age, of antislavery legislation and law enforcement, of civil society mobilization and religious calls to abolition. Digital media can be great tools of emancipation for victims of trafficking, saving them from "twenty-first-century slavery."[2] But traffickers also use them to coordinate, conduct illicit businesses, and punish those who dare to disobey, leading sometimes to fatal consequences.

The emergence of the digital industries also contributes directly to the continuation of "the classic form of slavery as well as feudal slavery based on rent and corvée slavery" especially in the eastern regions of the Democratic Republic of Congo (DRC).[3] This is where some of the most indispensable minerals for the global IT industry, such as cobalt and coltan, are extracted.

Christian Fuchs identifies "digital slavery"[4] as the first link in a much larger "International Division of Digital Labor" (IDDL).[5] Here, in the mines of South Kivu province, for example, 866 cases of slavery were documented by the NGO Free the Slaves in 2013 alone, of whom 23 percent interviewed were children.[6] The total number of the enslaved is estimated to be around 462,000.[7] While children are also found in the mines of other African countries,[8] the DRC stands out due to its "vast mineral wealth"[9] extracted by forced slave laborers toiling in the dark shafts underground: in 2010 they supplied 51 percent of the world's cobalt; in 2008, 21 percent of the world's coltan.[10] The human rights violations were so grim that George Monbiot, who writes for *The Guardian*, wondered: "Are the components (of my next phone) soaked in the blood of people from the eastern DRC?"[11]

Without Congolese conflict minerals, there would have been much less a boom in the world system of electronic gadgets. Although domestic factors are not to be dismissed, the global demand for iPads, Samsungs, and HP laptops is a main reason Congolese children and laborers are put to work, sometimes at gunpoint, always paid little more than basic life necessities to extract valuable minerals for the material production of present-day electronics.

This is undoubtedly slavery: there is violent coercion and the almost complete deprivation of personal freedom among the miners, adult or child. In a similar light, in December 2014, shortly after the release of iPhone 6, the BBC investigative journalism program *Panorama* found that Indonesian children worked in extremely dangerous mines to extract tin that probably ended up in Apple's products, an allegation that caused Apple to claim that the company was "deeply offended."[12]

Fuchs developed a chapter discussing horrible labor conditions at Foxconn, the world's largest electronics manufacturer, whose labor force concentrates in South China. But he chose not to call it outright slavery, even though he discusses "forced labor" at the factory, while arguing that the "slave-character" of the Congolese mines "is preserved" in Foxconn.[13] This choice of wording is not random. The more we study slavery, from ancient Greece to early modern Americas, from Africa to India to China, the more it seems impossible to pin down specific modes of slavery as a unified institution, or as a unitary set of practices that can serve as a universal yardstick. There were notable moments for popular perceptions of slavery to change abruptly, for instance, in both the United States and Britain:

> Until the 1760s, roughly speaking, black slavery was generally assumed to be a necessary and "progressive" institution, accepted or tolerated in cities like Boston, New York, and London, which were far removed from the booming peripheral zones of plantation agriculture. But during the next thirty years there occurred a profound change in the basic paradigm of social geography—a conceptual differentiation between what can only be termed a "slave world" aberration and the "free world" norm.[14]

Such alterations and subsequently different definitions of slavery are not uncommon. To discuss them all would require more space than is available here. Nonetheless, one can discern a few basic patterns or overarching themes from past slavery studies, which shall inform the general approach of this book.

· · ·

First and foremost, definitions of slavery are often fluid, contingent upon contexts and norms that are subject to change. Maids and eunuchs in domestic settings, artisans and apprentices in workshops of antiquity, gang labor in sugar or cotton plantations, maroons on castaway islands, inmates of concentration camps—change is constant in the way slavery exists and the way it is defined. The meaning of enslavement varies over time and across space. To interrogate issues of slavery under contemporary conditions of digital media is, in this sense, consistent with past intellectual traditions in that it poses fundamental questions about liberty and its deprivation that deepens our understanding of humanity itself.

It was with this spirit that research on slavery continued from the nineteenth century onward after the legal abolition of transatlantic slave trade involving mostly Africans: coolies from South Asia and East Asia, *mui tsai* (female domestic servants) in South China, inmates in Nazi concentration camps and Soviet gulags, blacks living under South African apartheid. The specific modes were so culturally and historically diverse that Claude Meillassoux remarked, "In the present state of research, there is really no general theory that allows us to identify slavery or the objective conditions for its likely emergence."[15]

Over the past few decades, many have attempted to produce a single theory that summarizes historical and contemporary modes of enslavement. But the result is never satisfactory due precisely to the diversity and contextual contingency of the phenomena. It is therefore essential to reckon that slavery can and does adapt itself to drastically different situations and, in so doing, it often becomes sociologically amorphous.

Attempts to create a precise definition for slavery may, in this sense, distract us from understanding the true operations of enslavement, including its latest permutation in the twenty-first century. Is this new slavery system identical or equivalent to that one in the past? Is it nothing but a throwback to ancient times, an anachronism that cannot capture recent change in the world today? Asking such questions may be counterproductive in that it assumes too much historical conformity in a liquid social formation.

Approached from another angle, slavery is essentially about the deprivation of one's freedom. Yet what freedom means is not a constant, objective "fact." Freedom from poverty, from fear, from want—we need only to go slightly deeper into these seemingly elegant components to find out that poverty, fear, and want are relative terms, too, whose meaning hinges heavily on cultural and institutional circumstances. There is no static or fixed definition for liberty. Ditto for slavery.

. . .

Despite the variation, a rudimentary feature of slavery is that it imposes a system of inequality upon those who were either born or made to be on the margins of society. In its classic form, the imposition usually works through physical violence, including the threat of using violence, be it state-sanctioned or extralegal violence as is present in underground economies. Yet violence is not the only means of imposing slavery; often, it is not even the most effective. As Orlando Patterson argued, the social control operates on a more regular basis through symbolic domination, cultural hegemony, and especially social alienation: "Because the slave has no socially recognized existence outside of his master, he became a social nonperson . . . a socially dead person."[16]

It is due to this cultural and social logic that the enslaved are often found to be foreigners, migrants, "aliens," whose state of subjugation stems from their lack of family and social-network resources more than from individual-level economic and political disadvantages. The factor of violent domination still matters, though, because physical vulnerability remains a key attribute of bondage, as can be seen in the case of young females who were among the first to become slaves. In ancient Sumer, more than five thousand years ago, the word for "slave girl" actually pre-dated the word for "slave."[17] In classic Chinese, "slave girl (nubi)" was synonymous with and more often used than "slave (nuli)"; the strokes on the left-hand side of the Chinese character for "slave" (nu 奴) also indicates its feminine nature. Slaves were historically, in this sense, female by default. As Patterson points out, women were "the main and preferred source of slaves in most slave-holding societies" in world history.[18]

Skin color was another notorious physical identifier: the darker the color, the more inferior with regard to servitude, and the more "suitable" for bondage. Although there were long periods when Caucasians suffered under captivity, it was those with other skin colors who had to suffer the most under slavery regimes based on racism, all the way into modern times. Without a doubt, black Africans are the most trafficked population in human history. Between 1500 and 1870, approximately twelve million of them were "exported" from the coast of Africa, mostly to the New World.[19] While skin color cannot predict physical strength, its daily functioning as racial identifier was to isolate the enslaved culturally and socially, as "a secular excommunication."[20]

Think about Foxconn. Like other Chinese electronic manufacturers, its labor force on the shop floor consists mostly of young migrant workers from China's rural hinterlands, including notably *dagongmei*, or factory girls. Cut off from their families and networks of social support, they are often found isolated and alienated in the factory zones thousands of miles from their natal communities.[21] Is it complete coincidence that the social and demographic profile of *dagongmei* overlaps with the slave girl in what became known as China's "gendered industrialization"?[22]

Even though these factory girls belong to the same Han ethnic group as Foxconn's Taiwanese managers, their accents and culinary habits are distinct, forming "quasi-ethnic markers"[23] that differentiate "northerners" from "southerners," "Mainlanders" from "Taiwanese." Although in the 2010s *dagongmei* are not punished violently as often as they were in the 1990s, the fundamental structure of imposed inequality persists through quasi-ethnic identifiers of shop-floor culture when workers are constantly subject to verbal abuse. Alienation and atomization remain widespread social ailments in the factory zones of electronics manufacture, following rather classic patterns of symbolic disempowerment facilitating social control.[24]

It is certainly not just factory girls, as Foxconn in fact has more male than female employees. But would a similar question emerge over complaints about how digital-media obsession estranges today's youth, making people loners, "mall rats," unable to relate themselves to others? Should we reconsider why digital capitalism has been so detrimental to our social ties, transforming citizens sharing communal life into individualized consumers, indifferent to neighbors close by but responsive to masters far away, to the cracking sound of their whips: another Facebook advertisement?

The answer to this question was laid bare by Antonio Negri long ago, in 1973: "The continuation of capitalism entails the creation of a 'productive subject' who does not act collectively."[25] Raewyn Connell applauds Negri for predicting the logic of late capitalism a full decade before Reagan and Thatcher's "neoliberal turn." Examined from a *longue durée* perspective regarding domination through isolation in slavery, Negri's articulation is of transhistorical explanatory power that makes sense in early capitalism as well.

・　・　・

The third theme in studies of slavery is often understated, sometimes deliberately forgotten, or carelessly buried in oblivion. That is the theme of resistance, in practice and in idea, which has been an integral part of slave history as much as the theme of domination. But because the enslaved were often either illiterate or deprived of their liberty to produce records that could last through long periods, archives and artifacts about slavery are usually imbued with the biases of slave masters, conquerors, traders, and bureaucrats. The conventional image of the enslaved is thus overwhelmingly partial. They are docile and submissive, dumb and helpless. Slaves are slaves. They don't resist—or so the ruling-class intelligentsia would like us to believe.

The myth of the submissive slave has long been debunked since Herbert Aptheker's 1943 book *American Negro Slave Revolts*.[26] Yet even in recent years, although abolition has become a more frequent topic in scholarly inquiry, it is still common that stories of antislavery struggles are told from the limited vantage points of the urban middle class, lawmakers, business leaders, and the consumer society.[27] Either the slaves are unable to resist by themselves or their resistance would be futile without "white saviors." This view is, however, utterly mistaken.

The entire history of all hitherto slave regimes is the revolutionary history of antislavery. As Peter Linebaugh and Marcus Rediker present systematically in *The Many-Headed Hydra*,[28] slaves—or what they call "the proletariat" in the temporal frame of 1600s to mid-1800s—have defied efforts to reduce them into other people's property. This is a "motley crew" consisting of Africans, Americans, and Europeans, both men and women, who fought against the enclosure of the commons, forced emigration onboard slave ships, exploitation in plantations and in factories. In so doing, they waged countless servile wars, food riots, mutinies, and general strikes. Some of these defiant acts have been immortalized by Shakespeare's play *The Tempest* and William Blake's poetry: "Tyger tyger, burning bright / In the forests of the night . . ."[29]

More than internal conflicts within the British Empire, slave revolts were characteristic of the entire Atlantic world, extending to the Indian and Pacific Oceans since the beginning of the nineteenth century. According to Robin Blackburn,

> The records of the WIC [Dutch West India Company] list fifteen major revolts aboard their [slave] ships in the years 1751–75, most of them occurring while the vessel was still close to the African coast. In 1770 the slaves, led by one Essjerrie Ettin, seized control of the *Guinniese Vriendschap*, but the Dutch warship *Castor* succeeded in recapturing it. On another occasion when an entire ship, the *Neptunius*, was seized, in 1795, an English warship suppressed the mutiny, though only by blowing up the ship.[30]

Note these were merely "major revolts"; there were countless more minor incidents: refusal to eat, collective singing, jumping overboard to commit suicide (we will return to this last act of defiance in chapter 3 when analyzing suiciding Foxconn workers jumping from tall buildings).[31] Some were more successful in affecting the trade of human cargo, others less so, but these were acts of resistance nonetheless. One estimate was that, between 1650 and 1860, such resistance altogether reduced the total number of Africans being trafficked to the New World by one million due to "rebelliousness by Africans on ship and the resulting efforts by European carriers of slaves to curb such behavior."[32]

The most notable revolution of the era took place in San Domingo (Haiti). Led by Toussaint L'Ouverture, a former slave, the slave army consisting mostly of plantation laborers succeeded in overthrowing their French masters and establishing an independent republic of the formerly enslaved. It was the first action of its kind in human history. Known as the "black Jacobins,"[33] these slave rebels were but one component of the "many-headed hydra" whose membership encompassed such a great variety of rebellious forces, be they pirates, witches, maroons, or heretics; be they Irish, African, South Asian, or Chinese. Interracial resurrection was a common phenomenon in archival as well as fictional representations of this history—for example, Amitav Ghosh's Ibis trilogy—*Sea of Poppies*, *River of Smoke*, and *Fire of Flood*—which connects the themes of resistance and domination from the Atlantic to the Indian and Pacific Oceans.[34]

So long as there is slavery, there is resistance—not only from civil-society organizations, well-off consumers, and elite abolitionists, but more crucially from the slaves themselves, who have, once mobilized, the greatest political will to break from bondage, as history has repeatedly shown.

. . .

Slave systems wax and wane due to economic and sociopolitical factors. The general pattern: when new empires arose—Islam, Mongol, the Eurocentric Atlantic system—there would be significant increase of slave population resulting from war, famine, or the new regime's endeavor to conquer new people and new land, and to propel new trade. In ancient Rome, up to 1.5 million slaves were estimated to have worked in a wide range of rural and urban occupations throughout Italy.[35] During the Islamic dynasties of 650–1900, close to twelve million sub-Sahara Africans were transported into Muslim markets, of whom eight million were delivered prior to the fifteenth century.[36] At the dawn of the Industrial Revolution, as Immanuel Wallerstein wrote about the peak of Eurocentric transatlantic slave trade in the decade prior to 1793:

> The shift [of slave raiding from a luxury export of gathered "surplus" to a veritable productive enterprise that entered into the ongoing division of labor of the capitalist world-economy] may be considered to have occurred in the eighteenth century with the steady rise in slave prices, reflecting the combination of the increased demand for slaves, the increased competition among European slave traders, and the increased difficulty in expanding supply at the same pace, all typical phenomena of a period of overall expansion in the world-economy.[37]

The expansion of slave systems was often accompanied by the deployment of new technologies in weaponry, transportation, and confinement, be they shackles of the lower deck used to constrain slaves physically or drugs designed to debilitate them mentally. Sometimes entire institutions for slave transaction, keeping, and suppression emerged, usually along major trade routes as well as the shifting boundaries of geopolitics. But as the expansion of empire slowed down, as the danger of disintegration increased along with chances of slave uprising, there would be attempts of abolition, decreed by the emperor, conspired by dignitaries or the propertied class, sometimes leading to civil wars when the enslaved fought, not for their masters any more, but for themselves.

This was how the Atlantic slave trade decreased after 1793. Again, according to Wallerstein, "the Franco-British wars [caused] a decline in this as in all other oceanic trade, and subsequently, the combined effect of abolition and the Haitian revolution kept the figures from ever going as high again."[38] When the Portuguese and Spaniards first brought slaves to the New World, the geopolitical fault lines separating the colonizers from native Americans were more easily penetrated. But with the rise of competing European slave economies, each armed with mercantilist state policies, war and conflict became frequent among the masters, which then produced increasing space for slave revolts. The zones of confrontation subsequently moved from margins of empire to its core regions until the world-system of slaves imploded.

Hence, there are, roughly speaking, two phases in the geopolitics of the imperial project, of which enslavement is a part. First, the fault lines are mostly exterior, outward-going at the verge of the expanding world-economy, where slave raids, slave trades, and slave imports take place. Then in the second phase, the lines of confrontation are drawn within the world-system, cracking inward, occasionally close to its core, where slave masters fight each other, where it is not uncommon for slaves to triumph and set themselves free.

Which phase are we in? Is our era of digital media still at the initial phase of empire expansion—into cyberspace? Into the developing regions of China (where the construction of huge factories requires massive land grabs) and into the conflict zones of of Global South (think, again, about Congo)?

Gone is the time of New World slavery. But are we confronting New Economy slavery today? Have we already gone beyond the phase of empire building, when abolition is about to carry the day? Or perhaps the vortex of New Economy is likely to produce even more disruptive geopolitical rivalry than in the past?

A vortex it is indeed, at least in economic terms. Since the beginning of New World plantation economies, it took a couple of centuries for sugar and tobacco to transform themselves from luxury goods to everyday necessities, even for wage labor. Yet in a similar process it took less than two decades for the wide diffusion of digital "luxuries" as a popular form of pleasure among working and underclasses, in slums and villages alike. The newly "discovered" wealth seems to be so readily extractable—comparable, some would say, to the legendary silver mines of Mount Potosí from mid-1500s to mid-1600s.[39] What would come next? Another era of mercantilism and subsequent wars in the new fault lines of geopolitics, and in cyberspace?

Then comes China, whose export-oriented model of economic growth has for many years been criticized for being "mercantilist," threatening to "wreck the entire post–World War II trading system" and challenging the global leadership of the United States.[40] One worrisome project, from the perspective of Washington, is what China calls the New Silk Road, also known as the Beijing-Moscow-Berlin (BMB) trade alliance being actively planned and pursued in the name of "One Belt, One Road," which may build political coalitions that destabilize U.S. interests in Eurasia.[41] Of course, not everyone would see the clash as inevitable. While Beijing keeps up its talk about "peaceful rising," optimistic analysts continue to argue that China and the United States have formed such an unprecedented "Chimerica" symbiosis that old-school geopolitics is no longer relevant.[42]

Yet by December 2014, China had accumulated an astonishing amount of $3.9 trillion foreign-exchange reserves as a result of its immense trade surpluses, more than three times as large as the reserves held by Japan, the world's second-largest holder.[43] This is certainly little more than a crude indicator, and it would be an oversimplification to equate China today with any of the classic mercantile states of the seventeenth and eighteenth centuries. But historically speaking, such national policies and sustained imbalance in global trade did cause mayhem while motivating colonial expansion, including the spread of slavery.

Will humanity in the twenty-first century be able to escape from this old curse of geopolitics? Answers to this question are fundamental because, without them, how can we be so confident in claiming that we have sloughed off every bit of the slavery legacies that exist at the very root of this capitalist world-system we inherit and inhabit? To uproot slavery, the human species probably has to put an end to empires and empire building. Otherwise, peace and freedom would be transient; dark ages may still return.

$$\bullet \quad \bullet \quad \bullet$$

Despite slavery's many forms and the fluctuation in slave population, another theme is fairly constant: slavery exists so that the labor of the enslaved can be extracted at minimum cost. No matter a plantation field worker, a household servant, or a child soldier, the essential goal is for them to provide labor—material or immaterial—to his or her "owner," who reaps the value produced without paying the full cost, as would have been the case with wage labor under *normal* market conditions. Slaves are put to arduous employment for the accumulation of capital. As Blackburn points out, "Etymologically the word capital derives from the Latin word for head, as in head of cattle. Slaves, usually all too literally, were regarded as human cattle—but they were also feared as potentially murderous wild beasts. They were known as 'chattel' slaves, another word stemming from the same Latin root as the words 'cattle' and 'capital.'"[44]

For the pursuit of monetary wealth, the institution of slavery does have its superiority, especially if one hopes to possess a large fortune in no time. Otherwise, abolition would have been much easier. It is not just simple efficiency plus minimal cost: slave productivity can be raised by increasing the total volume of work hours beyond the limits of wage labor.[45] Behold the Great Wall of China or the glitzy skyscrapers of Dubai;[46] the argument of cost effectiveness can be persuasive if one works from the often unstated premise that the sufferings of the enslaved do not count as economic "cost," a rather narrow and outmoded idea.

There were probably no better exemplary slave economies with more long-lasting global impact than the plantations of the Americas producing cotton, tobacco, coffee, and, most important of all, sugar. Before the Industrial Revolution, the slave-powered sugar plantation had been the most "efficient" in maximizing capital returns. It had thus "always been the favored child of capitalism," wrote Fernando Ortiz.[47]

When Christopher Columbus brought sugar cane to the New World in 1493, it took twenty-three years for the first shipment of sugar to be sent back to Europe.[48] From that point on, with the increasing input of labor power from Africa, sugar production surged. By one estimate, "New World output of sugar in 1600 was around 10,000 tons; by 1660 it was around 30,000. Sugar prices dropped by a half between the 1620s and the 1670s. . . . [In Britain,] the smaller towns and country folk could also occasionally indulge a sweet tooth."[49] And, as Ralph Davis notes, "After 1660 England's sugar imports always exceeded its combined imports of all other colonial produce."[50] Per-capita annual consumption of sugar among British citizens rose from four pounds in 1700–1709 to eighteen pounds in 1800–1809.[51]

The tremendous growth in sugar production was only conceivable as a result of further exacerbation of the Atlantic trade of "human cargo." It had to be the case because in most New World colonies, especially those specializing in sugar, the slave population could not reproduce itself due to malnutrition, disease, physical abuse, and harsh working conditions. Fresh "chattel" had to be imported to sustain the labor force and meet the need of production. According to Blackburn, the total number of Africans being trafficked to the New World was approximately 370,000 in the sixteenth century. It rose by more than five times to 1.87 million in the seventeenth century, which again more than tripled to reach 6.13 million in the eighteenth century.[52]

While fortunes were made and the sweet tooth grew in Europe, life for those toiling on Caribbean "sugar islands" was hell. The majority of them were field hands. They were organized in the "gang" system to perform the tough tasks of planting, manuring, and cane-cutting, for as long as their masters and supervisors dictated, under the scorching sun and the bloody whip.[53] "Perhaps only a tenth of the labor force was required in the mill and the boiling house," which was "most like a factory."[54] This was, however, a factory of horrendous conditions, full of punishing heat, loud noise, and occupational hazards. According to a seventeenth-century observer, "If a Mill-feeder be catch'd by the finger, his whole body is drawn in, and is squees'd to pieces. If a Boyler gets any part into the scalding Sugar, it sticks like Glew, or Birdlime, and 'tis hard to save either Limb or Life."[55]

For all the hard work, physical abuse, and peril endured, slaves received either nothing or a tiny fraction of the value they created, which would be deemed unfair should they become "freemen." Why didn't they leave? Because being enslaved meant they could not leave for jobs that were more rewarding; because the labor market was so peculiarly constructed that the laborer could no longer function as an independent actor by herself or himself. In other words, it was because they were under *abnormal* market conditions characterized by coercion, deception, and oppression.

Which brings us to labor conditions in Foxconn. Yes, the company uses a modern management system, where workers are supposed to receive a wage and can choose to leave, at least in theory. Yes, it tries to abide by China's labor law, albeit not always successfully, as will be discussed in chapter 3. Yes, an electronics plant of the twenty-first century has to look somewhat better than a sugar plantation of the seventeenth century. But could there be other answers?

That unlikely direction is what I shall explore. After all, both factory regimes are capitalist in nature. If one scrutinizes the substance of labor relationship at Foxconn, especially its implemented practices of recruitment and employee turnover, the situation is quite close to *abnormal* market conditions. At the very least, it does not qualify as *normal* market conditions in that the company, local governments, and other forces in the labor market (such as recruitment intermediary agencies and the vocational schools) have colluded to create conditions that reduce workers' choice and contribute, as much as possible, to the unfreedom of labor.[56]

As Pun Ngai et al. found through their definitive investigative research that Foxconn's labor management system "maximizes productivity and profits through highly intense and overtime work, low wages, violent discipline and atomization of the labor force designed to prevent resistance, at the cost of workers' dignity, health, even their lives."[57] It therefore makes sense to contend that labor conditions at Foxconn remain in the long shadow of slavery, a point that will be elaborated in the following chapter.

Could one say that the seeds of Foxconn tragedies were sown centuries ago, and oceans away, sprouting only suddenly in 2010 during the so-called "Foxconn suicide express"? Are these new and old plants of enslavement still being irrigated by the gadget I purchase or the content you create? Without digging out the deeper roots of slavery, will they sprout again, in the immediate aftermath of another recession? These are questions worth contemplating.

•   •   •

For a while, plantations supplied with "well-disciplined" slaves seemed to have solved the problem of production for the Eurocentric world-economy. But consumption remained, and continues to be, a daunting challenge. The upsurge of commodities is remarkable. But who's going to buy? Eric Hobsbawm points out that in the seventeenth century, as the New World's slave-powered economies took off, "the future industrialist required not an infinite willingness to keep scores of chefs, stucco artists, and perruquiers employed, but mass demand."[58] Writing more specifically about merchants selling sugar, Sydney Mintz points out that these "sucrose vendors have always been interested in patterns of consumption only in order to be able to change them."[59]

To this end, it is no longer suitable to rely on brute force, intimidation, and coercive measures of the law. Rather, the general pattern is that a hegemonic cultural regime has to be put in place for the stimulation of market growth. This system is essentially what Jean Jacques Rousseau refers to as the "conventions" that are used by the powers that be "to ensure them continual mastership"[60] vis-à-vis the enslaved. Via hegemony, they can—at least they hope—achieve domination via symbols, social practices, and ideological apparatus. The result is reduced choice and constrained "free will" for the less powerful and the less wealthy, in more or less deceptive ways via interpersonal or mediated channels of communication and persuasion.

There has to be a newfangled regime of (servile) consumption to match the marvelous regime of miraculous (slave) productivity. The goal of this new hegemonic system is to generate a new culture, even a new religion of consumerism, an indispensable pillar of the capitalist world-economy because, without it, the commodities from plantations could not have been turned into profits.

This is, however, a formidable task, not only because the growth in New World production was so immense. In the Old World, the wealthy minority already had their long-established ways of consumption, shaped by customs rooted in various European cultures, climates, and modes of local economy, be they agrarian, fishing, or manufacture. These were not easy to sway. The impoverished majority, on the other hand, had little purchasing power. As a result, their patterns of purchase were even more local, not to mention traditions of frugality from prolonged periods of economic scarcity. Even if many could earn more disposable income, why would they *want* the New World commodities?

*Want* is the key here, and a fundamental lesson from past scholarship is that *want* is elastic and manufacturable on a large scale. First, the commodities were not of the usual type. The most prototypical of them, like sugar and tobacco, were addictive, meaning consumption at one point often led the consumer to *want* more. Meanwhile, mercantile and other preferential policies kept the commodity prices artificially low with government subsidies and tariff protection.[61]

As discussed in Sydney Mintz's *Sweetness and Power*, new "rituals" arose in regularized dietary habits such as adding sugar into tea and ending a meal with dessert; so did new "ceremonial occasions" exemplified by "wedding cakes with their elaborate icings and figures."[62] Mintz analyzed the deep and long-lasting effects of sugar—and the tactics of increasing sugar consumption—for instance, on British diet. As a cultural anthropologist, his main interests were less about the culinary habits themselves than changes in cultural patterns in food consumption. Hence: "Vendors also understand that the patterns [of consumption] will not yield unless the conditions under which consumption occurs are changed—not just what is worn, but where and when, and with whom; not just what is eaten, but where and when, and with whom."[63]

Did the sugar vendors succeed? Yes. What was the key? For Mintz, it was "desocialized eating"; in other words, consumers were somehow persuaded to maximize their "freedom of individual choice" so that they no longer need to coordinate with other people to have a meal.[64] In so doing, their old *wants* of enjoying food as a collective activity with other human beings were reduced, replaced by a new set of consumerist *wants*. This pattern of food consumption being increasingly "desocialized" can be observed around the world, not just in the United Kingdom, well into the present time.

From the vantage point of slavery studies, the change toward desocialization clearly parallels Patterson's theme of "social death"[65] as discussed earlier in this chapter. There is of course obvious difference in that the "desocialization" of field slaves often took place much more abruptly, in a war or a court decision, whereas for the consuming masses the process took decades and generations through much less violent forms of persuasion, intoxication, and indoctrination. But the basic pattern of social atomization was consistent enough to support the suspicion that the deliberate shaping of *wants* leads to another kind of enslavement, in this case of consumers. It is not the same kind as the enslavement of trafficked Africans. But it is enslavement nonetheless.

This process of shaping and manufacturing *wants* relied initially on interpersonal communication, word of mouth, and small group gatherings. From the sixteenth century onward, new advertising techniques grew along with the ascent of the printing press, which played a prominent role in facilitating the growth of commerce and the consumption of imported goods in Europe.[66] But it was not only advertising: other genres of the press—novels, poetry, journalism—also contributed. The result was the making of a new subjectivity, a consumerist self, whose appetite could grow as fast as, sometimes more rapidly than, rising slave productivity in the New World.

The printing press was only a harbinger of what later became a full-scale industrial system of advertising and marketing, going beyond black-and-white printing to colorful images, moving pictures, radio broadcast, satellite TV, and culminating in the "ubiquitous" digital media that codify and commodify our social existence in this wonderful world of gadgets. Altogether this seems to be a truly remarkable *longue durée* historical process in the sense that, in not only the Old World and the New but also the entire planet today, consumerism has become such an unchallenged cultural norm in so many places that it would be absurd to imagine a "modern" people without consumerist propensities.

Again, how does this relate to slavery, and to abolition? First, the expansion of enslavement in the New World could only continue when consumerism expands in the Old World. The latter is a necessary condition for the former, just like the supply of African slaves. But growing consumerist culture in Europe was perhaps a more fundamental drive because the main goal of the Atlantic triangular trade was capital accumulation.[67] It is for this reason that antislavery consumer movements often play a central role in abolition endeavors throughout history.

Second, communication, cultural change, and and the rise of the media industry were crucial factors for capitalism to solve its consumption challenge by shaping and manufacturing wants through joyful intoxication that leads to social isolation. The main product of these advertising and marketing endeavors was the making of a new consumerist self, who constitutes as another peculiar kind of slave—in other words, "the ultimate slave."

· · ·

In his masterpiece *Slavery and Social Death* comparing dozens of slavery regimes from history and around the world, Orlando Patterson devotes a full chapter to those slaves who did not toil in poverty at the very bottom of the social pyramid. Instead, they were placed extremely close to the pinnacle of society while enjoying tremendous influence and affluence.[68] This is best exemplified by the Roman *familia Caesaris* (slaves and freedmen serving the emperor directly or indirectly) and the Byzantine and Chinese eunuchs (who dominated certain periods of Byzantium and imperial China).

These were people who occupied some of the most privileged political, administrative, or bureaucratic jobs of their times, supervising the royal palace or managing the imperial coffers. Yet Patterson nonetheless defines them as slaves despite their elite status because their power "was utterly precarious; it existed solely at the whim, feeblemindedness, or design of the master," in other words, the emperor who "needed persons who in law had no separate legal identity but were simply living surrogates of their masters."[69]

Legal standing aside, these upper-class slaves were found, very much like Africans trafficked to the Caribbean or female rural-to-urban migrants working in Chinese factory zones, to be socially isolated and "natally alienated."[70] Although at one moment they could command huge armies and possess tremendous wealth, the next moment their masters could appropriate all their fortunes "by the simple expedient of execution," as did Roman emperor Vespasian in the first century A.D. and China's Qing Dynasty emperor Jiaqing in the eighteenth century.

To what extent are those who populate the modern consumerist society still comparable to the precarious and alienated "surrogates of their masters," masters of capitalism? Are they, like the "ultimate slaves" of the past, psychologically dependent and servile?

The most intriguing lesson from Patterson about the dialectics of slavery is that, once viewed from a different perspective, once the constraint of cultural hegemony is removed, the "ultimate slaves" are also the closest to emancipation, by themselves: "It is difficult to dominate another person when that other person is either the main basis of one's power or, more frequently, the sole means of communication with the basis of one's power. Isolation is vulnerability; the control of communication is power. Sublation of the relationship immediately becomes a possibility."[71] It was not uncommon for the "ultimate slaves" to subvert the imperial world order by overthrowing, abducting, sometimes killing the emperor. This was how the Turkish mamluk kingdoms were founded in medieval Egypt, when more than fifty ex-slaves, including two females, turned themselves into kings and queens.[72]

How could this history inform a new movement of digital abolition? For one thing, the subversive potentials of these elite slaves come from their role in communication. The media systems that the capitalist world-economy has to depend on for the manufacturing of consumerist wants are, by the same token, also its Achilles heel.

No wonder the abolition movements of the eighteenth and nineteenth centuries were more effective than before due to the growth of the modern printing press and the subsequent emergence of inter-urban and transnational civil society. Big Sugar had to rely on Big Media, complete with their new instrument of Big Data these days, although one may still wonder: Who exactly are the "ultimate slaves" of Appconn?

· · ·

The last and most profound lesson from historical studies of slavery is its active role in the making of modernity. According to Marx's classic argument, the modern capitalist mode of production is a unique configuration of the bourgeoisie vis-à-vis the proletariat wage workers, a distinctively new and hence "modern" working class "who live only so long as they find work, and who find work only so long as their labor increases capital."[73]

However, recent historical scholarship, including Karl Heinz Roth and Marcel van der Linden's *Beyond Marx*, contends that this conventional Marxist approach is Eurocentric, built exclusively on the experiences of nineteenth-century working-class aspirations in the northern Atlantic system.[74] Whereas if one takes a truly global view from half a millennium ago to neoliberalism today, "the historical reality of capitalism has featured many hybrid and transitional forms between slavery and 'free' wage-labour. Moreover, slaves and wage-workers have repeatedly performed the same work in the same business-enterprise."[75] In other words, Marx underestimated the power and persistence of slavery, even though it is indeed an archaic mode of production.

This theoretical critique on Marx's flawed conception of slave labor is consistent with other historical work on the variation of slavery systems over time. And it was not just Marx but also Adam Smith, Auguste

Comte, Max Weber, and Ludwig von Mises—all these great thinkers associated slavery with traditions of backwardness, therefore unrelated or peripheral to modes of modern capitalism as they knew them. Yet according to Robin Blackburn, "of course slavery is indeed a very ancient human institution, but it has also been highly flexible."[76] "The Enlightenment was not so antagonistic to slavery as was once thought."[77] Well into the eighteenth century, "New World planters and Atlantic merchants were still in the vanguard of progress."[78] Blackburn continues,

> The slavery of the Americas not only presented many novel features. Its development was associated with several of those processes which have been held to define modernity: the growth of instrumental rationality, the rise of national sentiment and the nation-state, radicalized perceptions of identity, the spread of market relations and wage labour, the development of administrative bureaucracies and modern tax systems, the growing sophistication of commerce and communication, the birth of consumer societies, the publication of newspapers and the beginnings of press advertising, "action at a distance" and an individualist sensibility.

David Brion Davis goes further to claim that "in a sense, slaves were the world's first 'modern' people" in part because "the archetypal slave was a foreigner, an outsider torn from her or his protective family matrix by capture, treacherous sale, greed, debt, the threat of famine, or punishment for crime."[79] Indeed these "first peoples of modernity" explained as such could be found in the African slaves as well as the native American, Scottish and Irish, males and females in bondage. They have not only manufactured and serviced the external world of economic growth and infrastructure that became the material foundation of Industrial Revolution and modernity; they were also "manufactured" inasmuch as their subjectivity, their life and work, their mentality were shaped, too, as vital components of this new culture of consumerist modernity.

A captivating argument from Patterson is that "the history of freedom" has slavery as "its handmaiden."[80] This is because "our moral universe is a field of values that are in conflict not only with each other but with themselves" and that "inhering in the good which we defend with our lives is often the very evil we most abhor."[81] He continues: "In becoming the central value of its secular and religious life, freedom constituted the tragic, generative core of Western culture, the germ of its genius and all its grandeur, and the source of much of its perfidy and its crimes against humanity."[82]

Like it or not, in this epoch of digital media, we have inherited modernity full of its internal complexities and moral contradictions. Blatant or latent, slavery is a necessary part of modern times. Abolition, therefore, is a task perpetuated by modernity itself, socially, culturally, and politically.

## Guidelines of Law

The previous section has outlined, in a simplified manner, seven theses from historical studies of slavery that can serve as a conceptual foundation for this book. I have started to connect them with contemporary issues of labor (not only wage earners but also slaves and other forms of unfree labor), production and consumption, exploitation and freedom. But in legal terms, do conditions at Appconn—Foxconn, Apple, and the digital media industry as a whole—really amount to slavery, to such an extent that the characterization of iSlave is warranted?

The answer would be negative if one sticks to stringent definitions such as "slavery proper was characterized by a lifetime of enforced labor, together with a chattel status that was passed on to descendants."[83] But as discussed earlier, definitions of slavery vary significantly, and it can be counterproductive to apply the term rigidly. Using, for instance, the criteria of lifetime toil and heritage status, many internationally recognized forms of slavery would not qualify—human trafficking, labor camp, child soldier—because it is common for victims to be subject to coercion and forced labor for a limited period, like a few months or years; whereas in most parts of the world today it is rare for the inferior status to be passed directly onto children. Yet international bodies such as the United Nations Commission on Human Rights (UNCHR), media organizations like the CNN, and legal researchers still consider them "modern-day slavery," "twenty-first-century slavery," or "new slavery."[84]

To define slavery in legal terms, one must start from the 1926 Slavery Convention, the most foundational document. Signed in Geneva on

March 9, 1926, by member states of the League of Nations, the full name of the document was "The Convention to Suppress the Slave Trade and Slavery." As of 2013, ninety-nine countries had committed to participate in the Convention and its Protocol.[85] Article 1(1) of the Convention stipulates: "Slavery is the status or condition of a person over whom any or all of the powers attaching to the right of ownership are exercised." According to legal scholar Jean Allain, this parsimonious definition "is accepted as a norm of international law."[86]

The 1926 Slavery Convention marks a germane moment of interesting ideas. A member of the taskforce that drafted the Convention was Sir Frederick Lugard, a former governor of Hong Kong (1907–1912) and governor-general of Nigeria (1914–1919), who was representing the United Kingdom as well as the International Labor Organization (ILO). According to British government archives, he prepared the first draft of this landmark document.[87] In 1925 he also argued strongly to prioritize the eradication of "servile mentality"—a radical idea even by today's standard—which did not end up in the final text.[88]

Practically speaking, however, the 1926 Slavery Convention had relatively little impact until the 1990s due to the disintegration of the League of Nations and the mayhem of World War II. Three decades later in 1956, following the horrors of concentration camps, be they German or Japanese (in these some also saw Soviet gulag, South African apartheid, and colonization in general despite bitter debates that ensued), the United Nations took up the issue again and signed a treaty to both affirm the legal status of the 1926 Convention and extend it to cover new modes of enslavement, especially forced or compulsory labor. The title of the document is revealing: "The 1956 Supplementary Convention on the Abolition of Slavery, the Slave Trade, and Institutions and Practices Similar to Slavery." More emphasis is attached here to the elasticity of bondage and its contemporary variations as in "institutions and practices similar to slavery."

The Cold War made it difficult again to have unified worldwide action against slave systems. The collapse of the Berlin Wall and then the dissolution of the USSR started a brief period of the "end of history" celebrations—until history crashed again in the 1990s. On the one hand, the Soviet meltdown triggered an upsurge in human trafficking from the former Soviet republics and Eastern Bloc countries into Europe. Both the United Nations and the Council of Europe had to respond to this crisis. In Australia, the crime of pimps holding Southeast Asian sex workers as slaves also surfaced through the prominent case of *The Queen v. Tang* in 2008.[89]

On the other hand, ethnic cleansings in the former Yugoslavia and Rwanda necessitated the establishment of the International Criminal Court in 1998, which had to press charges against former military and political figures who had committed various crimes against humanity, including slavery. The "two primary streams [caused by increasing trafficking and ethnic cleansing] . . . joined together to give new life to the definition of slavery," "whose effectiveness has only recently gained traction" since the late 1990s.[90]

A key case was the trial of Dragoljub Kunarac in 1998. Following the breakup of Yugoslavia, Kunarac and his unit of the Bosnian Serb Army committed horrendous crimes, including most notoriously the Foča "rape camps."[91] As the International Criminal Tribunal for the Former Yugoslavia (ICTY) met in 1998 to prosecute Kunarac, "courts, particularly international courts, often grappled with the definition of slavery."[92] At the end, Kunarac received a sentence of "28 years' imprisonment for torture, rape and enslavement," which "marked the first time that an international tribunal had prosecuted sexual slavery."[93]

An unintended consequence of the ICTY hearings was a revival of interests in legal criteria that help pin down modern slavery. Judges, lawyers, and legal scholars revisited the 1926 and 1956 Conventions "in light of the requirements of criminal justice,"[94] only this time, general principles of international law would not suffice. Concrete methods of identification were in order. The renewed interests and practical needs paved way for the 2012 Bellagio-Harvard Guidelines on the Legal Parameters of Slavery (hereinafter the Guidelines), which is the most updated, comprehensive, and operable document for the definition of slavery from the vantage point of law. Given its importance, the Guidelines document is reproduced in its entirety in appendix 1.

. . .

For more than two years from 2010 to 2012, the Research Network on the Legal Parameters of Slavery took up the task of updating legal understandings of slavery into more practicable "guidelines" under historical, global, and contemporary circumstances. This is a group of twenty leading scholars and lawyers from universities in Australia, Ireland, South Africa, the United Kingdom, the United States, as well as two NGOs: "Anti-Slavery International" in London and "Free the Slaves: The Center of the Modern American Abolitionist Movement" in Washington, D.C. Members of the research network met, deliberated, and produced consensus during three symposia held in Oxford, Harvard, and the Rockefeller Foundation Bellagio Conference Center. The result was the Guidelines, which included ten recommendations on how to interpret the 1926 and 1956 Slavery Conventions in the twenty-first century.[95]

The Guidelines represent the best consensual basis among legal scholars and professionals in order to more precisely define "slavery and lesser servitude" in the contemporary world. Applying the principles of this document, one would see that labor conditions at Appconn do not always amount to "slavery" per se. However, it is rather common for the corporate policies and acts to qualify as de facto "institutions and practices similar to slavery," in other words, "practices similar to slavery" in simplified legal terms.[96] Sometimes instances of "practices similar to slavery" are found to be so numerous that should be seen as a system-level pandemic in the digital media industry.

It is unrealistic to use the next few pages to do full justice to this legal research network, given its interdisciplinary scope, intellectual rigor, and public policy commitments. For our purposes here, it would suffice to distill four insights from the Guidelines and the definitive book that explains and substantiates it, Jean Allain's *The Legal Understanding of Slavery*.[97] All of these insights extend from the 1926 Convention defining both slavery and the slave trade, whose cornerstone is Article 1(1): "Slavery is the status or condition of a person over whom any or all of the powers attaching to the right of ownership are exercised." Because legal language is known for its precision, there needs to be scrutiny of this elegant and seemingly straightforward definition in order to appreciate the underlying arguments of the Guidelines.

• • •

First is the emphasis on "status or condition." Status here refers to a formal arrangement of the law that matters greatly in the comparative history of slave regimes. Islamic law, or *Sharia*, for example, once facilitated the freeing of slaves to a greater extent than other medieval legal systems due to its "privileging the humanity of the slave over his or her status as property in many instances."[98] Such structural variation among slave regimes and the specific status of subjects therein were at one time crucial determinants for slavery.

However, due to the global success of abolition efforts in the nineteenth and twentieth centuries, it has currently become almost a "legal impossibility"[99] for one person to be formally and legally "owned" in any jurisdiction. Therefore, the main emphasis in practically defining slavery has to shift from one's legal status to her or his "condition" of life, of work, of the genuine experiences under particular economic, social, and cultural circumstances.

In the legal community, there has long been a demand to move beyond legal status in order to capture the substance of the actual relationship and practices. As Allison Gorsuch writes about cases of the "voluntarily" indentured in antebellum Illinois, "The question of whether the black indentured person was a slave might in fact be different than whether the black indentured person was held in slavery."[100] In other words, a worker may not be formally "owned" by anyone, but this does not prevent an individual or a company from holding him or her in slavery "conditions."

The same can apply to twenty-first-century situations in that, although slavery is forbidden by law in the DRC, Eastern Europe, and Australia, the legal arrangements on paper cannot preempt by themselves the possibility that slave-like conditions persist among warlord-controlled children, captives in the "rape camps," and triad-controlled immigrants. This is why "paradoxically, slavery can thrive when people believe it has been abolished."[101] For this reason, Guideline 5 specifies: "In evaluating the particular circumstances to determine whether slavery exists, reference should be made to *the substance and not simply to the form* of the relationship in question" (paragraph 3, emphasis added).

$$\bullet \quad \bullet \quad \bullet$$

Second, the 1926 Slavery Convention makes reference to the "powers attaching to ownership" not to "ownership" per se. This avoids defining ownership, an ambiguous term when applied to humans. By emphasizing "powers," this definition is broader in scope, while calling for more specific identification of particular "powers" within ownership rights. Hence, Guideline 2 specifies:

> In terms of slavery, the exercise of "the powers attaching to the right of ownership" should be understood as constituting control over a person in such a way as to *significantly deprive that person of his or her individual liberty*, with the *intent of exploitation through the use, management, profit, transfer or disposal of that person*. Usually this exercise will be supported by and obtained through means such as *violent force, deception and/or coercion*." (emphasis added)

This broader way of understanding slavery based on the "powers" rather than ownership itself has been characteristic of several court decisions, including the famous Australian case *The Queen v. Tang*.[102] Guideline 3, "Possession Is Foundational to Slavery," highlights the power to possess as a bedrock power to be reckoned with. Guideline 4 lists six "Further Examples" including (1) buying, selling or transferring a person, (2) using a person, (3) managing the use of a person, (4) profiting from the use of a person, (5) transferring a person to an heir or successor, and (6) disposal, mistreatment or neglect of a person.

None of the above applies to the charge, usually a moral one, of exploitation by one's employers, managers, or supervisors, whose control over the worker does not amount to possession.[103] Meanwhile, as Judge Hayne of Australia reasons, "powers attaching to the right of ownership" should be treated as powers exercised "as if it was possible to own a human being"; hence, "the exercise of such powers and the intention to exercise them are interconnected questions"; therefore, "it is not necessary to establish that the defendant had the specific intention to treat the complainants as slaves."[104]

Not considering intentionality, my observations are that Foxconn did treat its employees in similarly possessing manners. As Guideline 3 (paragraph 3) stipulates:

> Such control may be physical, but physical constraints will not always be necessary to the maintenance of effective control over a person. More abstract manifestations of control of a person may be evident in attempts to withhold identity documents; or to otherwise restrict free movement or access to state authorities; or equally in attempts

46

to forge a new identity through compelling a new religion, language, place of residence, or forced marriage.

Psychological control can be more effective and of more long-lasting effect, to the extent that "when such control operates, it will significantly deprive that person of his or her individual liberty for a period of time which is, for that person, indeterminate" (Guideline 3, paragraph 4).

That person feeling under "indeterminate" control was probably one of those Foxconn workers who chose to commit suicide in 2010. Is this conjecture true or false? Chapter 3 will introduce Tian Yu, a Foxconn survivor whose testimonies lend support to this suspicion.

Suicides are, of course, extreme cases—nowadays or in the seventeenth century among Africans enduring the Middle Passage. The next chapter will discuss more mundane conditions, such as how the company created tremendous difficulty for workers to quit; how student interns were used as inexpensive and involuntary labor on a massive scale; and how Foxconn basically disposed of its engineer Zhang Tingzhen after his debilitating work injury.

In the first occasions of Tian Yu and workers being unable to quit, unfair treatment did amount to possession, which imposed restrictions on the physical movement of the victims.[105] In the second, the plight of student interns constitutes "evidence of profiting from the use of a person [which] may include cases where a person is mortgaged, lent for profit, or used as collateral" as laid out by Guideline 4. The third case of the injured worker is another violation because, again according to Guideline 4, "disposing of a person following his or her exploitation may provide evidence of slavery." I shall return to this discussion in chapter 3.

Legal immunity is another important dimension with regard to the factory's "powers attaching to ownership."[106] Despite the high-profile serial suicides in 2010, despite dozens—if not hundreds—of cases in which Foxconn employees, ex-employees, and their families press charges against the company in Chinese courts every year, to my knowledge Foxconn never lost a law suit filed by its workers to bear civil or criminal responsibility. At the time of this writing, all the charges seem to have ended in vain, thus resonating with Rebecca Scott's remark:

> We may best avoid anachronism not by eschewing the use of the term "slavery" to describe the modern exercise of certain powers over hu-

man beings, but instead by examining the interplay of the legal and the extralegal in both historical and contemporary instances.[107]

• • •

The third crucial element of the 1926 slavery definition, which remains a spirit of the Guidelines, is a logical specification: "any or all." Legal identification of slavery does not require *all* such "powers attaching to ownership" to be exercised. So long as *any* of them exists, it can be deemed as slavery or practices similar to slavery.

Physical bondage, for example, can be absent as a condition in identifying slavery because the slave-owner sometimes can achieve stronger enslavement effect through psychological or sociocultural control. As Guideline 3 states: "While the exact form of possession might vary, in essence it supposes control over a person by another such as a person might control a thing. Such control may be physical, but physical constraints will not always be necessary to the maintenance of effective control over a person" (paragraph 3). This is reiterated in Guideline 5, "Making a Determination as to Whether Slavery Exists":

> The exercise of any or all of the powers attaching to the right of ownership just considered shall provide evidence of slavery, insofar as they demonstrate control over a person tantamount to possession (paragraph 1).
>
> The substance of the relationship should be determined by investigating whether in fact there has been an exercise of one or more of the powers attaching to the right of ownership" (paragraph 4).

This means the legal experts set the bar rather low for potential offenders to pass the test. If it can be established that the individual or company exercises any single one of the "powers attaching to the right of ownership" to another person, the allegation of slavery would be valid.

• • •

The fourth insight from Jean Allain's edited volume and the Guidelines has to do with slave trade and exchange, which is somewhat more controversial. Earlier I have dealt with the commerce of "human cargo," particularly the Atlantic triangular trade system. Such a trading network is essential to the motif of capital accumulation from past to present. Article 1(2) of the 1926 Slavery Convention thus defines "the slave trade" as

> all acts involved in the capture, acquisition or disposal of a person with intent to reduce him to slavery; all acts involved in the acquisition of a slave with a view to selling or exchanging him; all acts of disposal by sale or exchange of a slave acquired with a view to being sold or exchanged, and, in general, every act of trade or transport in slaves.

Note this old definition conceives the "commodities" being traded as "a person." However, in the twenty-first century, organizations such as Fight Slavery Now! and Slavery Today include organ trafficking as a subcategory of modern slavery.[108] Not everyone would concur with this position. While some victims are indeed enslaved for the purpose of commercially motivated organ removal, there is also argument that the trafficking in organs needs to be treated as a separate offense.[109]

Could enslavement occur when the objects of transaction are body parts? What about their time, their labor power, in the form of "slave-made goods"?[110] According to Kevin Bales,

> In Brazil, slaves are "recruited" in densely populated, economically depressed regions in the east of the country and then transferred up to 1000 miles to isolated forest camps to make charcoal. The charcoal, in turn, is shipped significant distances and used to produce pig iron and steel suitable for export. This steel is sold to Canada and the US, and the European Union imports nearly a million tons of Brazilian steel each year to produce everything from cars to buildings to toys. Investment from Europe and North America into Brazilian industry indirectly supports these slave-based charcoal operations.[111]

This is but one of the more prominent trades of "slave-made goods" that contributes to the continuation of what Bales calls "new slavery in the global economy."[112] Other examples in our time include "carpets, cocoa, cotton, timber, beef, rice, tomatoes, lettuce, apples and other fruit, shrimp and other fish products, gold, diamonds and other gemstones, shoes, clothing, fireworks, rope, and bricks," as well as coffee and the harvesting of "some sugar."[113] Bales continues with the now-familiar case at the root of the global digital industry: "In the Congo, armed gangs enslave and force local people to dig minerals such as coltan, cassiterite, wolframite, and tungsten. These minerals are sold to exporters who send them to Europe and Asia where they are used to make components needed for the production of cell phones, computers, and other electronics."[114]

Bales's "new slavery" argument is not without its critique. Patterson, for one, disapproves it because "[Bales] has defined slavery so broadly that it now embraces too vast a body of persons."[115] The Guidelines do not include a particular item targeting "slave-made goods," either. I, however, tend to agree more with the general approach of Bales (albeit not all his empirical assessments): only ending specific forms of enslavement will not suffice to meet the goal of eradicating slavery for good. Because slave systems are so flexible and ever changing, they are not limited to the forms that can now be observed and legalistically defined.

Moreover, slavery has to exist in a relational context. It continues not only because there is a slave, over whom a slaveholder exercises certain "powers." More crucially, and structurally speaking, enslavement exists because there is a larger system, regional or global, entailing such unequal relationships. This is an essential lesson from the history of slavery over the past half millennium that has great relevance to our investigation of iSlavery: Without consumption demand for slave-provided goods and services, the "slave trade" and the global problem of bondage would not have grown to such a scale and with such awful obstinacy. Only calling consumers "complacent" is not good enough to resolve the issue. A full definition of "slave trade" needs to include both the trade of slaves and the trade of slave-produced commodities for more effective abolition in order to eradicate twenty-first-century slavery.

· · ·

From the 1926 Slavery Convention to the Guidelines of 2012, the criteria for assessing enslavement status or condition have become more specific and practical. Criticism remains, no doubt, in the academy. The 1926 definition of slavery, as spelled out in Article 1(1) of the 1926 Convention, has, for example, been criticized as a "narrowly conceived Western approach which applies mainly to modern, capitalistic slavery in which the slave is quintessentially a commercial chattel."[116] Yet despite the debates and differences in intellectual traditions, participants in the drafting of the Guidelines share two spirits that shall be carried forward.

On one hand, as Jean Allain points out, the key is to capture "the essence of the lived experience of contemporary slavery."[117] For this reason, the Guidelines move "away from manifestations of *de jure* slavery [legally defined slavery] towards recognitions of *de facto* slavery [slavery in reality] with the obvious resonance this has for contemporary cases of slavery."[118]

In her comparative study of slavery cases in the 1810s and late 1990s, Rebecca Scott finds that de facto legal understanding had long held its explanatory power. "It is enslavement in this processual sense," she writes, "that modern international agreements prohibiting slavery seek to prevent."[119] This is why Guideline 10, "When Slavery and Lesser Servitudes are Present," stipulates:

> Accepting that both slavery and lesser servitudes such as forced labour or "institutions and practices similar to slavery" may be found *in substance* in a particular circumstance; the manner to proceed is by making *reference to that substance and not simply to the form,* and first ask whether there has been an exercise of the powers attaching to the right of ownership. If so, then the more serious offence of slavery is present. (paragraph 1, emphasis added)

On the other hand, the Guidelines, much more so than the 1926 and 1956 Conventions, are characterized by a palpable future orientation, which is particularly important for the discussion of iSlave. The Guidelines are designed to set a "gold standard," in other words, "a reference point for grounding any future study of contemporary slavery."[120] The document is more inclusive of all forms of captivity and therefore may "well apply to cases that have not yet been given sustained legal consideration."[121]

"We must open our eyes to the myriad forms that ownership may take in the twenty-first century."[122] This is precisely what I shall do with the critique in chapter 3 of manufacturing iSlaves at Foxconn and then, in chapter 4, with an argument against manufactured iSlaves in Apple and the digital industries at large. Given this future orientation, it is only natural to wonder: Do the Guidelines need further updates under the circumstances of today's fast-evolving digital media? Does slavery, conceived as such, exist not only along the assembly line but also in the data mine?

# Concluding Remarks

The history of slavery and its legal definition constitute a vast corpus of literature. It is only possible to give, in one chapter, nothing more than a summary treatment to the topic. In the preceding pages I have first examined a few of the most vital historical patterns of slavery from ancient to present times. I have shown that slavery takes a great variety of forms that are often mutating and elusive. But slavery's main purpose, especially since the early modern era, is relatively stable. That is, to impose inequality upon certain members of society—often alienated "outsiders," women, people of color—in order to extract value from the exploitation of their labor and/or body.

Suppression breeds resistance. Abolition constitutes an equally fundamental theme in historical accounts, which, along with the expansion and contraction of the capitalist world system, has led to the wax and wane of the slave trade amid great geopolitical upheavals. A pillar for this slave-powered economy is the creation of a new culture that sustains consumption through communication, mediated persuasion, and marketing. In so doing, modernity itself is transformed into a manifold complex of intrinsic self-contradictions between freedom and bondage, enlightenment and backwardness, humanity and brutality.

The legal scholarship, albeit originating from a rather different lineage rooted in the past century of world politics and international justice systems, is surprisingly consistent with the central themes put forward by historians of slavery. Moreover, the legal scholars have responded to the thorny issues identified in historical studies by offering tangible guidelines such as moving from de jure status to de facto conditions of slavery and highlighting the exercise of "any or all of the powers attaching to the right of ownership." Debates, such as the one between Patterson and Bales,[123] are likely to continue, although these scholars would both concur, or so I believe, that slavery—however defined—continues to overshadow human civilization, that it is imperative to apply the historical and legal understandings to critiquing the world's problems today.

# 3

# Manufacturing iSlaves

The historical and legal studies of slavery, at least in my understanding, offer several crucial insights for an inquiry into iSlavery and forms of enslavement in this era of digital media:

- Rather than pre-modern or anti-modern, slavery—especially starting from the Atlantic triangular trade—is part and parcel of capitalist modernity.
- It is common for slavery to mutate over time with extraordinary elasticity.
- Slavery works through sociocultural alienation and political-economic domination.
- Resistance and abolition are fundamental to the transformation of slavery.
- Slave systems wax and wane, resulting from and accelerating geopolitical change.
- The goal of slavery is to exploit the labor and/or body of the enslaved.
- Hegemonic consumption culture, relying on media and communication technologies, is a pillar of slave-powered economies.

- Slavery is better defined as de facto condition rather than de jure status.
- The substance of slavery is "the powers attaching to the right of ownership," such as possession, use, transfer, profit, and disposal.
- Slavery and "institutions and practices similar to slavery" exist if *any* of the aforementioned "powers" is found to have been exercised.

My task, from here on, is to apply this framework in examining twenty-first-century slavery and digital labor conditions. First, in this chapter, I shall conduct a critical assessment of iSlave conditions in its first basic form of *manufacturing iSlaves*, as exemplified by Foxconn workers in China. Then, this framework will be applied in chapter 4 to shed light on the second domain of *manufactured iSlaves*, as in Apple's business model and the New Economy of apps in general. This will be followed by a discussion in chapter 5 on slave resistance and abolition movements from antiquity to the present.

Conceptually, the manufacturing mode of iSlavery consists of all the labor force required in the productive processes of digital media industries. It can be waged or unwaged, formal or informal, handling mostly tasks of material manipulation. There are many modes of manufacturing iSlaves—be they Congolese mine workers or Indonesian child labor.[1] Even though the following analysis focuses on Foxconn in China, the world's largest gadgets manufacturer, the overall argument is global in its scope: despite advances in technology, severe conditions of isolation and exploitation have persisted, even deteriorated, not only at particular times and places, not only to certain individuals, but systematically at the level of the world system.

## Foxconn: The Long Seventeenth Century

In 1974, as Terry Guo (Chinese name: Guo Tai-ming) started Hon Hai, a small Taiwanese factory making plastic parts for black-and-white TV sets,[2] no one expected his plant to churn out half the world's digital gadgets four decades later. In 1985, Hon Hai created the trademark

"Foxconn" for purposes of overseas expansion, including setting up assembly lines in mainland China, where its first facility, "Foxconn Ocean Precision Computer Components Factory," started operation in 1988.[3] By then, Guo had already been known among his Taiwanese peers as a ruthless character: "You want his money, he wants you dead!"[4]

After a decade of meteoric growth, Foxconn eliminated several of its competitors and became a leading supplier for almost all major global IT brands around the turn of millennium. In 2001 Guo hired Michael Chung, a high-level executive from Apple, to start a special unit producing Apple products.[5] This was a decisive move. A decade later, Foxconn would draw "60 to 70 percent of its revenue from assembling gadgets and other work for Apple Inc."[6]

As the company was on its way to becoming the largest exporter out of China, Guo remained relatively unknown to the public due to his "super-low-profile."[7] But by 2005, when he became the richest Taiwanese tycoon, Guo had already acquired a peculiar reputation for aggressiveness and frugality.[8]

The decade following 2005 witnessed the descent of Foxconn into the world's most fatal and notorious sweatshop. In 2006 a British newspaper reported terrible working conditions and low pay in one of Foxconn's facilities in Longhua, Shenzhen, infamously dubbed "the iPod city."[9] After losing his wife in 2005 to cancer and a bitter battle against mainland Chinese reporters in 2006,[10] Guo turned into the very opposite of his previous public image. Holding hands with female celebrities, he became for about two-and-a-half years "Taiwan's playboy tycoon" favored by Chinese paparazzi.[11]

Meanwhile, in 2008, a newly sold iPhone in the United Kingdom was found to contain the images of a lovely Foxconn worker, known as "the iPhone girl."[12] No one could confirm her identity. The incident was likely a PR stunt. It seemed, for a while, that Foxconn and its owner had mastered the art of diverting attention from workers' life and work—until the suicide of Sun Danyong in July 2009.[13]

Sun jumped from the twelfth floor after being interrogated by Foxconn guards because he lost an iPhone prototype. The Chinese press investigated and exposed the tragedy thoroughly. Foxconn admitted managerial problems and suspended the head of its security unit from duty.[14] A senior manager responsible for making iPhones also resigned as a result of pressure from Apple.[15] Few could foresee though that the case was the harbinger of something much worse: in the first five months of 2010, fifteen young workers jumped or fell from tall buildings to kill themselves (table 3.1).[16] Thirteen of them died; two others suffered injuries, with one paralyzed for life.

TABLE 3.1   List of Foxconn workers who jumped or fell to death from high places in the first five months of 2010

|   | Name | Gender | Age | Location | Time | Reason |
|---|------|--------|-----|----------|------|--------|
| 1 | RONG, Bo | Male | 19 | Langfang | Jan 8 | Jump from 8th floor |
| 2 | MA, Xiangqian | Male | 19 | Guanlan | Jan 23 | Fall from building |
| 3 | LI, Hongliang | Male | 28 | Longhua | March 11 | Jump from 5th floor |
| 4 | TIAN, Yu* | Female | 17 | Longhua | March 17 | Jump from 4th floor |
| 5 | LI, Wei | Male | 23 | Langfang | March 23 | Jump from 5th floor |
| 6 | LIU, Zhijun | Male | 23 | Longhua | March 29 | Jump from 14th floor |
| 7 | RAO, Shuqing* | Female | 18 | Guanlan | April 6 | Jump from 7th floor |
| 8 | NING, Yaoqiong | Female | 18 | Guanlan | April 7 | Jump from high place |
| 9 | LU, Xin | Male | 24 | Longhua | May 6 | Jump from 6th floor |
| 10 | ZHU, Chenming | Female | 24 | Longhua | May 11 | Jump from 9th floor |
| 11 | LIANG, Chao | Male | 21 | Longhua | May 14 | Jump from 7th floor |
| 12 | NAN, Gang | Male | 20 | Longhua | May 21 | Jump from 4th floor |
| 13 | LI, Hai | Male | 19 | Guanlan | May 25 | Jump from 4th floor |
| 14 | Mr. HE (Given name unknown) | Male | 23 | Longhua | May 26 | Jump from 7th floor |
| 15 | Mr. CHEN (Given name unknown)* | Male | 25 | Longhua | May 27 | Attempted to jump but was stopped. Cut his wrist. |

* survived with injury

Source: SACOM, *Workers as Machines: Military Management at Foxconn* (October 12, 2015), 2, available at http://ow.ly/MDak5 (accessed on May 7, 2015).

The terrible "Foxconn Suicide Express"[17] of fifteen workers trying to kill themselves in five months was followed by activist campaigns, during which "iSlave" emerged as a powerful meme against corporate misbehavior.[18] Foxconn and Apple have been targeted by the press, labor organizers, Chinese authorities, international NGOs, as well as artists, including Mike Daisey, whose monologue "The Agony and Ecstasy of Steve Jobs" caused major controversy in 2012.[19]

Among the most visible campaigns is the joint investigative team of students and scholars from twenty universities in mainland China, Taiwan, and Hong Kong (henceforth, "the twenty-university joint team"). Along with talented students of my university, I have taken part in this network, whose key node is SACOM (Students and Scholars Against Corporate Misbehavior, a Hong Kong-based labor NGO). Since 2010 the team has released four major reports on Foxconn, covering a wide range of issues, from suicide and salary to work injury and union operation.[20]

Appconn, on the other hand, has kept denying the allegations. Terry Guo blamed suicides on workers' "personal relationships," "breakups" and "family disputes,"[21] while Tim Cook and his executives emphasized Apple's admirable endeavor in ensuring labor standards.[22] However, in May 2013, after a dispute over Foxconn's production quality, Apple moved part of its supply chain to Pegatron, another Taiwanese manufacturer, marking a rare moment of distancing itself from Foxconn.[23]

High-profile suicides continued at Foxconn well into 2015, including the death of Xu Lizhi, a worker-poet who jumped from the seventeenth floor.[24] He gained much posthumous fame. As Emily Rauhala wrote for *Time* magazine:

Factory life [at Foxconn] made Xu feel like a machine, a half-human with a "stomach forged of iron / full of thick acid, sulfuric and nitric." The same jig that forced workers' "skin to peel" replaced their human tissue with a "layer of aluminum alloy." He felt dehumanized, stunted, as if the work itself was stealing his ability to conjure language beyond "working words" like "workshop, assembly line, machine, work card, overtime, wages . . ."[25]

With the release of iPhone 6 in late 2014, Foxconn, along with Pegatron, was targeted by BBC's *Panorama* in an episode titled "Apple's

Broken Promises" for abusing workers by forcing them to work exhaustingly long hours.[26] The twenty-university joint team report of 2014, for instance, found that overtime work at Foxconn far exceeds China's legal maximum of thirty-six overtime hours per month. In the busy season of 2014, assembly-line workers were found to have performed 140 hours of overtime work each month, several months in a row, sometimes up to 152 hours in the most hectic month—4.2 times beyond the legal cap.[27] Despite the slowing down of China's manufacturing sector, it was still reported in January 2015 that Terry Guo "expect(s) his executives to meet 30 percent year-on-year increases and has a very forceful management style."[28]

The plight of Foxconn workers has been heatedly discussed. Yet so many basic questions remain: Are the workers really willingly exploited because they are better paid and/or have nothing better to do? Did they commit suicide simply due to psychological problems and breakups? Is it true that Foxconn has been unfairly targeted because it is associated with Apple Inc.? Colorful and controversial as the Foxconn story has been, it would be better not to devote too much attention to corporate spin, bloody fanfare online, or so-called "expert opinions" from those who never set foot in the factory. Instead, the spotlight should be on the de facto conditions workers experience, as will be illuminated in the following pages.

Again, one may ask: Why does this electronics industry of assembling digital gadgets deserve our scrutiny? The usual answers are often exclusively contemporary, lacking historical depth. Yet as Slavoj Zizek points out about "the dialectic of the Old and the New": "It is those who propose the constant creation of new terms ('postmodern society,' 'risk society,' 'informational society,' 'postindustrial society,' etc.) in order to grasp what is going on today who miss the contours of what is actually New. The only way to grasp the true novelty of the New is to analyze the world through the lenses of what was 'eternal' in the Old."[29]

Slavery, as discussed in the previous chapter, is one such "novelty" from the seventeenth century. It is still around in this century that we call the twenty-first. For, after all, the institutions and practices similar to slave systems centuries ago are not completely gone. They just assume different forms.

## Foxconn Feitorias

Labor sociologists examine factories through their "factory regimes"—structures of production and discipline that regulate activities in the workplace.[30] Some of these regimes are more "despotic," as they use more brute force, others more "hegemonic" in their reliance on co-optation and their manipulation of organizational culture. Ruled by the world's largest communist party, China, with its version of capitalism, has become a "museum of factory regimes" because it harbors many kinds of regimes that would otherwise exist in very different time and space, from the old socialist *danwei* work-units to restructured state-owned enterprises to new monstrous systems such as Foxconn.[31] But when China's leading sociologist Shen Yuan spoke about this "museum of factory regimes," he did not refer to the *feitoria*, probably the oldest "factory" in history.

The word "factory" only came into the English language since the late sixteenth century, and only after the Victorian era did its meaning stabilize as a social unit of industrial activities, especially manufacture.[32] Yet, late-medieval Portuguese already had the word *feitorias*—not as places of production but as trading posts, trading no ordinary goods but slaves. These earliest "factories" were not in Europe. They were, instead, located mostly along the "slave coast" of West Africa. Among the most notorious feitorias was Lomboko on the coast of Sierra Leone, operated by the slave trader Pedro Blanco. Steven Spielberg's 1997 film *Amistad* depicted the destruction of Lomboko.[33]

The feitorias served the capitalist world-economy long before the rise of industrial capitalism. Far from units of manufacture, these were, in essence, little more than prisons where slaves were gathered from African hinterlands, first in small numbers, then accumulated into the hundreds, to be traded onto European slave ships. For reasons of transportation as well as defense, feitorias were usually found close to major river deltas of West Africa, such as the delta of the Escravos River in today's Nigeria. Escravos was the Portuguese word for "slaves."

The geographic location of feitorias parallels that of Foxconn, whose largest and most strategic facilities in China were in Shenzhen of the Pearl River Delta and in Suzhou of the Yangtze River Delta despite its move into the inland provinces in recent years.[34] These plants carried out the equivalent function of gathering labor power from the hinterlands, although their products of export were not "human cargo" but the gadgets manufactured. Was this geographic similarity merely a coincidence?

The feitorias were, on the other hand, military strongholds. Their main function was to constrain slaves who were only recently captured and subject to bondage by sealing off the place from unsanctioned outside contact. The militarized nature of the feitorias was prominent, with their armed guards and jurisdictional independence from local authorities. This was highly comparable to Michel Foucault's analysis in *Discipline and Punish*, where he argues that torture and bodily punishment work more effectively in a space of isolated enclosure.[35] These systems of discipline, be they prisons or feitorias, clearly anticipate Foxconn's "semi-military management factory regime" known for the social domination and alienation therein.[36]

• • •

An open admirer of Genghis Khan, Terry Guo rules Foxconn as if it were an army. He borrows explicit terms from the Taiwanese military to name the rank and file of his manufacturing troops, whose total number exceeded 1.4 million in 2013 (slightly larger than all of the U.S. armed forces combined).[37] The central unit to monitor productivity is called *Zhanqingshi*, meaning literally "War Intelligence Office."[38] According to a Chinese book praising Terry Guo, "Visiting the Longhua campus [of Foxconn] in Shenzhen, you could feel the atmosphere of an army officer training school. . . . In the soccer field located at the center of factory buildings, new employees were practicing military drills. Five of them formed a row, chanting slogans loudly."[39]

Approaching Foxconn Longhua (which contained four hundred thousand workers in 2010, when most suicides occurred in this facility), one would find huge signs with bold Chinese characters, the kinds one would see near military bases in China, which read: "This factory area is legally established with state approval. Unauthorized trespassing is prohibited. Offenders will be sent to police for prosecution!" Of the hundreds of Chinese factory entrances I've seen, there is no other place with such intimidating signs.

I thought this was meant only to scare off journalists and members of the general public. But even a policeman complained to me in 2013, "You know what they did? They gave me speed tickets!"[40] This officer never expected to receive speed tickets because he drives a police vehicle. Yet he had to pay a fine for breaking Foxconn's traffic rules, suggesting that the enclosure of Foxconn feitorias was indeed beyond the jurisdiction of local government.

On the shop floor and in the neighborhood, Foxconn guards are known for their brutality toward workers and eagerness to bully them. In Longhua alone, there were once more than one thousand guards in 2010. During a survey of 1,736 Foxconn workers conducted in nine cities and twelve facilities during summer 2010, 16.4 percent reported being subject to physical penalty by guards, or managers using guards to threaten them; 38.1 percent had experiences of being detained by guards or managers; 54.6 percent felt angry about the way they were managed.[41] "If a guard sees something wrong with you," a worker said, "he'd come and give you a couple slaps in the face. It was very common."[42]

During the Atlantic slave trade, "violence cascaded downward, from captain and officers to sailors to the enslaved."[43] In a similar fashion, Foxconn organizes itself using a hierarchy of thirteen tiers, demanding employees to be obedient to their superiors.[44] Workers are sealed within this structure, where they are normally expected to report to their supervisors only. If they feel they are being abused or threatened by guards, and they want to call the police by dialing 110 (the standard police hotline throughout China), they cannot reach the local police. Instead, they reach Foxconn guards. The company, like the feitorias, is an independent kingdom in itself. This institutional setup can be deemed as similar to slavery, for it "restrict[s] free movement or access to state authorities."[45]

There are many horrifying accounts of Foxconn guards abusing workers, torturing, maiming, and killing them, which have spread like ghost stories. "There is an underground chamber where the guards dismember workers they killed. A friend told me he saw them taking body parts from there and tossing them into the sea."[46] "The guards were weirdly quiet last night after they went out to beat a worker named Liang Chao. They slept early without having some evening food, which was their routine. Then this Liang Chao became the ninth jumper."[47] It is hard to assess the validity of these accounts, whose psychological effect upon the workforce is, however, not to be underestimated.

Sometimes there is ample evidence about the brutality of guards, as in the case of Ma Xiangqian, who was "suicided" (*beizisha*) in January 2010.[48] Of the fifteen jumpers in 2010, Ma was the only one whose reason for death, according to police record, was "death due to fall from tall building" (*gaozhui shenwang*) rather than "death due to jump from high place" (*tiaolou shenwang*). Even though the police never announced Ma's case as murder, his sister told reporters of *Asia Weekly*:

> There are serious bruises on my brother's chest. His forehead is scarred, skin broken next to his eyes. Bloodstains are visible on his chest, which is severely dented and black-purple in color. What's more, the second autopsy found four nail holes through his scull. His medial calf has nail holes, too. Some silver-white metal pieces are inserted in his shoulder. A large wound is on his head. Six severe abrasions are found on his arms. A piece of meat is also missing on his wrist, now covered by a wrist band which I've never seen my brother wear before.[49]

These journalists saw photographic evidence of Ma's injury, while reporters from another news organization were able to confirm instances of guard brutality among victims in three different Foxconn plants. There, workers referred to factory guards as *jinyiwei*, or brocade-clad guards, the imperial secret police of Ming Dynasty known in Chinese history for their vicious torture and interrogation techniques.[50] This is how ordinary employees perceive those who run the twenty-first-century equivalent of the feitorias.

$\bullet \quad \bullet \quad \bullet$

I had a surreal encounter in 2011 with one of the guards in Foxconn's Guanlan facility in Shenzhen.[51] Because I went with students who called me "Teacher Qiu," a guard thought I must be one of the "teachers" supervising Foxconn's many "student interns" (a topic to be discussed in more detail in the next section). Well paid by schools sending students and labor-market intermediaries to work for Foxconn, these "teachers" didn't really teach, except when their students became less obedient and wanted to leave the factory.[52] Not infrequently these "teachers" need the guards to teach the disobedient students a lesson, not in class but in the back alleys.

This well-built guard thought I was one of the "teachers." He came to me. "Teacher Qiu, phone me if you need my help," he said and offered me his mobile number. Looking at me straight in the eye, he added, "But no need to call me if it's not big business." He made the hand gesture for money, indicating clearly that by "big business" he meant some considerable amount of cash. Does that mean he was offering to hurt people seriously if I want to hire him? How seriously and how much would it cost?

Astonished by his candor, I was speechless for a minute, as he started rambling about why he needs to "help" me. He said he was a seasoned migrant, almost killed during the 2009 Urumqi ethnic riots in China's Muslim northwest. "From then on, I've decided all I want to do in this lifetime is to fucking enjoy myself: to eat well, drink well, and find good female company."

He boasted about his gang activities in another city, which kept him busy fighting every other day, and he won most of the fights—or so he said, perhaps to assure me of his abilities. For him, it was exciting, lucrative, although it meant he was too busy to find girls. "But this year in Foxconn, it's not exciting at all because we cannot hit workers like before last year (2010, the year of Suicide Express). It's so boring." He complained, "Although I have free time now, more than enough time for girls, I find myself short of cash. This is why I need more business from you, Teacher Qiu!"

Again, I have no ground to judge if he was exaggerating or lying, although it was clear he was trying his best to sell me a violent service, disciplining my students so long as I paid him well. Wearing the Foxconn guard uniform, he looked relaxed and confident, talking to me in broad daylight at a major intersection of the dormitory area, a sign that he probably took this as "normal business." He was sincere in talking "business"—as if I had "powers attaching to the right of ownership" over "my" student interns.

This was nothing more than an intriguing anecdote, which needs to be taken against the backdrop of a widespread complaint: when workers lost their personal items in the factory, the guards almost never care to investigate.[53] Is it because they are too busy with their own "business"?

. . .

Besides physical penalty and bullying, there are other practices echoing slavery in its classic barbarity. *Factory Gossip* (*gongchang longmenzhen*) was an underground magazine edited by several Shenzhen workers, including Foxconn workers. Its seventh issue, published in April 2013, focused on the scandalous factory.[54] One essay discussed the aftermath of the suicide tragedies in 2010, when Foxconn promised to increase salaries, set up care centers for workers, and transform their strict hierarchy into "humane flavor management system (*renxinghua guanli tixi*)." But "Where is the 'humane flavor'?" the author asked. "How come I seldom smell it?"[55]

Another article cites a teenage worker who discussed Foxconn's hiring process and how he felt about it. Altogether he had to go through seven steps, including a written exam, interview, and physical examination. One of the steps was to check if the applicants had disabilities: "I felt I was stupid, being picked by others like an animal."[56]

A separate interview conducted in another Foxconn plant revealed more details. The worker interviewed was asked, during the recruitment process, to remove all clothing on his upper body and then to extend and retract his arms to show he had no physical disability. To prove he was not deaf or dumb, he had to shout his name loudly. "I had this feeling at the time that I was a commodity on sale. The master [*zhurenjia*, or the Foxconn manager] was looking for those who are physically healthy and strong, those he could purchase paying the price of two horses, whereas others do not even deserve to become commodities."[57] Here the analogy was palpable, although the worker did not mention the slave trade explicitly.

. . .

A common misunderstanding in public discussion was that Foxconn workers chose to stay, endure monotonous work and poor conditions there, which were in any case still better than elsewhere. Is this true? Can someone really choose to leave feitorias at will?

Difficulty in quitting one's job was a common problem among workers, especially when the factory is short on hands.[58] This was the case of a factory girl I interviewed who had to go through a long and arduous process to leave Foxconn in 2011.[59] According to China's labor law, workers do not need approval from the employer when they decide to quit. All they need is to inform the management. Yet the law was hidden from workers, who were instead required to obtain dozens of approvals. In her case, she had to approach more than three dozen supervisors, mostly strangers to her, and get a total number of thirty-eight signatures before Foxconn let her go. "Had I been a little less persistent," she said, "I probably would have never left there. It was so hard to get hold of the managers because they were busy. It was even harder to find them in different buildings because, as an ordinary worker, I didn't have the e-permit to enter. I had to wait many hours outside and sometimes could not get a single signature after a whole day waiting. It took me almost two months to gather the thirty-eight signatures."

This is but one method for the company to exercise control over workers, to keep them from leaving. Even though this is not done using shackles or chains, the result of reducing labor mobility and workers' legal rights is similar in substance. In this case of preventing the worker from quitting, both deception and coercion were involved. She was deceived to think there was no other way out except following Foxconn's rules. She was coerced because, otherwise, she would not have her wages back. Such measures of constraint "constitute control over a person in such a way as to significantly deprive that person of his or her individual liberty."[60]

Enslavement occurs "with the intent of exploitation through the use, management, profit, transfer or disposal of that person."[61] These "practices similar to slavery" are most evident in the cases of "students interns [*xueshenggong*]" at Foxconn. The aforementioned Foxconn guard mistook me for one of those "teachers" because every year so many interns were sent from vocational high schools to work on the assembly lines.[62] Due to seasonality, the total number fluctuates. In 2010, for instance, Foxconn had between 76,000 and 150,000 student interns at any given time, making it by far the world's largest internship program.[63]

China's 2010 education law stipulates that student interns cannot work for forty hours each week. Yet, in Foxconn Shenzhen, usually student interns had to work sixty hours each week.[64] Most of the interns are in their late teens or early twenties, although underaged minors as young as fourteen were found in the Yantai plant, for which Foxconn has formally aplogized.[65]

I interviewed a dozen student interns from 2010 to 2012. Most of them came from Henan Province in Central China to the Longhua or Guanlan facility in Shenzhen, South China. At school, their majors were business management, English, education, accountancy, Chinese medicine. In Foxconn, nearly all of them did one thing: make iPhone cases. None of them had a labor contract.[66]

The work was repetive, boring, and had nothing to do with their studies. No wonder most of them wanted to escape. It was most demanding for these teenagers who often had to stand there ten hours a day, maintaining the same body posture in order to work more effeciently. According to their male line-leaders, whom I interviewed, by the end of the first week, the constant standing and working would cause all female students to have sore legs so painful that they would cry. In the second week, the male students would be in tears.[67] But they had to be there because completing internship was a graduation requirement.

In 2012, Foxconn denied using forced student labor.[68] Yet in 2013 the violations—of Chinese law as well as Foxconn's internal regulation—were still found by a *Financial Times* report in Foxconn Yantai.[69] Another 2014 report by Earl Brown, labor and employment law counsel at the AFL-CIO Solidarity Center, and his colleague Kyle DeCant, concluded that these vocational school internships "violate the International Labor Organization's convention on forced labor" partly because the system "operate[s] under the menace of penalty by withholding diplomas when interns refuse to engage in their work assignments and by denying students access to complaint mechanisms."[70]

Student interns provide "flexible, cheap, and obedient labor."[71] This was, more precisely, a situation of Foxconn's borrowing or renting the labor power of the teenagers from their schools for the purpose of profit. The work was supposed to be educational, but the tasks had little to do with students' major of study. They were there because they had no other choice; because they accepted that their schools "possess" their time, and now that their teachers order them to work in Foxconn, they became the factory's possession as well.

Such use of "student interns" qualifies as "practices similar to slavery" because, according to the Bellagio-Harvard Guidelines: "In evaluating the particular circumstances to determine whether slavery exists, reference should be made to the substance and not simply to the form of the relationship in question."[72] "Evidence of profiting from the use of a person may include cases where a person is mortgaged, *lent for profit*, or used as collateral" (emphasis added).[73]

．．．

Whereas workers had to go through humiliating processes to get hired and the factory made it extremely difficult for workers/interns to quit at will, it could not be easier for Foxconn to lay off employees when deemed necessary. In December 2009, due to market downturn, Foxconn fired forty thousand workers at once all over China. This was not too difficult because the company avoided having direct contractual relationship with workers by hiring from job-market intermediaries, a practice that was also found in Foxconn's facilities in Turkey and the Czech Republic.[74] Other workers were either "interns" or workforce "provided" by state agencies in charge of labor export from inland provinces. These workers were conveniently rendered dispensable in the legal loophole because Foxconn did not directly hire them.

As for those who had a signed contract with Foxconn, the company also found ways to reduce their monthly salary to 500 yuan, or $73, thus coercing them to quit their jobs "voluntarily."[75] Ironically, market demand recovered at the beginning of 2010, and Foxconn laid off too many "disposable" workers. The company then announced thirty thousand job vacancies on the website of China's Ministry of Commerce in March 2010, less than four months after it fired forty thousand workers. "How could Foxconn hire and fire tens of thousands of workers at will?" analysts remarked. "How could Foxconn play with human resources in such an effortless way? What's the trick?"[76]

The trick was simple: evade legal obligation to employees, who were rendered, often unknowingly, into the ultimate "flexible labor." "This semi-militarized management system is really worse than real military systems," said a Foxconn worker, "because they can get rid of you anytime they want."[77] In this case, "anytime" includes times of market slowdown as well as times of work injury or vocational disease when workers became costly liabilities to the company, when their bodies, no longer worth exploiting, are discarded as during the nightmare of the Middle Passage.

## The Middle Passage

A critical parallel between Foxconn and the slave trade system in history has to do with the extremely poor conditions of living the enslaved have to endure. The filthiness, stinking air, and insecurity could be found not only on slave ships making the notorious Middle Passage to cross the Atlantic but also in Foxconn dormitories at the beginning of the twenty-first century.

Although feitorias were militarized enclosures, their hygiene was not the worst because the slaves had to be fed and protected from diseases so that they could be "tradable" anytime the slave ships arrived (which the feitorias' rulers often did not know until the actual arrival). The worst conditions of living were, on the other hand, found onboard the slavers, especially its "lower deck," when the ships journeyed to the New World.[78]

On the slave ships, the captain and crew usually stayed in upper deck or on deck, while the lower deck was used to store food, water, and trading goods, including "human cargo." Shackles prevented slaves from moving freely. Slaves were extremely densely packed, as depicted in the classic image of the slave ship, the *Brooks*, which "showed in gruesome, concrete detail that the slaver was itself a place of barbarity, indeed a huge, complex, technologically sophisticated instrument of torture" (see figure 3.1).[79] As English politician William Wilberforce told the House of Commons in 1789 about horrible conditions in the lower deck: "So much misery condensed in so little room is more than the human imagination had ever before conceived."[80]

Living conditions in Foxconn were better than the lower deck. At least workers are not physically locked up or chained down. But there are still similarities. First is the size and density. When undercover reporters

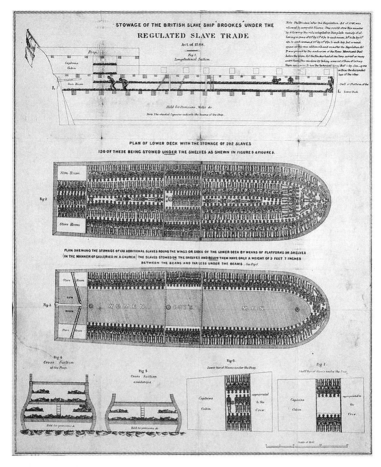

FIGURE 3.1   The slave ship *Brooks* and its plan of lower deck, 1788.
Source: U.S. Library of Congress (digital ID: cph.3a34658).

visited Foxconn Longhua in 2006, they entered the Peace Dormitory Building to see nearly three hundred workers packed in one huge storage room. They slept on three-level bunk beds in a crowded space without air conditioning.

According to a Foxconn worker, who lived there: "When I first walked in, I was truly shocked. It was summer time. The odor of sweat and dirty feet was suffocating."[81] The reporters noted: "The situation was appalling. Looking inside from the entrance, we saw a thick formation of bunker beds covering the entire dormitory. Although there were five windows and electric fans, we were still caught by strong unpleasant odor."[82]

These observations resonate with the lower deck of a slaver, known in historical records as "hot, crowded, stinking."[83] The slaver usually traveled along the equator to go from West Africa to the Americas; the Foxconn dormitories in Shenzhen were also located in the tropical zone of South China. Although Foxconn installed some electric ceiling fans, in general ventilation was probably not a whole lot better than the lower deck.

Fortunately, when the twenty-university team visited Foxconn in 2010, they did not see similar dorm conditions of several hundred people sharing one gigantic room. The improvement was likely a result from media coverage in 2006 about the "iPod City."[84] However, smaller dormitories did not prevent tragedies of suicide, yet another grisly reminder that today's world is still haunted by seventeenth-century slavery.

· · ·

Physical condition being merely one indicator, as Patterson argued, slavery works more significantly through social isolation and "natal alienation."[85] This was precisely what Pun and Chan found in what they term Foxconn's "dormitory labor regime," which was tightly interwoven with the factory production regime.[86] That is, in these dormitories, workers were intentionally shuffled and atomized so that friends, classmates, and colleagues on the same production line would be separated while off duty. Even married couples working in the factory were put on day and night shifts separately. A wife, for instance, could only see her husband two or three times a month.[87]

Only after the Suicide Express of 2010 did Foxconn start to change its policy to atomize workers by allowing friends, classmates, or those on the same assembly line to become dorm mates. Until then, the dormitories were little more than spaces of strangers subjugated in a system of "total management," designed to control workers around the clock so that their social ties can be severed to the maximum extent and their socializing activities reduced to the minimum.

In the film *12 Years a Slave* a heartbreaking scene is rendered when Eliza, a female slave, was separated from her children because they were sold to different owners. This was but one of countless instances when African slaves were forced to be parted, first from their families and relatives after capture, then over and again from their friends and shipmates, before and after the Middle Passage.

Of all these separations, a most important historical archive is the narratives of Olaudah Equiano, a slave boy.[88] After being snatched by raiders in central Nigeria, he was first pulled apart from his sister. Then he was sold multiple times, each time being uprooted from a new social environment he was just getting accustomed to. Finally, he survived the Middle Passage, making friends among his shipmates, who gave him "the small comfort of being together." But such "small comfort" was torn away once again when they reached the New World and had to go different ways.[89]

Separation and isolation are among the most quintessential experiences of being a dehumanized slave. This was true for African slaves centuries ago as much as it was for Chinese workers who had to live under the dormitory labor regime of Foxconn. Although there are notable differences in the degree and methods of coercion, the origin of such atomization was the same: essentially, these are efforts to structure a worker's life—not just work, but life in the holistic sense, 24/7, throughout the year—for the goal of profit maximization.

Under such extremely exploitative logic, workers' social lives are not only insignificant, they may even be seen as detrimental to productivity. Foxconn workers know it well: they are treated as machines that need no socializing. "Women are treated as men, and men as animals" was a common saying among the workforce. The consequences were thus similar to the isolation of African and African American slaves from each other. Living in atomized social conditions prevents workers from fully relaxing and recovering from their hard work; instead, it adds to their sense of insecurity, loneliness, and anxiety, undermining their psychological well-being.

· · ·

Among the most hideous crimes committed during the Middle Passage was the disposal of slaves deemed as liabilities with little or no commercial value. Sometimes slaves were tossed into the ocean because the ship carried too much "human cargo" and was short on supply of water or food, as shown in another horrible scene depicted in Spielberg's *Amistad*, or because the ship ran aground, as in the notorious case of the *Zong*.[90] More often it was because the slaves were sick or injured, requiring medical care.[91]

As the Guidelines specify: "Disposal of a person following his or her exploitation may provide evidence of slavery."[92] This could also be observed in some of the most well-known cases involving injured workers at Foxconn.

Zhang Tingzhen was a Foxconn technician who reportedly fell while fixing a lamp twelve feet off the ground on October 26, 2011.[93] Within ten minutes, he was in a Foxconn vehicle. The nearest hospital was less than two miles away, and there was little traffic. But it took ninety minutes for him to be hospitalized. The delay—which his families suspect was deliberate—almost killed him. After surgeries, Tingzhen survived but his left-brain had to be surgically removed. Having lost most of his ability to speak and think, he cannot work anymore.

Tingzhen's families expected Foxconn to accept its legal responsibilities. To their dismay, however, the company refused to do so because, although Tingzhen worked for Hongfujin, Foxconn's main subsidiary in Shenzhen, the company insists that he belonged to the Foxconn plant in Huizhou, a city where Tingzhen never set foot in.[94] But using Huizhou rather than Shenzhen standards, Foxconn could save roughly $55,000 in compensation.

There were many points of suspicion as the family was stonewalled when they did their best to learn about what happened, obtain evidence from Foxconn, and seek justice. They doubt the authenticity of Tingzhen's signature on his labor contract with Foxconn Huizhou because it does not look like his handwriting. They asked Foxconn to show Tingzhen's personnel files, his factory ID, and the surveillance video when he was injured. However, despite court order, the company cold-bloodedly denied access to all crucial evidence.[95]

*Yangcheng Evening News* reported on one of the case's court hearings and used a cartoon to illustrate the company's arrogant indifference. It depicted a Foxconn manager speaking condescendingly to the injured worker: "Sorry, you do not have a *de facto* employment relationship with me" (see figure 3.2).[96]

"They have lost all the conscience under heaven!" said Tingzhen's father, who had many brawls with Foxconn guards. When he reported to the police, he was laughed at. The police said, "You know what level of authorities they have connection to? You think they will care if I intervene?"

Far from an isolated case, I have met similar victims of work injury at Foxconn elsewhere. Another example is Yang Dan, who joined Foxconn in 2009 and was exposed to benzene, among other prohibited poisonous chemicals there. In 2014 she was diagnosed with leukemia, but Foxconn has been trying to evade their responsibilities despite court orders.[97] Several similar cases were depicted in the influential documentary film *Who Pays the Price? The Human Costs of Electronics*, produced by Harvard

FIGURE 3.2 Work-injury victim, Zhang Tingzhen, being stonewalled by Hongfujin, Foxconn's main subsidiary in Shenzhen.
Source: Yangcheng Evening News, December 19, 2013.

researcher Heather White and her colleague Lynn Zhang.[98] The victims were from Foxconn as well as other electronics contract manufacturers making iPhone as well as Samsung products.

Why is it so hard for employees with work injuries or occupational disease to receive basic care and compensation according to the minimum legal requirements of Chinese law? Some say it is the factory being too stingy; some say it is the local government being bought off; some say it is the workers being unskillful and their families too greedy. These claims may be partially applicable in different cases. But much more important, something larger is amiss: larger than the individual, larger than the factory, larger than China, larger than this strange modern world-system of digital gadgets. As Yuezhi Zhao points out, a key step is to "re-root" and "re-historicize" our understandings in a much larger conceptual framework[99]—which, for our purposes here, is slavery.

## Suicide Prevention Nets

Suicides—more than four centuries ago on the slave ships, or in Foxconn neighborhoods in 2010—result from extreme existential despair. It was, at the same time, an ultimate act of defiance to free oneself from that despair while denying the "powers attaching to the right of ownership." One criterion of slavery, according to the Guidelines, is that it "significantly deprive[s] that person of his or her individual liberty for a period of time which is, for that person, *indeterminate*" (emphasis added).[100] Using this definition, one does not have to be controlled for the entire lifetime to become a victim of slavery or "practices similar to slavery." It qualifies so long as one perceives that the enslavement will last for an unspecified period. This mental perception, created by systematic suppression, severe alienation, and a deep sense of disempowerment, leads to suicide.

Occurring from time to time in the feitorias, suicide was much more commonplace during the Middle Passage, when life was so miserable and the future so indeterminate. Hunger strike was almost incessant onboard the slavers to such a degree that Rediker sighed, "The Atlantic slave trade was, in many senses, a four-hundred-year hunger strike."[101]

Meanwhile, slaves also chose to "cut their own throats, with hard-edged tools, sharp objects, or their own fingernails."[102]

Another way of suicide was jumping overboard, which meant imminent death because many Africans were from the hinterlands and could not swim, and because the sailors discarded slaves—dead or alive—into the ocean such that sharks would follow the ships, anticipating. Yet the slaves threw themselves into the ocean anyway attempting to free themselves from the unbearable miseries onboard, to refuse being treated like animals, to return to their home villages, as many of them believed.[103] Such suicide jumps happened so often that it endangered the profit margin of the trade in human cargo, to such an extent that the captains made a special request: "Netting, a fencelike assemblage of ropes, would be stretched by the crew around the ship to prevent slaves from jumping overboard."[104]

Some attentive readers may ask, if the slaves were in shackles and constrained in the lower deck, how could they jump overboard? The reason was profit. In order to maximize the sales of slaves, the crew had to minimize death rates among slaves during the Middle Passage. One method was to bring the slaves on deck, ask or force them to sing and dance, so that they could stretch their bodies and inhale fresh air. It was often in such a "singing and dancing" session when slaves jumped overboard into the ocean. Sometimes the slaves had to first free themselves from shackles; sometimes they jumped with their hands cuffed. Some were immediately drowned or killed by sharks, others brought back by the crew to face more torture and humiliation.

The autobiography of Olaudah Equiano gave a vivid description: "One day, when we had a smooth sea and moderate wind, two of my wearied countrymen who were chained together (I was near them at the time), preferring death to such a life of misery, somehow made through the nettings and jumped into the sea: immediately another quite dejected fellow, who, on account of his illness, was suffered to be out of irons also followed their example."[105]

The "suicide prevention net" was among the most mind-boggling inventions from the transatlantic slave trade. The real goal was not to protect slaves from themselves but to safeguard business revenue. Since the trade was abolished in the nineteenth century, anti-jumping nets

FIGURE 3.3   Slave ship equipped with anti-jumping net as depicted by Olaudah Equiano, 1745–1797. Source: Robert Riggs, "Aboard a Slave Ship," *Life*, September 3, 1956, p. 57.

had become obsolete, almost completely forgotten—until they suddenly appeared again, atop Foxconn buildings where iPhones and iPads were made.

•   •   •

In summer 2010, Foxconn installed more than three million square meters of "prevention and protection nets" in its various facilities around China.[106] As shown in figure 3.4, these were made either from steel netting and erected on the rooftops of tall buildings to prevent workers from jumping (the term for these was "sky net") or from strong fabrics spread out like skirts in the lower parts of buildings in order to catch those jumping from windows (called "ground net"). All the staircases, windows, and balconies were also sealed using steel rods ("middle net"). From tall buildings nearby, these Foxconn anti-jumping nets look like fences of a vast concentration camp, floating mid-air.[107]

The emergence of suicide prevention nets is unprecedented in the entire history of industrial capitalism founded, supposedly, on a "free"

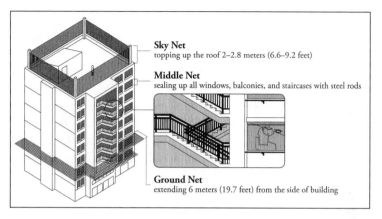

**Sky Net**
topping up the roof 2–2.8 meters (6.6–9.2 feet)

**Middle Net**
sealing up all windows, balconies, and staircases with steel rods

**Ground Net**
extending 6 meters (19.7 feet) from the side of building

FIGURE 3.4   A typical Foxconn dormitory building with anti-jumping nets.
Drawn by Kwan Kei Heung.

labor force. Terry Guo called the anti-jumping nets "a foolish solution, but a solution anyway."[108] However, from May to August 2010, workers continued to jump and commit suicide in at least four different Foxconn plants. In the last case, a female worker was indeed saved thanks to the "ground net" of her building.[109]

In August 2010, to reduce the scandalous effect of the nettings, Foxconn announced it would dismantle all of them and rely on the "web of human hearts" instead, meaning it would give workers more social and psychological care. Walking around the Guanlan plant in spring 2016, I still saw anti-jumping nets atop tall Foxconn buildings, attesting the throwback from twenty-first-century to seventeenth-century slavery reducing humans to objects of possession by their "owners."

• • •

Why did the suicides happen? Terry Guo and his associates pointed fingers at Chinese society and inappropriate media coverage. Above all, they emphasized the psychological problems of workers being too young, volatile, and egocentric.[110] One would wonder, though: Why doesn't Foxconn hire workers who are more mature? Why can't the company retain employees with more experience? Five years after the tragic

Suicide Express, young workers in their late teens and early twenties still account for the bulk of Foxconn's workforce in China.[111] Are they still in grave danger?

Another claim was that the company's compensation for employee death was so generous that the workers wanted to get it for their families.[112] There were more reasons to blame the deceased, while the shrewd corporate brains probably forgot to ask themselves: Would an egocentric kid jump from the roof just to make his or her family rich? Does this act of altruism make sense if the worker indeed only cared about himself or herself?

Guo famously declared that, although the number of jumping suicides might look high, it was actually not the case because his company has such a huge workforce. Quoting the psychologists he hired, Guo asserted Foxconn's suicide rate was "in fact slightly below the lower margin of national average."[113] Is this true?

There are a few fallacies here. First, Foxconn's number of suicides only included jumpers, which cannot be equated with the total number of suicide cases. Even in Hong Kong, a city more densely packed with tall buildings than Foxconn's factory zone, jumpers usually only account for half of all completed suicides.[114] Among attempted suicides, other methods such as poisoning, cutting, or hanging are much more common.

Back in 2007, there were reports about Foxconn workers hanging or poisoning themselves to death, but such cases were peculiarly absent from the 2010 Suicide Express figures—likely because they happened within the dormitory regime in ways that were much more private, hence more easily hidden from the public. Otherwise, the actual total number of suicides among Foxconn workers must have been significantly higher than the reported cases of jumping or falling. This should be common sense, although most reporters covering the tragic events failed to see the not-too-nuanced difference between "jumpers" and "suicides."

Second, national average was too crude an indicator. As in other countries, suicide rates in China are considerably higher among senior citizens and in rural areas, but among young members of the urban workforce they tend to be much lower. A more sensible comparison should be with the suicide rates of young urbanites instead of the national average as a whole. This is especially the case because, if we examine the age of the deceased in table 3.1, it is clear that, except for a twenty-eight-year-old victim, all the other fourteen were no more than twenty-five years old, the best time of life. Six of them were teenagers.

Most important, according to *The Economist*, China's suicide rates had declined dramatically since the late 1990s.[115] Paul Yip, a renowned suicide researcher, praised China: "No country has ever achieved such a rapid decline in suicides."[116] Yet, even in the 1990s when a spike of national suicide rates was recorded, there was no such Suicide Express in any Chinese factory. Should national statistics be referenced, would 2010 be the least likely to have become such a tragic year? Or perhaps it is instead the case that, rather than "slightly below the lower margin of national average," as Terry Guo claimed, Foxconn's suicide rates were indeed an anomaly in the context of China's national trends?

Liu Huashan, an independent psychology professor, provided an alternative estimation.[117] First he calculated that the average suicide rate among Chinese university students (a more comparable demographic group than the national population as a whole) is between 2 and 4 per 100,000 people each year. But in May 2010 alone, six people killed themselves in Foxconn Longhua. Extrapolating this figure, he concluded that the annual rate of suicides would be 24 per 100,000 for Foxconn as a whole. In other words, Foxconn's suicide rate, even using jumping cases only, would be six to twelve times higher than the average rate among college students.

One may see this comparison as inappropriate because college students are understandably less pressured and better taken care of than factory workers. That is perhaps correct. However, while a smaller difference may be within the acceptable range, this margin of six to twelve times higher is simply too wide to be normal. Otherwise, if Foxconn's 2010 suicide rate is "close to the lower margin of national average," does it mean the company should be rewarded before and after 2010 for its suicide rates being truly exceptionally low? What about other other factories in China, including other Taiwanese-owned factories, whose suicide rates are far below Foxconn's? Why did others never even consider erecting "anti-jumping nets," following practices of enslavement that was only "normal" during the Middle Passage?

. . .

It is unfair, though, to blame Foxconn as the only culprit. Although the company does stand out with its military-style management system, unparalleled size, and unique installation of suicide prevention nets, researchers have also traced the harshness of its system to pressures from Apple Inc.[118]

The problem of employee suicide is notable in other companies of the IT industry. Huawei, China's leading telecom brand, had three instances of jumping suicides between August 2007 and February 2008.[119] Samsung, the preeminent Korean corporation, also lost two workers who leaped to their deaths in January 2011.[120] These were far fewer than Foxconn's Suicide Express, when fifteen workers committed suicides in five months. But for some reason, employees of the global digital industries, of Appconn as a whole, indeed seem to be more suicidal compared to most other sectors.

A similarly gruesome case would be the string of thirty-five suicides at France Telecom / Orange over the two years from 2008 through 2009, and another "suicide epidemic" involving ten Orange staff from January to March 2014.[121] These tragedies involved a variety of suicide methods, such as stabbing and poisoning, not just jumping. Under public pressure, the French authorities under Sarkozy intervened, and the company's president and CEO, Didier Lombard, had to resign in 2010. In 2012, he "was placed under formal investigation for psychological harassment" that caused the suicides.[122] Even though the case was closed in January 2015 without indicting Lombard, the accusations against him "may return to court."[123]

Comparatively speaking, what did China do? How did the Communist Party of the People's Republic compare vis-á-vis the supposedly right-wing politicians in France? Foxconn enjoys decidedly more impunity in China than France Telecom did in France. There is a geopolitical reason behind the political and economic dynamics of Taiwan-Mainland China interactions, which will be discussed in chapter 5.

There is also a reason with regard to the global system: while the "suicide epidemic" of France Telecom peaked during 2008–2009, Foxconn's Suicide Express went out of control in early 2010. Could this timing be more than coincidental? Analyzing France Telecom suicides in a Durkheimian framework, Sara Waters contends that the root reasons are to be found in finance capitalism.[124] This can in part explain why the Foxconn suicides and the France Telecom tragedies happened around the same time. It also makes one wonder: Would the companies be less fatal if Foxconn or France Telecom / Orange were not listed on the stock market?

Before the Global Financial Crisis, hospitals in Longhua were filled with Foxconn workers who "merely" lost fingers or fingertips at work. They outnumbered hospital beds and had to sleep in the corridors. But 2010, the year of suicides, was the post-crisis year when Appconn, including all major global IT players, pushed hard to maximize profit in order to make up losses in the 2008–9 recession.

Boom-bust-boom: the pressure fell on Foxconn, which then passed it downward through its military-style management system to *buquanxu* workers at the very bottom of the hierarchy. The term *buquanxu* originates from the Taiwanese army: it's the lowest rank. Most jumpers in 2010 belonged to this rank, including Tian Yu, probably the most famous of Foxconn survivors who once attempted suicide.

## A Testimony of Tian Yu

Why on earth did so many workers choose to end their lives? Answers to this question should preferably come from the victims themselves because the social meanings of suicides "must be constructed by the individuals committing them and by others involved through their interactions with each other."[125] Sadly, most of the suicidal workers have passed away. Although some left behind words that were released by Foxconn to confirm the company's claims about the reasons of suicides (for example, psychological illness or the company's high compensation for employee death),[126] these were little more than an exceedingly partial and selective snapshot of reality.

Fortunately, there is one such survivor, an exceptional window through which invaluable insights can be gained on the social and mental world of Foxconn workers who attempted to take their own lives. Her name is Tian Yu, the fourth and the youngest among reported cases of the Foxconn Suicide Express (table 3.1). She was seventeen when she jumped on March 17, 2010, from the fourth floor of her dormitory building, which is in fact six stories from ground level because the first two stories are used as warehouse. After twelve days in coma, she miraculously woke up—although, due to severe spine injury, she will have to spend the rest of her life in a wheelchair. My research team was lucky to find and talk to her in the hospital, keeping in touch with her and her family.

There are admittedly only limited grounds to take Tian Yu's experience as representative of all the other deceased. However, at least her case suffices to dismiss the company's blaming of workers' individual vulnerabilities as the main cause of tragedy, to show how Foxconn's management system was the main culprit due to its "institutions and practices similar to slavery."

. . .

Tian Yu was born in rural Hubei in Central China. Although her parents went out as seasonal migrant labor when she was young, she grew up a happy girl in a caring family (care from grandparents and from parents when they were home) with the company of her siblings as well as classmates, among whom she made good friends. Growing plants was her hobby. She also liked to laugh while socializing with her peers.[127] There was no sign whatsoever of her being psychologically challenged before she left for Foxconn Shenzhen at the beginning of 2010.

Tian Yu's story has been told many times in Chinese media, scholarly publications (including my own), and my short documentary film *Deconstructing Foxconn*, produced in 2010 for SACOM and the twenty-university investigation team.[128] When my research team interviewed Tian Yu in summer 2010, she was still a minor. Her parents encouraged her to talk to us, but she was somewhat reluctant. Over the years, the family declined many more interview requests so that Tian Yu could forget the traumatic experience.

The following testimony was, however, from 2013 when she had become a twenty-year-old young adult. She told the filmmaker Tu Qiao that she was ready to share what actually happened to her. The interview became the basis of a full-length Chinese-language documentary *Fly to Ascend*,[129] and the following quotations are lifted directly from this interview.

Some additional background information: Tian Yu left home around the time of the Chinese New Year. She took a train ride of about nine hundred miles to become an ordinary worker in iDPBG, Foxconn's special unit for making Apple products. Her job assignment as an "outside-checker" (*waijianyuan*) was to scrutinize the external appearance of glass screens, to assess if they were scratched, tainted, or irregular. Working under glaring lights that hurt her eyes, Tian Yu has to repeat a single mechanical body movement twenty-eight hundred times a day—at least that was the design of the assembly line.

The first day they took me to the assembly line. We had a look and would be on the shop floor the next day. The Full Technician [*quanjianyuan*] gave a brief explanation about the job, and you were put on the assembly line. As I was a newbie, he said, "If you have questions, ask others nearby." But others were all busy working, how did they have time [to talk] to you?

In the beginning I worked slowly. For each backlogged pile [of screens], I shouldn't be the only one held accountable because there were two outside checkers. But every time they accused me for working slowly, and I couldn't do anything.

When we started working each shift, the line leader would give an admonitory speech. He would say he did not only reprimand me, he would do that to us all. All of us on that assembly line stood there, listening to his rebuke.

For once, a disqualified product was checked by the other checker, who approved it. As she was not sure, she double-checked with the Full Technician, who said okay. So it passed the check. But in the end, at the checkpoint of IPQC, it was not passed. But the line leader said it was my responsibility. . . . He often scolded me, probably because I was more obedient.

I never cried (after being wronged). At the end of day, after working night shift, I was so exhausted and really sleepy upon taking a shower. How could I have time to cry or even think about it?

As a newbie, I was timid. Fresh from school, I did not have much social experience. I would not know how to argue (with the line leader). I did not think about confronting him. I never had that thought. I was too obedient.

Human beings for sure couldn't compete with a machine. You take a screen from the line, check it, and put it back. How can human match the speed of a machine? I kept wondering. On the assembly line if those people in the front work quickly, those after them must follow the speed and make a lot of items.

You know, when the assembly line starts moving, you literally work non-stop.

As for the whole factory beyond her assembly line, Tian Yu was most struck by the massive hiring at Foxconn. While the company often presents these hiring sprees as evidence of workers being so eager to work for them, Tian Yu, looking from the inside, saw this as the very opposite: the real reason was because workers were so eager to leave the factory after they get a taste of the assembly line and Foxconn's merciless management system. Tian Yu also confirmed that the company was indeed keeping workers from leaving by asking them to get approvals and, in so doing, infringing on workers' legal rights of free movement.

They [Foxconn] hire constantly, very much so. In the only month when I was there, another group of new workers were hired after me. Then yet another group came. So many people were hired. I don't know whether it was because too many people had left before the Chinese New Year or what other reason.

If they [workers] couldn't get approval to quit, they left anyway without receiving the monthly pay. They were bored, exhausted and did not want to do it any longer.

Immediately before Tian Yu talked about her attempted suicide, she talked about her social life in Foxconn being highly estranged, lonely, and helpless. The record of her dormitory shows that she had seven roommates. None of them came from Hubei, her home province. None of them worked in her unit iDPBG. These eight people belonged to seven different units of the factory.[130] Such a management system atomizes workers in ways that echo Patterson's sociological analysis of slavery and its "social death." Tian Yu continues:

Before entering the factory, I thought I could make friends, like at school, where classmates [would be] hanging out together, where we could chat freely, even make fun of each other. Something like that, so close and natural. And then I went to a strange new city, without school buddies. It was like, though living in the same dorm room, we [workers] didn't bind. There was no exchange among our hearts. Once in the factory, there wasn't such talk. I don't know why, there wasn't such special [opportunity to talk to fellow workers]. It might be because I didn't know how to talk to them. We were not familiar. We were like familiar strangers.

In the end, I was broke. With my cell phone lost, and I wanted to ask why I couldn't get my salary. After all, I had worked for a month there, but nobody told me how to collect my pay. I asked the line leader. He [didn't seem to care] and told me the pay bank card was in Guanlan. I was a newbie indeed, knowing nothing, just a rookie. I didn't know if he was truthful or not. I thought he, as a line leader, was not likely to lie to me. So I believed him and stupidly took the bus [to Guanlan.]

There, at Guanlan, I didn't have any idea how to get my salary. I simply ran from one building to another, getting nothing in the end. Nobody cared. There wasn't a way, completely no way. You were full of grief. And when you were back, you again went from one department to another. And I didn't know. I felt strongly, with so many things adding together, and I collapsed.

When I came back, it was really late, with dorm lights all off and others asleep. I lied down, feeling so . . . frustrated and infuriated. I lied there thinking, I didn't know what I was going to do. I really didn't think of going to work. Not at all. So the next morning, I did the irrational thing.

Anyway I myself wasn't even aware of all these [matters]. At that moment, my brain went blank, real blank. I didn't know what to do. To call my father—that thought really didn't cross my mind. To have a meal—how can I think of that? Anyway, there was no sense . . . then I woke up and found myself in ICU (intensive care unit).

When Tian Yu repeated that her brain "went blank, real blank," she was describing precisely a state of mind when one's liberty was deprived "for a period of time which is, for that person, indeterminate," quoting from the Bellagio-Harvard Guidelines.[131]

After Tian Yu spent a few months in a Shenzhen hospital, Foxconn hastily gave the family a lump sum of $29,000 as "humanitarian compensation." In exchange, the Tian family had to agree that the company was no longer responsible and shall not be subject to negative media exposure. "It was like the way we buy or sell a commodity," said Tian Yu's father.[132] As such, it concludes yet another tragedy at Foxconn.

## Concluding Remarks

This chapter, "Manufacturing iSlaves," is the first prototype of twenty-first-century slavery in the context of digital media industry. I have examined herein the conditions of work and life in the world's largest electronics manufacturer, Foxconn, including a brief history of the company; its suppressive factory regime from the guards to the "anti-jumping nets"; its harsh working conditions, from its semi-military management system to excessively long overtime hours; and the subsequent alienation and "social death" of workers. Evidence from primary and secondary sources, from fieldwork and interviews, and from Foxconn workers themselves, are rather consistent in exposing the underbelly of not only Foxconn but also Appconn, including the global gadgets production system as a whole. Despite the huge scale of Foxconn, its labor predicaments are indicative of an even larger regime gone wrong.

As Patterson argued, slavery as a global institution was "firmly established in all the great early centers of human civilization and, far from declining, actually increased in significance with the growth of all the epochs and cultures that modern Western peoples consider watersheds in their historical development."[133] The recent turn to a new epoch of digital media, powered by Chinese manufacturing iSlaves in such deplorable conditions as exist at Foxconn, is yet another instance in this long shadow of slavery, cast from history to modernity.

Structurally speaking, Foxconn today is comparable to that of the feitorias centuries ago, serving the role of concentrating and exporting labor power from the periphery to the core regions of the capitalist world economy. As Barbara Solow noted, "The mere existence of imperialism or colonialism does not explain how the metropolis exploited the periphery, as some would have it: It was the coerced labor of African slaves that allowed Europe to benefit so greatly from its conquests in the New World. When we assess the distribution of those benefits, we find that although the race went to the swift, the glittering prize was hammered out by African hands."[134]

Undeniably there are numerous differences between the production regimes of the seventeenth and the twenty-first centuries, changing from African to Chinese hands, from sugar plantations to electronic assembly lines, from West India Company to Foxconn, from the Atlantic to the Pacific. But at the very least, the comparative exercise explicating this new analytical category of manufacturing iSlaves should be taken as an attempt at several clarifications that are metaphorical as well as practical, historical as well as contemporary.

First, we have to dismiss the claims that our iPads, computers, and smartphones simply represent progress; that digital media is all about intangible content and immaterial wealth; and that it is okay for Foxconn to exploit its workers in China, while consumers the world over pay cheaper prices for these gadgets. Seen from historical and legal standpoints, this is absolutely not acceptable because the social and moral cost is simply too high.

Second, it is fundamental to recognize that all the gadgets have to be produced as part and parcel of our "modern material world,"[135] that every single one of them comes into being with concrete social and environmental costs.[136] Can there really be a cyberspace if all our computers (one particular type of material objects) disappear? How can Facebook and Twitter operate if we discard our smartphones? Will the global knowledge economy continue to exist without these physical objects: servers, fiber optics, and satellites?

Much of the cost invested in this planetary communication infrastructure cannot be measured in monetary terms alone: there is liberty and dignity, justice and social ties. Without a full consideration of the cost at large, the crude logic of profit maximization, of putting a price tag on everything, is leading to slavery-like institutions and practices, which are not only ongoing but deteriorating.

In this chapter, we see at Foxconn a full range of "the powers attaching to the right of ownership," including possession, use, transfer, profit, and disposal of ordinary workers, of student interns, of injured employees. Here, we see plights reminiscent of the Middle Passage—even though the sufferings are far from identical—as well as epic tragedies like the Foxconn Suicide Express, when the obsolete practice of "protecting" the owners' "human cargo" using "anti-jumping nets" was revived after centuries in oblivion.

In retrospect, this unprecedented string of suicides at Foxconn was so much more than individual attempts to relieve pain, so much more than personal insanity, as the company would like us to believe. The suicides can also be interpreted as a subliminal collective endeavor to expose the unbearable conditions that manufacturing iSlaves have to endure. They constitute a defiant act of resistance, too.

Let me close this chapter with two direct quotations from Foxconn employees themselves, both shedding additional light on the de facto conditions of iSlavery. First, a reflection from *Factory Gossip*, the underground workers' magazine commenting on Foxconn's deceptive outlook and its brutal, arbitrary, and often absolute power of management.[137]

> I suddenly realize that Foxconn is like an imperial palace. The buildings look so grand and beautiful from outside, behind the high walls of enclosure. Talk about high salaries is blown out of proportion. But inside, the security is so tight and the hierarchy so dominant. Employees are like slaves and palace maids. The line managers and slaves often die in the hands of eunuchs without ever knowing what happened. The rare case of survival depends, entirely, on good luck!

When Durkheim famously attributed suicides to anomie, he meant precisely a chaotic and unpredictable social existence of absolute disempowerment.[138] The above paragraph narrates such a state of work and life within Foxconn; so does another blog entry, put online in the midst of the Suicide Express. This is a poem revealing workers' emotions, how they see themselves, how they view the meaning of life, and how they understand the unfolding of the tragic events inside the massive factory:[139]

> Only death proves we were alive,
> Perhaps to Foxconn employees,
> Or similar workers [called peasant-workers in China],
> Only death proves we were alive,
> Only desperation proves we are.

Authored by an anonymous Foxconn worker, this poetic blog entry mysteriously vanished three days after it appeared online.

# 4

# Manufactured iSlaves

Yang Ni (pseudonym) is a seventeen-year-old from Huangshan, a small city in East China. He grew up in a family of textile workers who struggled to make ends meet. Yet, in early 2011, Ni longed desperately for something trendy. Asking his parents to buy him an iPad but without success, he solicited help from relatives, but failed again. Meanwhile, the iPad "turned into a vogue in his school. Look at his friends playing with iPads all day, discussing its functions and usage, he felt like an excluded outsider. . . . He then searched online for ways to earn quick money."[1]

On May 5, 2011, Ni returned home looking pale and sick. His mother was surprised to see him carrying an iPad 2 and an iPhone 4, both brand new. Even more shocking was a scar 4.3-inch (11cm) long on his abdomen. It turned out the teenager had sold one of his kidneys for $3,500 (22,000 yuan), which he used to buy the coveted gadgets.[2]

Following a recorded pattern of working-class internet users relying on QQ (the popular Chinese instant messenger) to sell blood for cash,[3] Ni also used QQ to find a buyer. He managed the logistics via digital media, although he didn't know the buyer in fact sold his kidney for $35,000 (220,000 yuan), of which he only received 10 percent. He was told, via QQ and in person, that losing a kidney would not harm his health. But now he was diagnosed with renal insufficiency so severe that he would qualify as having a category-three disability in China. Ni probably will not regain his full health for the remainder of his life.[4]

Is this case too extreme? Maybe. Still, there are even worse instances of organ trafficking in India and the Philippines, where "entire villages sell organs, rent wombs, and sign away their bodies after death—not only under duress, but also in mutually agreeable transactions."[5] Yet Ni's case is certainly most troubling in light of reports from 2011 to 2013 from various Chinese cities about schoolgirls entering the underground sex trade in order to purchase iPhones. In Shanghai, a young couple sold their baby daughter and used the money to buy an iPhone.[6] In December 2012, an elevator advertisement in an IT Mall of Kunmin, southwest China, proclaimed, "When selling kidneys becomes a habit, you get everything you want from iPhone 5."[7] Is this black humor, or does it represent practices similar to slavery, through a consumerist twist?

. . .

In his masterpiece *Discours de la servitude volontaire*, the sixteenth-century French philosopher Étienne de La Boétie explained why enslavement could prevail over so many people, for so long: they, the enslaved, "must either be driven by force or led into it by deception."[8] Throughout history, the use of brute force is common in systems of bondage, whereas at Foxconn, even though one does not see forceful oppression on a daily basis, the factory keeps an army of guards who threaten to use violence when needed. Physical punishment is frequently exposed, sometimes within the jurisdiction of Foxconn management, sometimes outside, scarring the collective psyche of the workforce.

Yang Ni's enslavement was, however, not "driven by force." He was instead "led into it by deception"—deceptive information about the value of his organ, the harmlessness of the surgery, and, above all, the magic power of the i-device. Historically, such deception varies in its form, content, and the length of time required for it to be effective. In contemporary digital cultures, the substance of this process is about the production of *manufactured* iSlaves. While the forceful subjugation of *manufacturing* iSlaves takes as its aim that those enslaved shall work hard, make money for, and/or provide comfort to the "masters," the parallel process toward *manufactured* iSlaves tends to be more subtle, albeit with long-lasting pernicious consequences, for it molds people's subjectivity, their desires and dreams, not only individually but more often on a collective basis, through friendship networks and peer pressure.

Manufactured iSlaves represent a deceptive, prevalent, and indispensable mode of iSlavery that operates in the realm of cultural consumption. It refers more specifically to those who are constantly attached to their gadgets, playing games, updating "status," and "liking" other people's updates. In reality, few routines of this ephemeral technoculture, of mundane ways to spend time online while having fun, would qualify as modern-day slavery using definitions from human rights groups and international organizations. How do they, nonetheless, constitute another major form of twenty-first-century slavery? Only by making a conceptual leap can one make sense of digital enslavement through consumer cultures and of Yang Ni's tragedy beyond odd instances of individual insanity.

Making this argument is, however, not too difficult, partly because, in China as in the United States, pundits have long noted the malicious consequence of Apple fandom, calling it the Cult of Apple.[9] Henry Jenkins, the leading expert on fan cultures, once discussed the Latin root of the word "fan," as in *fanaticus*, meaning "orgiastic rites and enthusiastic frenzy" as well as "possession by a deity or demon."[10] In most of his writings, Jenkins puts more emphasis on the "participatory culture" of fan communities online, its liberating effects especially via social media challenging corporate constraints, and the subsequent chances of creativity and empowerment. Mark Andrejevic has, on the contrary, disagreed by proposing to understand the fan cultures as "free labor" suffering from "social network exploitation."[11] Similarly, Christian Fuchs views such "participatory culture" as another way that "allows companies to outsource paid labor time to consumers or fans who work for free."[12]

•  •  •

To better situate the manufactured and consumption-oriented mode of enslavement in relation to both manufacturing iSlaves and other modes of labor at large, figure 4.1 provides a schematic overview, on

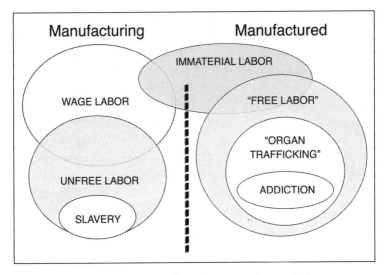

FIGURE 4.1    From manufacturing to manufactured iSlaves:
Conceptual connections.

which this chapter will elaborate. It shows that, although there are many connections, overlaps, and parallels, manufactured iSlavery also occupies distinct positions in this contemporary structure of labor, extended through social media.

On the left is manufacturing labor such as workers on the assembly line of Foxconn and similar factories. Under normal conditions as assumed in classic Marxian analyses or defined in terms of Chinese law, all Foxconn workers should belong to the modern workforce of wage labor, those who exchange their laboring time with the factory owner for salaries and benefits. Yet, as discussed in the previous chapter, it was rather common for such normal market conditions to become a façade that conceals unfree labor on and off the shop floor. Examples include the so-called "student internship programs," "voluntary" overtime work, and illegal obstacles that prevent workers from quitting jobs. In the worst case, unfree labor would descend to de facto status of slavery when anti-jumping nets were erected, injured employees disposed of, and despairing workers left in an indeterminate period of psychological limbo, which led to self-destruction.

On the right are manufactured modes of iSlavery in the immaterial domain. There are, of course, immaterial processes in traditional factory work as well. But for the manufactured modes, their immateriality is more pronounced and definitive in the absence of physical enclosure and, more important, in the ways by which value is generated. As Tiziana Terranova pointed out in her classic essay in 2000: "Free labor is the moment where this knowledgeable consumption of culture is translated into productive activities that are pleasurably embraced and at the same time often shamelessly exploited."[13] Compared to wage labor, "free labor" is a much diffused system of exploitation, which also camouflages more blatant modes of Big Data manipulation, sales of metadata and user profiles, in what one may call "digital organ trafficking," a metaphor to be elaborated in the following discussion.

The worst form of unfree digital labor in the immaterial realm is addiction, when one's subjectivity becomes fully captured in the consumerist mode designed and promoted by corporate marketing, as in the case of the Apple Cult. Free will is, under such circumstances, minimized to the extent that people are turned into slave-like entities under totalizing hegemonic control.

• • •

The allure of the Apple Cult, like most cultural phenomena since "the age of mechanical reproduction,"[14] must first be produced. This is a peculiar process of "manufacturing consent," a term used as book title for both Michael Burawoy's *Manufacturing Consent: Changes in the Labor Process under Monopoly Capitalism* and Edward Herman and Noam Chomsky's *Manufacturing Consent: The Political Economy of Mass Media*.[15] While the former is an organizational-institutional analysis and the latter a societal critique, both raised the hard question of why ordinary people at the grassroots level often fail to oppose the ideologies of the ruling elite and, in so doing, grant voluntary consent to their own enslavement? Herman and Chomsky's answer is mass propaganda. Burawoy uses a combination of factors at the workplace, be they technological, political, or sociocultural, especially corporate predominance over the shaping of industrial relations. Together, these authors demonstrate that the effectiveness of consent-manufacturing efforts lies not just in the system of power out there but inside the mental and ideological self-imaginations of the working people as well.

It is this generalized pattern of "manufacturing consent" that I shall apply in understanding the manufactured, consumerist mode of iSlavery. Despite the growing army of free labor, "virtual marketing" and online fan culture nonetheless need professional care to some degree. Apple, for instance, is the world's most valuable company not only because it sells smartphones and tablets, accessories, and songs, but, more crucially, because it creates and sells desires—to look cool, feel rich, be a member of what Richard Florida calls the "creative class."[16] Desires to have something sleek and fashionable, something all the sexy people also have, "something that makes you special," something like the iPhone, "an easy status symbol (for China's new rich who aren't feeling secure) to show they've made it."[17]

The educational game, *Phone Story*, which was banned in the Apple App Store, offers a sarcastic illustration for this craze of i-fandom. After the first two stages of the game, which deals with Congolese mine workers and Foxconn Suicide Express, respectively, the third level of the game starts with this voice order:

> Then, you purchased this phone. It was new and sexy. You've waited for it for months. No evidence of its troubling past was visible. Did you really need it? Of course, you did. We spent a lot of money to install this desire in you. You were looking for something that could symbolize your status, your dynamic lifestyle, your unique personality—just like everyone else.[18]

I will discuss the operations of this game in more detail toward the end of chapter 5. Meanwhile, admittedly, Apple's competitors, including Samsung and Xiaomi, all tried similar marketing tactics, although their following seems to be far less fanatic to qualify as "cult." Apple, in this sense, truly stands out, for it does not just design gadgets and have Foxconn manufacture them. It also designs dreams and has advertising agencies, PR firms, news media, and ultimately—you and me, crowdsourced—manufacture and circulate these dreams, "installing" the wants in each other. The professional dream makers, marketers, and amateur fans do not wear dull factory uniforms. Their main job is not about the production of something tangible. Rather, it's something immaterial that they manufacture, circulate, substantiate.

## Consumption, Geopolitics, and "Organ" Trafficking

The previous chapter zoomed into *manufacturing* iSlaves, whose king-pin, in the context of China, "the world's factory," is Foxconn, especially during the tragic moments of the 2010 Suicide Express. Broadly speaking, *manufacturing* iSlaves includes others suffering under modern-day slavery, such as those extracting minerals for the making of electronics.[19] Ni's tragedy, on the other hand, compels reflection beyond the mines, the factories, and the material links of the global commodity chain, into the terrains of consumer culture and immaterial labor—not only consumption to meet the needs and wants of consumers but, more important, through a vital process for the system of slavery to generate profit and realize its goal of exploitation.

As learned from the history of slavery, "African hands" have been essential to the capitalist world economy since the seventeenth century because there was growing demand for their output: slave-produced commodities such as sugar, tobacco, and cotton. From a *longue durée* perspective, the increase of production by slaves in the New World had to be accompanied by the rise of consumption markets in the Old World. Otherwise, the Atlantic trade would have been unsustainable had the expansion been one sided, with the growth of production by slaves only.

This means, figuratively speaking, one's habit of consuming sugar, like one's love of the iPhone, has to be cultivated via cultural practices maneuvered and social relations reconfigured, as Sydney Mintz noted in explaining the prevalence of the "sweet tooth" through mundane daily activities, key rituals like wedding ceremonies, as well as "desocialized eating."[20] There needs to be, more profoundly, the making of a new mentality toward certain commodities, toward other people, toward oneself, and a new culture of consumerism, all hinging upon modern media and marketing industries as well as communication through interpersonal and small group channels. Ni's more wealthy classmates were, in this sense, part of this social machinery manufacturing servile consumerist wants, while they were manufactured iSlaves as well.

In other words, my critique is not about the predisposition of some individuals to suppress and exploit other people so much as the entire global system that allows such individuals to prosper. This is, conceptually speaking, a system of enslavement that spans more than four centuries from the Eurocentric capitalist world-economy of the 1600s to present-day "Appconn," a global empire of dominance through hardware and software, content and services. Essential to both organisms of historical capitalism, Atlantic or Appconn, is the role of system-generated consumption markets serving as a pillar of the world-economy, which is as indispensable as production apparatuses.

• • •

But who gets to produce, who gets to consume? Why do certain groups have to toil and be forced to the margins of this problematic global system, at least by design? Why would others attract commercial and cultural attention as they become raw materials to be molded into the new consuming subjects, be they the working classes of the Old World centuries ago or China's new middle class in its booming megacities today?

Many factors matter, from trade policy and nation-building efforts to geopolitical dominance, from religious affinity to racial, ethnic, and gender stereotypes. Fundamental parameters are also set by the prevailing conceptions of time and space that are contingent, often unconsciously, upon technological conditions as represented by such devices as the mechanical clock, the telegraph, and the fiber-optic cable. While specific configuration varies, from a bird's-eye view the general pattern is the domination of the Global North over the Global South, of the West over the rest, as Anthony Smith maintains in his 1980 volume *Geopolitics of Information*.[21] Moreover, in recent years, as Vijay Prashad points out, the domination has deteriorated into an "obscene" situation of the supposed "locomotives of the South" pulling the "wagons of the North," with "sales of commodities and low wages to workers accompanying a recycled surplus turned over as credit to the North."[22]

It is against this spatial and historical backdrop that one can conceive the notion of manufactured iSlaves as a dynamic and dialectical formation of labor. The North/South boundary has been shifting, of course, given the volatility of digital capitalism.[23] In the aftermath of the 2008–2009 global financial crisis, large swaths of Western populations (in Detroit, for example) fell from their Northern status, while the new rich, especially in Asia, joined the ranks of global power elite. This is not to deny that the patterns of geocultural formation, of where the centers of consumer culture should be located, almost always depend on existing patterns of geopolitics, on the cyclical rise and fall of politico-economic empires as well as cultural and ideological hegemony.

In a way, this is not too different from the old division of labor in the Atlantic system, when Africans were trafficked to the Americas to produce sugar while Europeans were encouraged to indulge in their sweet tooth. The price could be prohibitive for a black slave to imitate the consumerist lifestyle. In this sense, it was anything but coincidental that Ni in a small Chinese city had to pay a much higher toll than his counterparts in small-town America to realize the intoxicating dream of consumerism due to the prevailing geocultural and geopolitical patterns of capitalism, both across nations and within.

•  •  •

There is another layer of interpretation regarding Ni's tragedy that illuminates the manufactured mode of iSlavery. As discussed in chapter 2, a hallmark of slavery is to extract value from the exploitation of someone's labor and body. But what is body, exactly? Ni sold part of his body: a kidney, which is not the same as an African body for sale in the 1600s or an East European or Southeast Asian body in contemporary sex trade, when conventional bodies and/or body parts were subject to enslavement.

What about social media that extend our body? Is today's human body really functionally complete without the gadgets, the data, the cloud? What about these extended, immaterial parts of our body—can they become subject to "institutions and practices similar to slavery," defined again in de facto terms?

For years, Chinese technology pundits have called the mobile phone a "fifth limb" (diwuzhi), which not only extends the functionality of our four limbs but also becomes a new organ of the modern human body.[24] Ever forgot to bring your phone? Then you probably have felt that sense of incompleteness in your "normal" social functioning, especially if you use a smartphone and have developed a habit of using it for all sorts of tasks, informational, social, or just to kill time.

Meanwhile, corporeal metaphors have gained currency as gurus in the West start to talk about the 'third skin'":[25] besides our biological skin and the layer(s) of clothing we wear, we are now surrounded by the data we generate through our social media updates, locational data, searches, purchases, and likes. It's part of us, or more precisely, of *the informational me* in that you and I produce these data interactively through our routine behavior, sometimes deliberately, sometimes unwittingly; it is intensely personal—arguably much more so than clothing, the "second skin"—in revealing our tastes and curiosities, our biometrics and social networks, the way we act and think, consciously and subliminally.

This "third skin" and the "fifth limb," however, often belong to someone else. If you clicked "agree" when you installed your app, chances are that the data you generate will either be shared from your gadgets or stored in the cloud, administered by Apple, Google, Dropbox, some tech company whose name you never heard of, or various state surveillance agencies, such as the NSA.

Our "skin" becomes their "property"; so does our "limb." Our labor in growing and renewing these informational "body parts" becomes the origin of corporate profits as well as police tools to spy on us. In many cases, for so many working-class people in China, for instance, this is not even voluntary, as the telcos or gadget brands would pre-install applications that cannot be deleted from the device. Hence, although there is little physical pain inflicted as during the Middle Passage or Yang Ni's suffering, are we nonetheless basically forced to wear these intangible shackles—a "wireless leash," as I once called it when analyzing mobile messaging services[26]—just to get by in this new social world of Big Data? Do we really have a choice? Isn't this a new mode of bodily exploitation, albeit not in a Congolese mine but in the data mine?

In classic conditions of slavery, people tend to be enslaved by scarcity, which is, to a great extent, still true for manufacturing iSlaves at Foxconn. They have to work long hours for fear of not earning enough. But to most of us today, are we enslaved by the apparent abundance of countless apps, of all the consumer "choices" (which marginalize the "choice" of not consuming), of not only our wants but also our needs to make sense of the world given the overwhelming profusion of information overload and the tyrannical tempo of digital capitalism?[27]

Manufactured iSlaves operate through strategic tension between perceived abundance and artificial scarcity. This chapter analyzes how the technological novelty of using digital media to extract free labor is, sociologically speaking, not new. In terms of the basic political-economy structures, it deepens the fetishization of audience commodity, as Dallas Smythe had long argued,[28] while continuing an archaic legacy of global capitalism: using addiction to create stable, even growing, market demand through voluntary as well as involuntary servitude.

## Digital Labor, Immaterial and Individualized

How do manufactured iSlaves come into being? How can a hegemonic consumption culture, centering on and sustained by the latest media technologies, be possible? This is unlikely the result of a single master plan. Instead, the digital reincarnation of consumerism results from a series of systemic crises in the world-economy, from the end of Fordism to the dot-com bubble burst, from the 1997 Asian financial crisis to the global crash of 2008. The overall contour is accidental, post hoc, and opportunist, like the "capitalist world stumbled towards neoliberalization."[29]

For a more comprehensive understanding of manufactured iSlaves, including its multidimensional relationship with digital labor, one needs to engage with two distinct yet equally important strands of thought from Italy, one being autonomist, the other feminist. This will help address the productive and reproductive tensions in the transformation of cultural hegemony, thus shedding light on the genesis of manufactured iSlaves.

First, in the early 1970s Antonio Negri already foresaw the new roots of servitude, more than a decade before the neoliberal turn of Reagan and Thatcher. Analyzing how the establishment would respond to the crisis of Keynesianism, he contended in *Red Notes* that capitalism would need "a project that is qualitatively different," one that separates production from circulation, aiming at creating a "productive subject" who does not take collective action or form solidarity.[30] Later with Michael Hardt,

Negri emphasized the revolutionary potentials of this new and diverse mass of the "multitude," ready to be unleashed against "empire."[31] This line of work widened the door for English-language readers to the autonomist Marxist idea of immaterial labor.

The next chapter will further illuminate the rebellious aspects of Negri's thinking in a Chinese context of online and offline struggles. Before then, it suffices to point out that his conceptualization departs from previous Marxist labor concepts in two significant ways. One is its immateriality, whose decisive implication is that the Foucauldian modes of oppression through bodily discipline and physical enclosure—like the situation in Foxconn—have become obsolete, whereas the main site of social control has shifted to the sphere of subjectivity and the mind.

The other is the individualized nature of this "productive subject," which echoes unmistakably Orlando Patterson's sociological definition of slavery as "natal alienation."[32] Even the most esteemed and most pampered consumerists do not really own their subjectivity as in the cases of Roman *familia Caesaris*. Instead, their wealth and honor can be deprived at any time, due to their isolation and fundamental lack of social power, akin to the "ultimate slaves."[33]

Along the tradition of autonomist Marxism, Maurizio Lazzarato more precisely delineated "immaterial labor" as one who "produces the informational and cultural content of the commodity."[34] He identified several "classic forms" of immaterial labor, as in "audiovisual production, advertising, fashion, the production of software, photography, cultural activities." These "classic forms" converge, in that

> they combine the results of various different types of work skill: intellectual skills, as regards the culture-informational content; manual skills for the ability to combine creativity, imagination, and technical and manual labor; and entrepreneurial skills in the management of social relations and the structuring of that social cooperation of which they are a part. This immaterial labor constitutes itself in forms that are immediately collective, and we might say that it exists only in the form of networks and flows.[35]

Lazzarato shares Negri and Hardt's optimism about a world revolution. Written in 1996, his essay examines those who are on the payroll of ad agencies, TV stations, and software companies. Working under increasingly precarious conditions, they are paid to create narratives and mental images in order to convince others to buy the idea of a new product, identify with an old brand, and adopt a particular lifestyle of consumerism. They produce commercials for the consumerist enslavement of others, as they themselves become "Net Slaves," a term used by commentators Lessard and Baldwin as both an accusation and ridicule to capture their despicable modes of work in front of networked computer screens.[36] Here, one can still see Lazzarato's immaterial labor as a variant of *manufacturing* iSlaves in an extended sense because they are paid to produce commodities and desires for others to consume, although they probably internalize the intangible products and the values they embody much more than Foxconn workers could afford for the tangible gadgets they assemble.

• • •

Making this "immaterial labor" argument in emerging markets like China is, however, more difficult. Although for decades Apple has been known for its media prowess since its iconic "1984" commercial, it has not made the kind of investment in China as it did in the West. Unlike its U.S. operation, Apple did "minimal advertising" in China, at least until 2012,[37] probably because commercials from domestic computer and phone makers had saturated the screens, airwaves, and printed spaces. Much of the Chinese media system is state controlled and prone to nationalistic outbursts targeting foreign brands.[38] It is hence a strategic advantage for Apple not to boost its mass media visibility in countries like China.

Under such circumstances, it makes strong sense to highlight the feminist origins for the conception of immaterial labor, which offers an arguably more important, yet often forgotten, conceptual formulation, especially for issues of reproductive labor via digital media. In a seminal 2007 essay Leopoldina Fortunati maintains that "the true promoters of the discourse on immaterial labor have been feminists,"[39] whose endeavor could also be traced back to the 1970s. Unlike Lazzarato, Fortunati situates classic forms of immaterial labor in the domestic sphere and the domain of social reproduction that traditionally involve women who carry out unpaid care work.

Fortunati's theorization has a few distinct characteristics unrecognized in the autonomist tradition, which however have tremendous bearing on not only the Chinese reality today but also the landscape of social-media "free labor" globally. First, female laborers such as housewives are seldom put on payroll. Second, their work includes as its central components the labor of affection, communication, sex, social support, and networking. Third, from household appliances to old and new media, technological invention and diffusion (or the slow speed of certain technological progress) are conceptualized as integral to the historical process of "machinizating" immaterial labor. "The mass possession of these intellective technologies represents an important ground for political experimentation and for a new theory and practice of communication, as well as a strategic moment of self-valorization."[40] Such conceptualization can easily incorporate internet and smartphones as more recent examples from the same historical trend.

Fourth and more important, rather than a break from body politics, Fortunati's notion of immaterial labor subsumes the corporeal dimension without the usual presumption to look up to labor that is non-physical, with an air of celebration or admiration. Here goes one of her sharpest critiques of Negri and Lazzarato: "Material labor is scorned and devalorized, while immaterial is valorized. But it is on the body that the system has launched its most radical attack. . . . [E]veryone, without exception, is subjected to the process of the machinization of the body, increasingly hybridized by means of machines."[41]

One needs only a small conceptual leap to connect Fortunati's body machinization thesis with the metaphorical references to our "third skin" and "fifth limb" as being in digital shackles and on wireless leashes. After all, as I have argued along with Melissa Gregg and Kate Crawford elsewhere, the distinction between body and mind, between the material and the immaterial, has fundamentally blurred under conditions of contemporary digital media.[42]

Finally, there is also an explicit geopolitical emphasis in the concept of immaterial labor, which Fortunati highlights. In an earlier piece, she identified the tendency that the Global North is becoming home to the bulk of the popularly desired "immaterial labor" developments, whereas material production has been relocated to the Global South, to places like China.[43] In "Immaterial Labor and Its Machinization," she continued: "Globalization separates the material elements from the immaterial ones of the same production process. The latter very often remains in the (post)industrialized countries while the former is located in developing countries, which brings the international division of labor to another level."[44]

Published in 2007, the basic spatial pattern outlined in this article persists, while much has also changed since the financial crisis of 2008–9. Immaterial labor has diffused further from the core regions of Global North. The result is, however, far from a level playing field because, although ordinary residents of the Global South can now join the ranks of manufactured iSlaves, the accessibility of the consumerist dream in fact increases their vulnerability and, more profoundly, their dependence on the cultural hegemony of the North. Digital media play a vital role in producing these new dependents and reducing them to little more than dispensable surrogates in the form of the individualized consumer, the ideal capitalist subject Negri contemplated four decades ago.

•   •   •

Back to the case of Apple in China, much of the company's prominence in the Chinese market did not come directly from its professional advertising or marketing campaigns, although China accounts for more than one fifth of Apple's total global sales.[45] A main reason is the perceived scarcity of Apple products, which has everything to do with mind management and the manipulation of habitual social memory.

Due to corporate strategy (which works against Chinese consumers as Fortunati points out in her geopolitical note) as well as Chinese imports policy, the release of Apple products in China had, for a long period, been slow and in limited quantity. The result is what Chinese marketers call "hunger marketing" (ji'e yingxiao), resulting mostly from word of mouth, online and off. You want what your friends crave. You want it even more badly when the products are in short supply.

Fueling the craze, Apple only had six stores for the vast country by summer 2012, compared to more than two hundred in the United States. The result was that four of the six Chinese stores sold more Apple products than any of the U.S. stores.[46] One not only has to queue up much longer to buy an iPhone in Beijing, but sometimes one has to get literally into fist fights. By the first quarter of 2015, Apple for the first time was selling more iPhones in China than in the United States.[47]

The rise of Apple Cult in China offers "a lesson in how to prosper without really trying," wrote Hannah Beech in *Time* magazine.[48] The secret is crowdsourcing, voluntary work, fan sharing—in other words, shifting the workload away from the paid immaterial labor *à la* Lazzarato. Although these "classic forms" are still around, they tend to be less visible and less costly as promotional duties are no longer carried out in the office towers of Shanghai. Instead, they become "fun" tasks heatedly discussed in the chat rooms of unpaid amateurs, enthusiastic fans, women, volunteers, and little helpers like those in Yang Ni's high school showing off their iPads.

An update is clearly in order when it comes to unpaid Apple enthusiasts providing "free labor." Trebor Scholz's *Digital Labor: The Internet as Playground and Factory* tackles this task by presenting an impressive collection of essays prepared by some of the most influential authors on the subject.[49] Although it's mostly about the western world and doesn't really examine China, the trends explicated are quite relevant.

As Scholz's book title shows, a fundamental change from Lazzarato's "immaterial labor" to today's "digital labor" is the further blurring of boundaries between "playground and factory," a tendency quite consistent with Fortunati's analyses. For the professional media workers and fashion designers, they may feel at times that their workplace—the image factories so to speak—is *like* a playground. But *like* a playground differs from actually *is* a playground, when they are off duty, hanging around with friends, or playing games with kids, for which they are not paid. For immaterial labor, the distinction between work and play has long started to blur, as signaled by Julian Kücklich's notion of the "precarious playbour,"[50] but it is still possible to differentiate the two. Yet as Scholz and colleagues maintain, the distinction has evaporated for various kinds of digital labor today.

Increasingly, manufactured iSlaves are way more than just *playing* with their gadgets. They are *working* as well, for Apple and other corporations selling products and services while extracting Big Data from user's free labor. Yes, they remain consumers. But their consumption behavior, their attitudes and gestures, their laughter and gaze, also manufacture Yang Ni's consumerist obsession when he watched his classmates play and talk about their iPads. And not only at school: when he went online, he was bombarded even more by posts and pictures of his friends sporting their latest gadgets, conversing about the new functions, comparing the latest games.

Yang Ni's selling of his kidney was, in a bizarre way, among the ultimate acts of "prosumption." In order to join his rich pals in their digital playground, he submitted himself to two systems, one being the illicit trade of organ trafficking, the other being the "image factory" of countless news organizations (where the immaterial labor professionals still work) and online discussions that had repeated his story thousands of times. While consuming the gadgetry, he also consumed his kidney and health to produce a most tragic, and much circulated, marketing ploy for Apple, in China and worldwide.

## Addiction and Enslavement

From ancient times, people dominated by drugs constitute an archetype of the enslaved, especially among voluntary servitude. It is not too great an exaggeration to claim that addiction—to alcohol, to opium, to sugar, to computer games—reduces human beings to slaves from within. As Le Boétie noted, this was the strategy used by Cyrus, the Persian king, when he captured Sardis, a city of legendary wealth, whose residents rose up against him:

> It would have been easy for him to reduce them by force, but being unwilling either to sack such a fine city or to maintain an army there to police it, he thought of an unusual expedient for reducing it. He established in it brothels, taverns, and public games, and issued the proclamation that the inhabitants were to enjoy them. He found this type of garrison so effective that he never again had to draw the sword.[51]

Since the beginning of the early modern era, micro individual-level addiction and disempowerment have materialized in a larger system of macro inequality. This is most clearly demonstrated in the classic case of sugar being bought and sold in the Atlantic system, which historically traded many other commodities. But besides African slaves, sugar stands out as the most well-known product of the transatlantic trade, in part because it is an addictive substance; in part because it looks so "pure," so "problem-free," and tastes so nice; in part because, while the manufacturing slaves of African origins had to toil in the sugar plantations of the New World, the manufactured slaves of Europe's new working classes gradually developed a stable "sweet tooth" and, along with it, an insatiable market demand.

Sugarcane was first domesticated in Asia, and for many centuries large-scale sugar cultivation and production followed the Koran until crusaders returning from the Holy Land brought sugar to Europe, where the sweet substance acquired the status of an extravagant rarity. When King Henry III of England ordered three pounds of sugar, he had to add: "if so much is to be had."[52] The situation had not changed much until the 1600s, when sugar remained a luxury for super-rich aristocrats.

Back then, to most Europeans, sugar was like newly released iPads in China at the beginning of 2011 when Yang Ni sold his kidney. Ordinary people had seen or heard about it, but to taste it one had to pay a dear price. That was also the social status of electronic devices just decades ago for the majority of humanity, who had never placed a phone call. But as Sidney Mintz demonstrated in *Sweetness and Power*, things started to change with the expansion of New World plantations and the import of African slaves.[53]

As the seventeenth-century Atlantic slavery system gained traction, sugar became increasingly a working-class commodity. Factory workers began to take tea breaks while putting sugar into their cups. In so doing, not only was the natural system of the New World transformed into even larger and more numerous sugar plantations but the cultural system of the Old World was also fundamentally altered.

Can one still imagine European cuisine without sugar? This blurring between nature and culture is Mintz's greatest insight, which can also be applied as forceful enslavement blends with addiction, paving the way for voluntary servitude. To what extent is this happening in today's digital culture/nature? Does the latest trend in immaterial labor suggest that the addictive power of expropriation has become more pervasive and more profitable than ever before?

Yes, millions of Africans were shipped across the Atlantic for all kinds of work: growing cotton and tobacco, working in mines and households. But sugar was undoubtedly the most important product for the European market. In contrast, although in the triangular trade system New World sugar could theoretically also be sold directly in exchange for slaves in Africa, this rarely happened. Instead, according to David Eltis, throughout the early modern era, textiles remained the dominant imports for West Africa. By selling slaves, traders in West Africa also bought alcohol (especially rum, a by-product of sugar processing), tobacco, and firearms, but these imports were not more dominant than in other world regions.[54] This comparison confirms, from another angle, that the emergence of European "sweet tooth" was not a "natural" process simply because all humans like things sweet. It was instead a selective process of artificial "manufacture"—in this case, of culinary cultures.

Who benefits the most from this selective "manufacture" of culture? Not the slaves, of course. Not even the sailors, who were often abused by their captains. As historian Svend Erik Green-Pedersen investigated, the average death rate for European sailors during the period 1777–1789 was 33 percent, much higher than African slaves, which stood at about 15 percent.[55] Many sailors could not survive the voyage, and their bodies were simply discarded along the way, buried sometimes by the Africans they once brutalized.[56]

The European proletariat were not benefited, either, even though they could drink tea with sugar, maybe plus a dessert. Few of them could realize the global impact of their enhanced sweet tastes. Few knew at the time that this is an addictive substance and that consuming too much of it would harm their health. The ultimate beneficiary is, unsurprisingly, the new capitalist world-economy, because by changing the lifestyle of common people, starting from taste buds, it achieves a stable demand and predictable dependency.

Meeting this demand is big business. It entails a vicious cycle of coercion and exploitation, trade and addiction, creating unprecedented levels of profit maximization, culminating in a new empire. This history of sugar was telling, but it was not unique. Kevin Bales, an antislavery expert who took part in the drafting of the Bellagio-Harvard Guidelines, uses the example of Brazilian pig iron and the steel industry to illustrate similar processes of long-distance dependency going hand in hand with slavery practices, as discussed in chapter 2 in this volume.[57] Despite critique from Patterson, my take is that Bales does not exaggerate his allegation, which does more than point out the pervasiveness of our indirect contribution to modern-day slavery. He highlights the scope of the problem rooted in global structures of trade as much as in our daily consumption habits, addictions, and voluntary submission to such a regime of unequal power relations. In so doing, he confirms this old argument by Col. Patrick Montgomery, secretary of the Anti-Slavery Society: "Slavery will cease only when human rights in general are effectively protected."

• • •

Leading the charge into cyberspace, Andrew Ross made a poignant reference to new ways of exploiting free or token-wage labor on the internet as "expanded prison labor programs."[58] In reality, there is indeed an imperceptibly thin line between voluntary donation of one's time and addicted behavior beyond control. On the surface, it appears that the fans, volunteers, and digital laborers have a choice not to play online, inasmuch as Chinese workers can be seen as having the option not to join Foxconn. But is there really such a choice? Does the process of individual decision making depend more on free will than on systematic incentives or structural constraints? For many Chinese migrants, choosing not to work for factories like Foxconn would mean hunger, eviction to the street, or being unable to buy a ticket home. Choice is nothing but a deceptive façade when one can choose only from this or that sweatshop, neither of which has an independent union; when one can select to play only this or that online game, both of which are owned by profit-driven corporations.

As Nancy Holmstrom wrote sarcastically: "Persons who have no access to the means of production other than their own capacity to labor do not need to be forced to work by chains and laws."[59] In the factory zones, a migrant worker cannot really afford the financial risk of skipping assembly-line work. At school, teenagers from working-class families, like Yang Ni, had to suffer from being socially excluded by their iPad-waving peers. The two types of iSlaves—manufacturing and manufactured—therefore share much in common, as both can be seen as manifestations of voluntary servitude structured under macro forces of alienation.

Such seemingly "voluntary" action, including addiction, previously spread more slowly, sometimes serendipitously. Yet nowadays such diffusion is not only faster but also much more manipulated by commercial interests with the rising army of immaterial labor. The fundamental political economy, however, remains largely the same. Christian Fuchs's critique of Facebook is most relevant here, although this critique is applicable to other social media platform as well: "Facebook labor creates commodities and profits. It is therefore productive work. It is, however, unpaid work and in this respect shares characteristics of other irregular workforces, especially house workers and slaves, who are also unpaid."[60]

Fuchs notes the main difference between free labor on Facebook and slaves: "slaves are the private property of slave masters, by whom they can be killed if they refuse work." In his critical analysis that connects classic Marxian theory with the thinking of Dallas Smythe, Fuchs continues using the material measurement of time for Facebook users: "One hundred per cent of their labor time is surplus labor time, which allows capitalists to generate extra surplus value and extra profits."[61]

Like Fuchs, Mark Andrejevic argues that the business model for targeted ads online—what Ethan Zuckerman calls "the Internet's original sin"[62]—is based on companies exploiting free labor of users, including their personal data, whose commodification may or may not be something that users are aware of.[63] "If consumers are generating value, we can interrogate the conditions that structure who is compelled to surrender the economic value generated by their activity and who benefits."[64] Otherwise, continued commodification and privatization of the social media platforms lead to "the next stage of the colonization of social life by commerce and marketing."[65]

Andrejevic refers to Ian Ayres's 2007 bestseller *Super Crunchers* that envisages, "Super Crunching will predict what you will want and what you will do"; "firms sometimes may be able to make more accurate predictions about how you'll behave than you could ever make yourself."[66] Both Andrejevic and Ayres see grave danger in the rapidly expanding computing power of big corporations, which also have much stronger capacity now than ever before in extracting user-generated content (UGC), making use of Big Data, and imposing its data "violence" via intellectual property rights regimes enforced by not only lawyers and courts but also by dedicated computer codes and algorithms.

What neither of them has asked, but what one should ponder after revisiting the historical lessons of sugar, is a different set of questions: If cyberspace is today's New World, is UGC the new sugar? Who's the equivalent of England's new working-class—now having a "sweet tooth" for UGC? Who's becoming addicted? Are corporations like Apple and Google now becoming too obsessed with Big Data? Is the new sugar of UGC causing corporate obesity, making them less sustainable? As individual companies, they have tasted the sweetness of "free labor." But as they become addicted, are they also developing new kinds of dependency, vulnerability, even voluntary servitude—but serving whom?

FIGURE 4.2 "First mobile phone sidewalks in China," Chongqing, Sichuan Province, June 2015. Courtesy of Weiwei Zhang.

For decades, a popular sci-fi imagination about the future of human–machine interaction has been the cyborg, as our bodies absorb high-tech parts that enhance our physical and/or psychological functionality. Yet the tragedy of Yang Ni's selling his kidney, shedding light on the lot of today's manufactured iSlaves, seems to suggest the very opposite: it's not about adding things to our body. Rather, it's about hollowing us out, removing an organ from within, removing human spirit.

The consequences of this process are twofold. On the one hand, manufactured iSlaves would descend, at length, into the trap of voluntary servitude. On the other hand, the value of that extracted organ, that commodified part of the informational me, would ascend—it would get harvested by the powers that be, to be transferred upward along the hierarchy of social class—hence the detachment of manufactured iSlaves from their digital selves. Addiction becomes enslavement.

## Tyrannical Time

While the functioning of manufacturing iSlaves, as in Foxconn, depends on spatial structures of physical and social enclosure, the most fundamental dimension for the operation of manufactured iSlaves is, arguably, time. No matter how specific forms of slavery mutate, the exploitative relationship based on "powers attaching to the right of ownership" invariably aims at possessing and profiting from the value-generating hours, days, months, or years of service provided by the enslaved. Digital media may have changed the working units into minutes, seconds, even fractions of a second as consumer attention flashes through the Apps and online content. But these are, nonetheless, still temporal units of labor power.

The basic importance of time was long evident in historical analysis of slavery. Robin Blackburn was among those who did the actual calculation, for instance, regarding year 1800, when

> Britain acquired the produce of around one million slaves, each working for an average of 2,500 to 3,000 hours in the year and producing crops worth around £18. . . . Thus sugar, tobacco and cotton which had cost the slaves 2,500,000,000 hours of toil was sold by metropolitan merchants or manufacturers to consumers who, in order to afford

these purchases, themselves had to labour for hundreds or thousands of millions of hours for their employers. At retail prices these consumers had to pay a gross sum that could not have been much less than £35,000,000 around the turn of the century.[67]

Using similar methods, my estimation is that for Foxconn's 1.4 million employees, if on average each of them work ten hours a day and 340 days a year, the total hours would add up to 4.76 billion—in other words, nearly twice the total amount of slave labor power the British Empire was able to muster in 1800. Although without an indicator for per-hour productivity, this rough comparison can at least partially put things into perspective when it comes to the total size of manufacturing iSlaves.

The next question: How much time have manufactured iSlaves spent on their coveted gizmos? According to Global Web Index, a major marketing research team focusing on digital consumers, the average daily time users worldwide spent online via their gadgets (PCs, laptops, mobiles and tablets) had increased to 6.15 hours in 2014, of which 1.72 hours are spent on social network sites each day.[68] Meanwhile, as of December 2015, Facebook has a total of 1.59 billion monthly active users, of whom 1.04 billion are daily active users.[69] Calculating these daily active users only, assuming that they maintain their activity level throughout the year, the total hours of labor power for Facebook would reach a whopping level of 652,912,000,000. This is more than 261 times larger than the input from the plantations to the British Empire in 1800. It is also more than 137 times larger than the size of labor power accumulated along Foxconn's assembly lines, although here only Facebook is counted, not other social network platforms!

In abstract terms, these numbers may not be too meaningful. But think about it—when you have to sit in front of a computer screen ten hours a day, when you hold your hand-held device for so long and so regularly that your arms start to hurt, when your neck and backbone become stiff after working/playing around the clock: it is not only your bodily posture but also how long you do these things without a break. Even though this cumulative time may well be intangible, this constitutes a material dimension because it confines bodily movement and the materiality of everyday experience. Understanding time as a material object, even a material commodity that can be exchanged, monetized, accumulated—this is a foundation for Marx's labor value theory, when factory owners could extract surplus value by producing commodities more efficiently below the average "socially necessary labor time."

Time is an elementary unit to measure the materiality of labor, including digital labor. Extending this insight from the conventional factory to advertiser-supported media systems such as TV in the 1970s, Dallas Smythe proposed the notion of "audience commodity":[70] when one watches TV with commercials, one's time of watching TV becomes the commodity being produced, valorized, and sold to advertisers.[71] Building on Smythe's critique, Mark Andrejevic argues that a similar process of audience commodification has occurred online in today's digital cultures, where "exploitation" is deepened because we are not only watching but also being watched.[72] We are not only participating but also *self*-generating as codes of surveillance and UGC provide advertisers with more, and more precise, information about what we do, what we want, and how we can be "manufactured" to want things we may or may not need.

· · ·

For manufactured iSlaves, exploitation along the temporal dimension goes far beyond the sheer amount of time. It is, as Judy Wajcman contends, more profoundly about the tempo, the quality, and the discipline of time, which have undergone dramatic change under conditions of digital capitalism.[73] The overall trend is acceleration, which is a cultural trend as much as an institutional arrangement materializing through the design of digital technologies. Instead of a historical novelty, this trend follows an age-old pattern since the Industrial Revolution. While we are "at a pivotal juncture in the evolution of technology," writes Wajcman, "industrial regimes still set the contours of our lives."[74] Quoting Ben Agger, Wajcman concurs that it makes sense to see the contemporary world as being governed by "iTime," in other words, "a manic, compulsive, deeply compressed time 'weighing heavily on the person who always has too much to do, not enough time to do it.'"[75]

iTime is the temporal regime that pulls the strings behind iSlaves. Wajcman's analysis centers on the "time–pressure paradox," in other words, the "lack of congruence between the amount of free, discretionary time available to us and our contemporary feelings of harriedness."[76] This can be seen in many aspects of social and professional life, but it is most acutely evident in relation to digital media. Not long ago, with the spread of computers and other intelligent, supposedly time-saving and productivity-boosting technologies, "sociologists talked of the 'end of work' and wondered with some apprehension how the vacant hours would be occupied. Instead, the iconic image that abounds is that of the frenetic, technologically tethered, iPhone- or iPad-addicted citizen."[77]

This paradox of time offers another insightful angle to appreciate the critical notion of manufactured iSlaves: we are ironically losing control over our time while pursuing the latest technological tools to maximize "efficiency" and "convenience," goals that are often defined in consumerist modes that can be very time-consuming to pursue because they tend to be moving targets. Underneath the apparent utilities of perpetual connectivity, the hidden corporate logic of social media and Big Data is to shift the locale of power away from individual users, especially if they are addicted.

Such a logic of time-pressure paradox is not only embedded in the software, the databases, and the "services" of surveillance and targeted advertising that follow the informational me wherever we go. It is also deeply ingrained in the hardware of the gadgets, too. Wajcman writes, "The social determination of time is built in to those technologies, just like the size of the screen is, or the power of the processor."[78] A primary mode of this "determination" has to do with how long a device can function normally before it has to be replaced.

Several years ago, before iPhone conquered the world, Nokia was known for designing its handsets as durable goods that are "made to last" with minimal environmental cost.[79] But with the latest smartphones, be they from Apple, Samsung, or Google, the average designed longevity of the gadgets has quickly declined. You are lucky if your smartphone can remain functional after a couple years of usage. Most people have no choice but to look for a new phone and follow the quick cycle of the industry due to the device's "built-in obsolescence":

The vast expansion of the market for consumer electronics, such as computers, cell phones, televisions, tablets, and MP3 players, is paired with an unprecedented speed of built-in obsolescence and product abandonment. We expect instant delivery of products of all kinds, and then discard them with equal speed, typically without a thought about the conditions of their production or the waste they leave behind. Indeed, one reason that time seems scarce is because it is impossible to consume the vast array of products and services on offer. Whether or not we view human desires as inherently insatiable, contemporary consumer culture is certainly characterized by excess. Symptomatic of this is the endless upgrading of smartphones and a World Wide Web that can be surfed indefinitely.[80]

Here, Wajcman draws an explicit connection between the design logic of obsolescence and the vital role of consumerism as a cornerstone of digital capitalism. She argues, however, against the view that this system is omnipotent and deterministic, leaving no room for agentic action and alternative possibility. While the technologies carry various tendencies of enslavement, Wajcman hopes also to debunk "the notion that we have all become cyber-serfs, technologically tethered workers with no control over our own lives."[81] Instead, she proposes that the solution lies in "temporal sovereignty," in other words, "the ability to choose how you allocate your time,"[82] which can also be enhanced using digital media: "Time may appear inherently egalitarian, in that everyone has just twenty-four hours in a day, seven days a week and twelve months a year, and this will remain the case in the epochs to come. However, temporal sovereignty and sufficient leisure time are important indicators of a good life."[83]

This is a more sophisticated approach toward technology and time, which goes beyond the usual celebratory or gloomy accounts of how digital media will inevitably liberate or enslave us. Alternatives to tyrannical time are possible so long as one is aware of the pitfall and makes efforts to avoid it. Otherwise, if one is careless and just goes with the technology "flow," the likelihood of enslavement would remain high.

Wajcman's principle of temporal sovereignty is consistent with Douglas Rushkoff's argument in *Program or Be Programmed*.[84] A concrete example would be the Fairphone project in the Netherlands, which designs smartphones in democratic and socially responsible ways to counter the "fast fashion" of digital device. The social enterprise behind Fairphone was named "Europe's fastest growing startup of 2015,"[85] a key case to be discussed more in chapter 5.

## Concluding Remarks

This chapter started with the tragic story of Yang Ni, who sold his kidney to buy an iPhone and an iPad. This is an unusual yet most telling case for the second mode of digital enslavement, not in industrial production but in cultural consumption and "prosumption," not the manufacturing but manufactured iSlaves, not forced labor but voluntary servitude. Although this chapter cannot provide an exhaustive account of manufactured iSlaves, it does offer a systematic way to examine the related phenomena from several historical and comparative perspectives.

Figure 4.1 sketches out the conceptual contours from manufacturing to manufactured iSlaves in relation to other modes of labor, free or unfree, including wage labor. Unlike manufacturing iSlaves who tend to concentrate and be isolated in selected factory zones, the landscape of manufactured iSlaves is much more global and diffused. It resembles a world order of consumer cultures and a new level of commodity fetish, serving as a pillar of the digital capitalist world-economy.

The immaterial forms of exploitation can be critiqued from multiple theoretical standpoints, be they autonomist Marxist, feminist, or critical political economy. Historically speaking, it is not uncommon for various slave systems to co-exist, forming symbiotic relations with each other, which is also the case for manufacturing and manufactured iSlaves. Although the geopolitical patterns have their contemporary specificities, the results converge in the rise of consumerist conformity in both digital "organ trafficking" and the spread of addiction among young people.

Manufactured iSlaves with their labor power—call it digital, immaterial, or informational—reside in not only western countries but also increasingly in more affluent regions of the Global South. The time and value they generate feed into the expansion of the gadgets market while providing raw materials of UGC for corporate profit making as well as state surveillance. Geopolitically, this vicious cycle leads to deteriorating trade and labor imbalances, deepening social divides, and worsening environmental impact. Can there be a different path?

The answer is yes if one realizes the fundamentally cultural nature of this technosocial regime. To quote Sidney Mintz again: "It is not our human nature that is universal, but our capacity to create cultural realities, and then to act in terms of them."[86] There is nothing natural about the allure of consumerist technologies, which are rendered through mechanisms of addiction into fetishized objects of digital capitalism due primarily to the voracious need of the world system for market expansion. David Harvey also argues that cultural hegemony and technological diffusion only become possible due to "a mix of consent and coercion,"[87] which echoes Burawoy's as well as Herman and Chomsky's "manufacturing consent" theses.[88] It is therefore imperative to look beyond the dichotomy of coercion and deception while developing a more holistic account for the seemingly voluntary consumerist laborers, who are nonetheless cultural artifacts under duress.

In important ways, this hybridized mode of enslavement is comparable to organ trafficking. While one can speak of UGC as our "third skin" and smartphone our "fifth limb" metaphorically as our "body parts," the power relations underneath are far more realistic and structurally constraining. I do not own the informational me, or, more precisely, my digital "body parts." The Big Data generated from my search results, Twitter conversations, and biometrical movements end up being owned, managed, and mined by corporate entities and state agencies behind closed doors. They control my data "organs" with impunity. Seldom are they held accountable if things go wrong. Like organ trafficking, the value of these Big Data assets tend to travel upward through the hierarchy of social class to serve, ultimately, the rich and the powerful.

At one level, Big Data marks a new hegemonic culture that is infinitely more individual than models of mass consumption in the industrial era. Jacob Silverman writes, "I share, therefore I am—more interesting, more sociable, more desirable, more myself."[89] But at another level, it is also more macro, more panoptic, more disempowering, and reflecting more geopolitical dominance than in the past.[90] Too often, people see only the individualized molecules of the former but forget the collective, structural devolution of the latter. This is a serious symptom of myopia, an ailment encouraged by the cultures of social media.

Toward the end of her critique against iTime, Wajcman concludes: "The 'i' word is practically an intoxicant."[91] The intoxication needs no further belaboring when it comes to the evanescent consumer cultures, of crowdsourced marketing campaigns, and of the myth of "free labor" *a la* Terranova.[92] The pending questions are, how could such a global system of iSlavery be possible? Are there meaningful acts of resistance against it—from within and without?

# 5

# Molding and Resisting Appconn

Appconn—the global digital empire of hardware and software, of content, services, data, and culture—generates, necessitates, and dominates iSlave in both its primary modes, manufacturing or manufactured. By this point I should have dispelled the myth of digital media leading "naturally" to a more humane and just society. But how and why has Appconn emerged with such devastating consequences that parallel slavery? Can it be resisted—by the enslaved?

As discussed in chapter 2, resistance is essential to the history of slavery from the very beginning. It took many forms such as singing and dancing, stealing, sabotage, hunger strike, suicide. The enslaved rebelled and waged wars against all odds. They ran away, became pirates and maroons, built their own economies, communities, and cultures. Although not all acts of resistance succeeded—indeed, many failed—the human experience of slavery as a whole would be seriously incomplete without acts of resistance, a main subject of this chapter.

Another focus of this chapter is geopolitics, which provides basic conditions for and is shaped by vectors of resistance. As discussed previously, Appconn is characterized by innate contradictions between labor and capital, production and consumption, efficiency and sovereignty. The spatial and temporal dynamics of Appconn produce its antithesis, online and off, concentrating in what Samir Amin would call a "tempest zone," where "people on the peripheries [are] . . . ridding themselves both of the illusion that development is possible in the context of capitalist globalization and alternative backward-looking fantasies, and coming up with alternatives for a breakthrough that measures up to the challenges and opportunities of our time."[1]

Writing similarly on a global level, Wallerstein reminds us: "The 'culture,' that is the idea-system, of this capitalist world-economy is the outcome of our collective historical attempts to come to terms with the contradictions, the ambiguities, the complexities of the socio-political realities of this particular system." He continues: "Since it is obvious that interests fundamentally diverge, it follows that such constructions of 'culture' are scarcely neutral. Therefore, the very construction of culture becomes a battleground, the key ideological battleground, in fact, of the opposing interests within this historical system."[2]

By "alternatives" and "opposing interests," Amin and Wallerstein understood more than simply the enslaved populace. Various state actors, commercial entities, sectors of civil society, and concerned citizens can all take part in the movement of resistance as much as they did in supporting and molding Appconn by acting as manufacturing or manufactured iSlaves, unfree labor, overseers, investors, and complacent consumers.

Indeed, slavery and antislavery co-exist in global and regional contexts that abound with colonialism, racism, and sexism, which is as true in cyberspace today as in plantations of the past. This means that forces of imperialism and identity politics often result from and exacerbate existing social inequalities, which shape patterns of resistance as well as domination. Congolese miners extracting minerals under gunpoint, Foxconn workers manning assembly lines in the shadow of suicide-prevention nets, "Chinese gold farmers" being ridiculed in massively multiplayer online role-playing games:[3] these are anything but random occurrences, just as it was more than a coincidence for New World sugar fields to be cultivated primarily by African and African American labor.[4]

The key factor here, especially when it comes to China and the geopolitics of information, is the role of the state, which conditions both Appconn and acts of resistance by providing basic institutional molds and responding to the subsequent politico-economic and/or sociocultural crises. In this chapter, I shall first provide an overview of the state-capital and state-society relationship before having a focused discussion on the different types of worker-generated content (WGC) online, the practices of social media on the picket line, and possibilities of alternative development involving citizens, consumers, and civil society groups, as they did in past resistance and abolition movements. Overall, the approach follows Eugene Genovese's *Roll, Jordan, Roll*, where he explains the internal workings of paternalistic slave regimes in the Old South before illuminating myriad forms of slave resistance, struggling for voice, respect, and freedom.[5]

## Who Made Appconn?

A decade ago, I wrote about the internet in China as "technologies of freedom in a statist information society."[6] Most analyses of contemporary China indeed start and/or end with an examination of Beijing's policies. Yet in this account of iSlavery, why has the state so far been peculiarly absent?

This is, of course, not true. One could delve only slightly into the rise of Appconn to see that the Chinese authorities play an essential role, as much as mercantile policies and empire-building geostrategies molded seventeenth-century slavery and the Atlantic triangular trade. Even when the state deregulates—in other words, decreases its involvement and commitment—it nevertheless creates an enveloping environment for the market, society, and polity with certain prevailing principles, especially under neoliberal rubrics.

Why did China become home to Foxconn? Is it only because China has cheap labor? Why not other developing countries whose labor cost is but a fraction of China's?[7] State policy, regarding minimum wages for instance, is one decisive factor. Basic infrastructure also matters, along with policies for welfare, training, and education, as well as workers' rights to organize, bargain collectively, strike, and picket. It is in these realms that one can clearly see, despite the rhetorics of New Economy, an uncanny return to old politics, to the interplay between capitalist and statist logics, be they competitive or corroboratory.

Simply put, China is home to Foxconn because the Chinese authorities have provided the most accommodating conditions for Appconn. Note Appconn's new growth model has outcompeted the established model of Wintelism (Windows and Intel) with its fabless factories and "electronic manufacture services."[8] No wonder Dan Schiller long regarded China and the IT industry as two "poles of market growth" for global capitalism, although he cautioned that China's state behavior is also a fundamental source of instability.[9] This is more so in recent years given Beijing's initiatives of One Belt, One Road—a super-mega-infrastructure that is supposed to unify Eurasia through the land-based "Silk Road Economic Belt" and the oceangoing "Maritime Silk Road"—as well as the AIIB (Asian Infrastructure Investment Bank).[10] But is this the entire story?

Both Yuezhi Zhao and Yu Hong argued for more in-depth and more complete assessment of China's state-led development initiatives, including especially their internal contradictions. Different interest groups in the ministries, state-owned enterprises, private firms, and different regions of the country often fight bitterly with each other.[11] The power of Beijing is sometimes also exaggerated both in its geopolitical capacities beyond Chinese borders and in its ability to suppress insurrections within.

A reality check is necessary. Yes, China has become the world's largest exporter and the world's largest economy calculated by purchasing-power parity.[12] Yet in some of the supposedly most aggressive frontiers of China's global expansion, its influence has been seriously overestimated. Africa, for example, was called alarmingly "China's second continent."[13] But in 2014, Japan alone accounted for $3.5 billion of all the $4.2 billion project funds Asian countries have invested in Africa, of which Chinese investment comprised only a small part.[14]

As for the much touted BRICS alliance, which is often suspected to be under Beijing's influence, yes, "there is no question that the realm of information and communication has figured prominently in the ongoing contestations over the evolving global order, and the BRICS countries, in their singularity or in collectivity, have been on the forefront of these struggles."[15] But as Yuezhi Zhao demonstrated, Beijing's leadership in the BRICS alliance is feeble and inconsistent. One example is the BRICS cable project, designed to promote Internet connectivity among the five countries and to challenge Anglo-American dominance in global communications. There is, however, little substantive progress beyond the initial hype. Zhao concludes,

> There is enough ground to believe that profound geopolitical differences, entrenched economic interests, US pressures, as well as the enduring power of the US-state-led and Western-media-supported, "democracy v. authoritarian," "freedom v. control" ideological framework, have prevented the BRICS countries from even appearing together or co-hosting a potentially counter-hegemonic meeting on global Internet governance.[16]

Global power shift does not occur overnight. Even more fundamentally, Beijing's seemingly unique role in hosting Foxconn and, in so doing, helping foster Appconn is decided not just by itself but at a higher level by the operational logic of the global commodity chain. The so-called "global race to the bottom" in world manufacturing, starting from the footwear industry, has long prioritized worldwide relocation of productive capacities to Asia since the end of World War II.[17] In East Asia, the neoliberal discourses of "crisis economy" have also long been ingrained in the region's developmental state tradition, following Japan's policy encouraging multimedia industries since the 1990s.[18] The combination of global and regional conditions proved particularly conducive to the growth of factories like Foxconn, whose ascent is explained at least in part by macro-historical imbrication of the capitalist world-economy beyond the control of any nation-state, including China. As Folker Frobel and colleagues pointed out:

> The development of the world economy has increasingly created conditions (forcing the development of the new international division of labour [i.e., NIDL]) in which the survival of more and more companies can only be assured through the relocation of production to new industrial sites, where labour-power is cheap to buy, abundant and well-disciplined; in short, through the transnational reorganisation of production.[19]

This NIDL is arguably the deepest root structure that undergirds Appconn and iSlavery.[20] There is a global logic here not only spatially but in its temporal dimension that influences Foxconn's production cycle, which is ultimately not dictated by Beijing. The real power lies in the world system. Analogous to the Atlantic trade functioning as "the pacemaker of global exchanges from the sixteenth century to the nineteenth,"[21] today's world-economy of Appconn plays an equivalent role in setting the pace for not only the global digital marketplace but also Chinese initiatives on the ground. There are, of course, disruptions and internal conflicts as in transatlantic rivalry among Old World empires and fledging powers of the New World. Competition, confrontation, war—these are also hallmarks of world-system dynamics.

The remaining questions are: What will be the geopolitical fallout of today's transpacific rivalry? Will the China-U.S. showdown be as peaceful as the "friendly antagonism" between Japan and United States in the 1980s? Or will it turn out to be much more devastating due to the disparity, animosity, and self-destructive tendencies of the iSlave regimes?

· · ·

Popular Chinese press has long celebrated the "triumph" of Foxconn in becoming the world's largest electronic manufacturer and extolled the personal qualities of Terry Guo, the Foxconn owner, who became almost as legendary as Steve Jobs. Most of this coverage, however, forgot Foxconn's long record of failures, and the Suicide Express was but one of them. For many years, the company tried to diversify itself from the electronic manufacture service business by investing in software development, audiovisual production, retail, automobile, content, and its own brand of electronics.[22] But all these efforts have fallen through, and Foxconn remains stuck with its old business model at the bottom of the digital media value chain (again comparable to the feitorias in West Africa). Why did Foxconn fail in its new ventures beyond manufacturing? Was it due, at least in part, to insufficient state support?

A peculiar pattern since the turn of millennium is that Beijing's favorable policies ended up fostering Taiwanese tycoons much more than industrialists from Hong Kong, South Korea, Japan, or the West. When Apple decided to divert some of its orders away from Foxconn, it chose Pegatron, yet another Taiwanese-owned, export-oriented company using mostly Mainland Chinese workers.

An old report from 2001 was revealing: Yu Youjun, the mayor of Shenzhen, brought two groups of officials to visit Taiwan, after which they concluded: "Taiwan's minimum wage prevents its factory owners to make a profit. Hiring Filipinos is a dead end. The only solution is to relocate to Mainland China." Commentaries at the time were explicit: "China hopes to leverage the power of these big companies [in electronics manufacturing] so that the Taiwanese government will be more cooperative."[23] Here, China's ambition to fold Taiwan in was manifest. Beijing's generosity toward Taiwanese investment was, in this sense, merely instrumental for a larger, geopolitical goal toward the reunification of Taiwan.

It is, however, erroneous to assume that Foxconn is under firm tutelage of the Chinese authorities. Over the years, the company's ties with high-level officials in Beijing seems to have weakened. Until 2003 it had enjoyed almost complete support from the Jiang Zemin administration while growing exponentially into the world's largest contract manufacturer of electronic gadgets.[24] But the lawsuit in 2006 against *First Financial Daily*, as discussed in chapter 3, ended with Beijing effectively vetoing Foxconn's aggression. It conveyed a clear message from the Hu Jintao leadership that they refused to lend unreserved endorsement to Foxconn as before.

Another watershed moment came in 2010 during the Foxconn Suicide Express. This was the year when China surpassed the United States to become the world's largest manufacturing powerhouse, a historic moment not seen for 120 years since the United States took the No. 1 position from the United Kingdom in late 1880s.[25] It was also the year of Asian Games in Guangzhou, whose official motto was "Safe and Sound Asian Games [*ping'an yayun*]." Beijing authorities had all the reasons to prevent the unprecedented spate of suicides in 2010. Yet they failed.

Chinese authorities conducted their investigations of the fatal events. First, the Shenzhen government sent multiple teams to Foxconn, including the vice mayor and the city's police chief.[26] Their conclusion was that the suicides resulted from "a unique problem during a period of rapid industrialization, urbanization, and modernization. Its deep-seated reasons are found in individual factors of the employees, the enterprise, and society at large."[27] Similar to Foxconn's position, the

Shenzhen municipal government downplayed faults in the company's management system itself.

Beijing central government intervened on May 27, 2010, when the fifteenth suicide occurred in five months. A team of more than two hundred officials led by Mr. Yin Weimin, head of the Ministry of Human Resources and Social Security (MHRSS), was dispatched from Beijing to Foxconn Shenzhen. It included members from All China Federation of Trade Union (ACFTU, the official union), MHRSS, and the Ministry of Public Security (MPS). Their inspection lasted ten days. The full report remains outside the public domain at the time of this writing.

Yet in November 2010 Mr. Jun Guo, a high-level ACFTU official, leaked findings from their investigation: Foxconn asked workers to do more than one hundred hours of overtime shifts each month, well beyond the legal maximum of thirty-six hours; its semi-militarized management system exerts too much pressure on workers, not only during work hours but when employees are off duty. In conclusion, Foxconn had to take responsibility for its "severe management problems."[28]

Beijing's intervention was effective in changing Foxconn's rhetoric and some of its practices. Right before the Beijing team arrived, on May 26, Terry Guo spoke confidently that the suicides had nothing to do with the company's management and that the main reasons for the incidents were workers' "innate personality and their ability to manage their emotions."[29] But soon after the Beijing team left, Guo spoke again, this time with a rare touch of humility, quite different from his usual arrogance, sounding slightly apologetic: "If I broke the law, put me in jail. If I don't, clean my name. After ten days of investigation, I'm not arrested. Therefore, there was no conspiracy. They analyzed individual incidents. We can say, after in-depth scrutiny by this team of more than two hundred officials, I can say we passed."[30]

The growing friction between Foxconn and Chinese authorities is also evident in that the company relied increasingly on the news media, including social media, to steer public opinion. Had Foxconn enjoyed complete support from Beijing as in the Jiang Zemin era before 2003, it would not have hired PR spin doctors to divert public attention. There would probably have been no "iPhone girl" or Terry Guo's high-profile womanizing operations around 2008 either. This media campaign played well with a long track record of Chinese media organizations, especially the market-oriented urban press. As Yuezhi Zhao comments: "In fact, the news media, given their own institutional setup and operational mechanisms, are often guilty of the same superficial, manipulated, and one-sided research and analysis that have contributed to a policy-formation process detrimental to the interests of workers. They are the main channels of propaganda for government officials and factory managers, and they play a major role in amplifying neoliberal reform ideas."[31]

The mediascape is at the same time a cultural battlefield. In February 2015, the same ACFTU official, Mr. Jun Guo, spoke up again against Foxconn's management problems. In response, the company issued a high-profile public statement titled "We Are Not Perfect, but Please See Our Progress," defending itself while accusing the ACFTU of drawing too hasty a conclusion and that Mr. Jun Guo needed to conduct more investigations on the shop floor.[32]

Spurring much debate in the press and in cyberspace, this confrontation was but one of the latest incidents showing how oversimplified it is to deem Beijing as nothing more than a neoliberal state whose choices are limited to assisting Appconn. On the contrary, without Beijing's support and the tolerance of Chinese authorities, iSlavery would have grown much less rapidly. This dependency on the Chinese state is, undeniably, another of Appconn's vulnerabilities.

.   .   .

Despite occasional clash, Beijing's policies have shaped the corporate behaviors of electronic manufacturers and IT companies as well as patterns of worker resistance. An equally crucial, but often underestimated, factor in conventional analysis of geopolitics, is the role of local state, i.e., the provincial and municipal governments, even the district, township, and village-level authorities.

As discussed in chapter 3, a main reason for the Foxconn Suicide Express in 2010 is the estrangement of workers due to the factory's semi-military management system, dormitory regime, and its large number of new recruits. Even if local officials chose not to intervene on the shop floor and in dormitories, the huge influx and concomitant exodus of workers must have created a major impact on local labor markets.

Meanwhile, Foxconn's explanation—and local governments like Shen-zhen concurred—was that suicides happened due to workers' young age and lack of life experience. Why, then, does Foxconn have so many new workers, who are more vulnerable? Why doesn't it retain more experienced ones?

Because the company fired so many experienced employees during the recession years of 2008–2009 as the local state turned a blind eye. But when Foxconn was short on hands, local governments, such as those in Henan Province, were so eager to supply Foxconn with young workers, including student workers, that they made this task their "No.1 project" out of all their work priorities.[33]

Had local state agencies enforced Chinese labor law such that Fox-conn could not have hired and fired workers at will, this would have stabilized the workforce and prevented it from being mostly young inexperienced workers. The failure of local state agencies in this regard means they should share at least part of the blame for the Suicide Express.

Massive layoff is, however, not the only way of crisis management. As Vaclav Smil noted, the Germans responded to the 2008 downturn differently: "The acceptance of smaller wage increases (or even wage freezes) by German unions in return for guaranteed employment, as well as a decision of many owners not to fire workers during a time of slumping demand but to retain a skilled labor force in anticipation of an economic recovery, helped make the country the only economy with falling unemployment."[34] In other parts of China (for example, Dongguan), workers accepted pay cuts to keep their factories from going bankrupt.[35] Yet in Foxconn, they laid off forty thousand workers so "effectively" and "smoothly" that it became a "role model" for human resource managers as Chinese-language trade magazines marveled at it.[36] As Pun and colleagues point out:

> The production management regime is more than a result of Foxconn's own efforts. It would also be impossible without the support of government authorities and transnational capital. The GDP-oriented growth model often leans towards capital gains at the expense of workers. First, export was the priority in the nation's macro economic policy. Under this framework, China uses the low cost and low rights of labor to attract domestic and international capital input. It was against this background that Foxconn achieved swelling profits.

Second, it's unlikely for a pro-capital local state to safeguard the legal rights of workers. This is most clearly the case when they connive with schools to send students to Foxconn for their "internship."[37]

Indeed, the making of Foxconn is a joint venture of many parties, of which the rationale of local state deserves more attention. In recent years, Beijing central government has put more emphasis, at least rhetorically, on sustainable development and social justice. Although local governments followed suit, GDP growth remains a key criterion in assessing their performance. Hence they have a seemingly insatiable appetite for overproduction, for export-oriented accumulation because that is where growth happens most quickly. This logic is most appealing to big companies, who "became more and more adept at imposing sometimes costly technological innovations on reluctant customers, often aided by state regulation that tended to favor large firms rather than small because the costs of regulatory compliance usually diminish with scale of operation."[38]

This observation from David Harvey applies not only to manufacturing iSlaves but also to manufactured iSlaves as well, including the media, advertising, and the latest Big Data industries, although in industrializing economies such as China it is still companies like Foxconn that dominate. Even though the factory's sweatshop nature is an open secret, official categorization still says it is a high-tech company eligible for policy perks. GDP-wise, hosting one Foxconn can be equivalent to hosting hundreds of smaller factories. There is little surprise that local officials chose the easier route given Foxconn's size and political clout. What one does not know is: How many smaller enterprises went bankrupt due to this choice of the local states, and how many jobs were lost along with them? Are they much more than the 1.4 million jobs Foxconn creates in China? The answer is probably yes.

Local governments have gone all out to serve Foxconn, not just in Shenzhen, which built a special customs building inside Foxconn to facilitate its exports.[39] As the factory accelerates its relocation into Chinese hinterlands in recent years, the competition among local governments intensified, for example, between Chengdu and Chongqing.[40] Wuhan built a dedicated railway and six power substations for Foxconn.[41] Township governments such as Qingkangtang, Guizhou Province, set up booths in rural markets and disseminated DVDs to help Foxconn recruit workers.[42] Chengdu, in a record time of merely seventy days, constructed eight huge building complexes for Foxconn—also known as the "iPad city"—where occupational hazards abound.[43]

Even Beijing's grand ambition of Eurasian integration through One Belt, One Road can be seen as at least in part resulting from local state initiatives. Years before the official beginning of this mega-infrastructure project in March 2014, the Chongqing municipality had already shipped four million HP notebooks, all made by Foxconn, to Duisburg, Germany, via freight trains during 2011–2012.[44]

How do workers see this move into the hinterlands? Does the relocation lead to more humane management because the new plants are closer to workers' homes? Foxconn workers see it as little more than a new trick to take advantage of incentives provided by local states, from tax breaks and cheap land to the provision of even more affordable labor. As workers wrote in their own magazine, *Factory Gossip*:

> Without exception, new plants in the hinterland used the old tactics as in the early years of the Shenzhen facilities: using guards to intimidate workers, "caring only about the result, not the process," causing acute confrontation between different divisions of workers, advertising deceptive salaries that sound good but is actually lousy . . . This management strategy of "stick plus (fake) carrot" could easily sway workers' hearts. It could also lead easily to "mass incidents." [45]

In Chinese, the term "mass incidents" is a coded expression for large-scale demonstrations, work stoppage, sometimes violence. These are collective actions of defiance when resistance takes place among large groups of workers. In so doing, they transform China into a more jagged landscape of geopolitical struggle among local states, Beijing central government, the multinationals, and a new working class through the making of network labor.

There is much difference among the contending forces, all of which, however, share one thing in common: they are built upon the failure of the Chinese authorities to eradicate practices similar to slavery. As stipulated in the Harvard-Bellagio Guidelines, "the State has at minimum the positive obligation to bring about the end of either the status or condition of a person over whom any or all of the powers attaching to the right

130

of ownership are exercised."[46] It is this failure that molded Appconn in a deep, structural sense, while sowing the seeds of resistance.

## Worker-Generated Content (WGC)[47]

Slavery takes myriad forms; so does resistance. The global history of slavery is punctuated by violent uprisings like the Haitian revolution of 1803.[48] So is working-class struggle in China by such events as the Tonggang incident of 2009, when workers killed their factory boss in an outburst of collective anger.[49] But overall, as Eugene Genovese argued convincingly, incidents of bloodshed were more an exception than the rule as more mundane instances of resistance occur alongside the accommodation of exploitative regimes in the everyday work and life of the enslaved.[50]

Among workers and activists there is sometimes a tendency to despise those who choose to resist domination through their poetry, folk songs, music, theatrical performance, and online videos—because they are not confrontational enough, because talking is, allegedly, easy. Point well taken, yet I disagree. If one defines slavery not simply as regimes of violence and suppression but more fundamentally in Patterson's terms as "natal alienation" and "social death," it follows that the first act of resistance is precisely about preserving and/or reconstructing the social ties through the most appropriate means of content creation and sharing. "Isolation is vulnerability; the control of communication is power."[51]

One example is the London Correspondence Society (LCS) that was instrumental in connecting the "motley crew" of the Atlantic proletariat in the 1790s—"Irish, Welsh, English and Africans"—against various forces of enslavement: "enclosure, capture, and imprisonment."[52] Their main weapon of resistance? Correspondence, writing letters to each other, before meeting occasionally in pubs and squares. The seemingly "non-confrontational" talks via letters and meetings generated such powerful radical ideas for democracy and antislavery that they made the conservatives tremble, who had to arrest leaders of LCS and charge them with high treason. Ideas and cultures of solidarity are probably more effective than brute force in dismantling the social foundations of slavery. The conservatives know this, so do the radicals.

Given our focus on digital media, which is much more widespread among young workers, it is crucial to note that these new-generation migrant workers, especially those in manufacture and service sectors, are less united, confrontational, and militant compared with their elders in state-owned enterprises and the rural villages. While those of older age still remember and try to continue practicing Maoist politics after they are laid off or facing illegal land grabs, young workers are much more individualistic, consumeristic, and prone to seductions leading toward manufactured iSlavery. Even when collective acts of violence broke out, as in Foxconn Taiyuan (Sha'anxi guards versus Henan workers, September 2012), Foxconn Zhengzhou (assembly-line workers versus quality-control employees, October 2012), Foxconn Yantai (Guizhou versus Shandong workers, September 2013), or earlier in Xuri Toy Factory of Shaoguan (ethnic Han versus Uyghur workers), there were infights among employees of different regional and/or ethnic identities and across internal divisions of labor rather than organized against the ruling elite or the factory itself.

This is why there needs to be a new analytical category of WGC (worker-generated content), by which I understand the alternative expressions, social networking, and cultural formation beyond the scope of UGC (user-generated content), the latter of which is governed by corporate goals and/or the logic of state surveillance. More than a subset of UGC made by workers, the notion of WGC sensitizes us to the critical juncture of class differentiation, power, and content production and, in so doing, opens up extensive spaces of voice, struggle, and solidarity at the grass roots. The naming of "worker" rather than "user" highlights the need to rethink and redefine the creative subjects of our digital era beyond existing Silicon Valley terminologies.

Occurring in cyberspace and beyond, WGC is, in a way, comparable to African singing and dancing during the Middle Passage and on plantations. To unacquainted observers, it may appear to be meaningless, chaotic, crude, repulsive, or, at best, entertaining. But for insiders, it can be immensely spiritual and poetic, gratifying and powerful, defiant and fun. Consistent with established patterns of working-class ICTs, the production and circulation of WGC are based on the existential needs of the information have-less for such basic life necessities as employment, housing, and family as well as self-expression, dignity, and community.[53] This differs considerably from middle-class kids and manufactured iSlaves adopting a new app or UGC service simply because it is trendy, while they discontinue using it because it is "out."

As a result, issues of the offline world, especially livelihood, as well as issues of resistance, are often seamlessly woven into WGC. The agents of change in WGC production include mostly ordinary workers, although activists, NGOs, and informal groups of concerned workers and/or citizens are important, too.

In the past, workers such as those in Foxconn seldom appeared in media coverage. When they did, they seldom spoke. Often, managers spoke for them; officials spoke for them. It was hard to hear their voices, except through NGO reports, conveyed with their own predispositions. Yet with the diffusion of inexpensive digital media, especially affordable camera phones, mobile internet, and social networking services, there has been a major increase of self-expression and participation in public discussion among Foxconn employees and grassroots workers elsewhere, whose voices are increasingly heard online, sometimes further amplified by traditional mass media.

More than a uniquely Chinese development, this echoes a global phenomenon whose impact we are only starting to comprehend. Similar technological and social transformation has been recorded, for example, in the "pavement internet" discussion among South Africa's information have-less (striking mine workers at Marikana, more specifically).[54] Meanwhile, Michael Brown, Eric Garner, the Walter Scott shooting, McKinney—reactions to these incidents of police brutality against African Americans during 2014–2015 were all triggered by smartphone videos shared through social media. They constitute a new genre of resistance, which sets an agenda for public debate and sociopolitical mobilization among the oppressed and the general public.

For many years, similar practices have been fermenting in Chinese cyberspace. The struggle takes place through acts of official crackdown, violent clashes, as well as more peaceful strikes, protests, and negotiations. While the camera phone plays a constant and indispensable role, the social-media platforms involved are perhaps never heard of outside China. Even middle-class Chinese may have stopped using them, but they remain popular among the information have-less.

First, Qzone (or *QQ kongjian*), a blog service provided by Tencent, is arguably the first WGC platform, widely used among workers for a full decade since at least 2005. Its content includes mostly diary entries and photographs. But since 2012, the total volume of WGC has exploded because many workers, including those at Foxconn, started to use the microblogging service Weibo, China's equivalent of Twitter.

Technology offers no more than partial explanation for why WGC has grown by leaps and bounds. The upsurge in recent years has to do with a new wave of collective action among workers, which has swept the nation since the Foxconn Suicide Express.

In May 2010 alone, there were at least seventeen major strikes involving bus drivers, textile workers, as well as assembly-line laborers across China.[55] A Reuters photo in May 2010 showed at least ten workers in Nanhai—all female—using their camera phones to take pictures of the factory guards—probably all male—as an act of deterrence.[56] The dramatic image makes one wonder: would politics of labor become more feminine, less dominated by hegemonic masculinities, due to the spread of digital media?

Foxconn workers also built solidarity among themselves through WGC. In April 2012, approximately two hundred employees of Foxconn Wuhan threatened to jump from their factory rooftop if the company kept neglecting their demand for a wage increase.[57] Images taken by the strikers themselves spread via social media. The event turned out to differ qualitatively from individual acts of suicide. Instead, it became a collective behavior that successfully pressurized Foxconn to increase wages.

Another incident took place in January 2014 when a small-scale protest in Foxconn Shenzhen went viral via Weibo among workers in different parts of China. Following each other's Weibo account, they discussed overtime wages in different Foxconn facilities across the nation, the usefulness in appealing to labor union, and ways to bring more public attention to their collective cause. All the conversations were in the public domain and easily retrievable.

Equally vital is the growing vibrancy of labor advocacy groups in China, who have in recent years invested strategically in capacity building among workers, especially in multimedia production and social-media networking. This is commonly done through lectures and training workshops conducted by NGO staff, university teachers, or students. Occasionally, this is also organized as open sharing sessions among workers who have already accumulated valuable experience or who have the reputation for using social media to support workers' rights.

Besides knowledge transfer in technology know-how, an arguably more crucial function of the labor activist groups is to draw connections between online activities and concrete cases of struggle, such as an ongoing walkout or a pending law suit. Also important is that the sessions and their follow-up discussions on social media would lead workers to the rich cultural repertoire for working-class expression—for example, the long literary tradition known as *dagong shige* (migrant-worker poetry) that has accumulated in South China for more than three decades.

The influence of labor NGOs, and of WGC at large, is, however, not to be exaggerated if one takes the dominant UGC as comparative referent. Still, most people, including most workers, engage in UGC activities with little interests beyond those of a socially isolated digital consumer. The more daring ones, on the other hand, must face mass media censorship, internet surveillance, and other means of social control, including the danger of imprisonment. The impact of WGC is increasingly visible, but it has not reached the level to compete with dominant modes of prosumption.

A main limitation is that WGC is often image driven because most workers hate verbosity when they type Chinese characters. With the help of a camera phone, they weave together their narratives using still images and sometimes videos with no more than a few words. But these images and videos are open texts with ambiguous, sometimes contradictory meanings. A scene of violent confrontation—for instance, between guards and workers—can be interpreted as a heroic act of resistance. It can also be framed as a justification that workers need to be further disciplined or that violence is acceptable, even expected, when an argument arises in the factory zone.

Where will WGC lead us? The answer to this question is likely to become a cornerstone for the future of Appconn, and of iSlavery, in our globalized digital culture. Although prospects for progressive change fall in the realm of "politics without guarantee,"[58] alternative modes of expression and instances of empowerment have indeed sprouted in the new territories of WGC. The question arises over how to conceptualize it systematically. A typology is in order.

Applying the procedure of property space analysis introduced by Howard Becker,[59] figure 5.1 presents a logically exhaustive typology of WGC. This means that although instances of WGC have grown along with its diversity, which is likely to multiply with future acts of resistance, all empirical possibilities are contained in this two-by-four typology. The goal here is to capture the essence of alternative development—alternative vis-à-vis the old political economy of UGC—along three dichotomous dimensions, namely: collectivity, activism orientation, and empowerment effect.

Yes, subjects of WGC production include workers from all walks of life: factory or call-center employees, waiters or domestic helpers, NGO staff or activist-workers. They have very different skills, experiences, social and cultural capital, regional and/or ethnic identity, and class consciousness. But their online activities are either conducted collectively or

| | | Collectivity | | | |
|---|---|---|---|---|---|
| | | + | | - | |
| | | Empowerment | | Empowerment | |
| | | + | - | + | - |
| Activism orientation | + | 1 | 2 | 5 | 6 |
| | - | 3 | 4 | 7 | UGC |

FIGURE 5.1   A typology of worker-generated content (WGC).

individually, either with or without an activist goal toward social change, and they either empower or do not empower workers.

Logically speaking, there is neither possibility outside the property space of this two-by-four typology nor instances of one case falling into multiple cells. The dots in figure 5.1 represent, in a rough estimate, the total number of cases that have been observed and/or recorded. The dark box of UGC is the domain of manufactured iSlaves, which still accounts for the bulk of everyday online behavior among workers. It does not involve collective production, activism orientation, and has no empowerment effect—at least this is my working definition of UGC—meaning it does not count as WGC.

More specifically, the first dimension of collectivity differentiates the producer as a collective WGC agent from an individual user—"natally alienated," as Patterson would say. Although self-organized worker groups remain hard to come by, NGOs such as Shenzhen's Tiny Grass, known for fostering worker photographers, have increased their communal presence online.[60]

The second dimension defines the process of production and sharing as either activism or mere recording. Activist WGC strives to change people's perceptions, attitudes, behaviors, and/or public policy. Simple recording of what one observes or mere expressions of one's feeling lack this intentionality.

Third is the empowerment effect, meaning one has to go beyond online discourse and see whether the content and social interactions lead to real change in shop floor politics, individual cases of grievance, collective action, factory management, and/or state policy—making differences not only online but also in workers' everyday life and work. The very opposite of empowerment would be rhetoric that sounds progressive but does not challenge the status quo, which in the final analysis serves the interests of what Jodi Dean calls "communicative capitalism."[61]

The following is a list of the main types of WGC with some brief examples and discussions:

1. *Collective activism with empowerment.* From perspectives of solidarity building and the formation of effective resistance cultures, this is

the most desirable type of WGC, although its actual occurrence remains sporadic. An example is the twenty-university joint investigation team that produced not only the influential series of reports on Foxconn labor conditions since 2010 but also led to long-lasting social-media platforms like iLabor.org. With explicit movement goals, it has led to tangible change in the behaviors of the factories. Another case in point, led by grassroots workers and their families, was the campaign to protect Tongxin Experimental Elementary School in a community of migrant workers on the outskirts of Beijing.[62]

2. *Collective activism without empowerment.* This type is not uncommon in high-profile cases of worker struggle. Due to the size and prominence of Foxconn and Apple, there have been several instances involving injured Foxconn workers such as Zhang Tingzhen.[63] Using photographs, videos, and text messages, labor activists and fellow workers helped raise public awareness of their suffering and the difficulty of their families in seeking legal compensation. The collective efforts were only successful in raising media and public attention and fell short of bringing about substantive change in either improving the victims' current conditions or changing corporate and/or state behaviors. Another important case is the forced eviction of Tiny Grass Workers' Cultural Home in Shenzhen.[64]

3. *Collective production without activist goals but has empowerment effect.* There is no good example in this category. Empowerment probably does not happen if the enslaved remain content with the status quo.

4. *Collective production with neither activist goal nor empowerment effect.* This is most commonly seen in media literacy training sessions (for example, regarding social media, photography, and multimedia production) held in NGO offices, community centers, and universities. Although such training may serve as basis for future activities by providing technical know-how and social networking resources, it is not empowerment per se.

5. *Individual activism with empowerment effect.* Due to structural constraints against collective formations online and off,[65] the cost has become very high for Chinese people to come together even using digital media. But individuals with grievances or advocacy goals nevertheless keep producing and sharing WGC by themselves and, occasionally,

they succeed. This was the case of numerous pictures and videos shot during factory strikes and circulated online, to great social effect, such as the 2010 Nanhai Honda strike and the success story of occupational disease victim Zhang Haichao.[66] Another prominent case is Zhang Jun, the worker-activist, who used high-impact videos during the Ole Wolff strike of 2009, resulting in China's first independent workplace union born out of an industrial action.[67]

6. *Individual activism without empowerment.* There are countless examples in this category, as victims of enslavement and those who cannot stand the injustice anymore choose to act by themselves to protest, confront the powers, protect their legal rights, and/or throw light on the origins of their sufferings. But without collective formation, chances are they cannot have much influence. Mr. Lu, a former Foxconn employee, filed a lawsuit against the plant in spring 2013. He made an unedited video in his family living room; it was more than forty minutes long. He distributed hyperlinks to this video via Weibo but ended up losing his case, which received little public attention.

7. *Individual production without activism orientation but with empowerment effect.* So far no empirical example can be found for this logical type of WGC.

To sum up, resistance to Appconn spurs alternative WGC expressions, which is not only about online content but also about ways to create and collaborate, the modes of production in digital environments, and the real-world effects against alienation, suppression, and the deprival of workers' voices.

More than a unitary occurrence, WGC comprises a heterogeneous space of new possibilities in resistance, whose diversity is only partially appreciated in this typology. The multiplicity of media practices reflects diversity in workers' employment conditions, everyday life, and sociality, not merely face to face but increasingly online, especially in camera-phone-equipped labor networks that are extending their influence through social media. This is particularly noteworthy when the goals are noncommercial and advocacy oriented, despite the fact that only a fraction of them have succeeded in bringing about empowerment effects beyond the discursive level.

Undeniably, the world of digital media is still largely dominated by UGC. Like past acts of resistance prior to a major slave uprising, today's WGC stays on the margins and deep underneath the seemingly perpetual cycles of manufacturing and manufactured iSlaves. Burgeoning as it is, WGC remains an inchoate arena of culture and democracy. There are many online images of workers dancing Gangnam Style or dressing up as Angry Birds, trying to reclaim their unpaid wages, but none of them succeeded in reaching their goal. There are many camera-phone videos of fighting among ethnic groups in the factory zones, leading to severe rioting and bitter divides within the working class. Yes, more voices in cyberspace, but who actually is listening?[68] How do different groups make sense of WGC?

Before history reveals more answers to these questions, at least one should reckon that the emergence of WGC, with its internal diversity, is an important harbinger of change—from individual struggle to class formation, from mere recording and self-expression to voices of advocacy and activist pursuits, from disappointing failures, over and again, to the ultimate triumph of humanity. It is, at the very least, more promising to look for alternative futures of digital media in the realm of WGC outside the old box of UGC.

## Social Media on the Picket Line[69]

The Yue Yuan shoe factory strike in Dongguan, involving more than forty thousand workers during April 2014, was among the biggest collective actions in China in recent years.[70] The world's largest manufacturer of branded athletic footwear, Yue Yuan is, like Foxconn, Taiwanese-owned. For many years it had failed to pay the full social insurance contributions for the workers' retirement plan as required by Chinese labor law, and the local government turned a blind eye. When Dan Levin from *New York Times* reported on the event, he found something noteworthy and highlighted it in his headline: "Plying Social Media, Chinese Workers Grow Bolder in Exerting Clout."[71]

Figure 5.2 shows one of many images from the Yue Yuan picket line, circulated to me via WeChat, the most popular social-media platform in China since late 2013. This is a handwritten poem by an anonymous

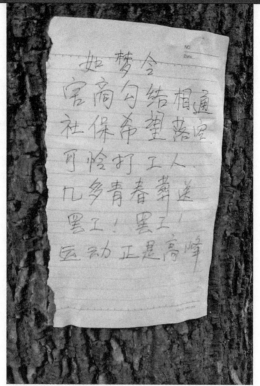

图1：如梦令·罢工

FIGURE 5.2  "A brave and bold *dazibao*": photograph of a picketer poem circulated via WeChat on April 24, 2014.

(author's translation):

*Officials collude with bosses,*
*Insurance becomes our losses.*
*What a pity, workers—our youthful years just a fuss.*
*Strike! Strike! The peak of labor movement is upon us.*

picketer, posted on a pine tree. Someone took a photo of it, using her or his camera phone, and named it "a brave and bold *dazibao*." Meaning literally "big-character poster," *dazibao* was the dominant format of grassroots political communication popularized by Chairman Mao himself during the Cultural Revolution of 1966–1976. The rhythmic structure of the poem, on the other hand, is called *rumengling*, a poetic format that has been around since Song Dynasty a millennium ago.

Plain and simple as it looks, this image makes several substantial revelations about the conjuncture between social-media activism and picket-line struggles in twenty-first-century DNA (digitally networked action). First is its uniqueness. While massive strikes had been associated mostly with mass-circulation press and broadcast media in the history of industrial capitalism, it is in the industrializing regions of Global South, such as China today, that one witnesses digital networks intertwining with picket lines in such creative ways as captured in figure 5.2.

Second is the blurry boundary, if there is a meaningful one at all, between "talk" and "act," between writing poetry, producing content, and being physically on the front line of struggle, in the volatile moments of labor uprising.

Third are the multiple layers of cultural meaning woven together into a thick tapestry of political expression, traditional or contemporary. Song Dynasty rhyme, Maoist label, camera-phone image, social-media sharing. Elements of diverse cultural traditions and technological tools are brought together to highlight the injustice of the system and sound a rallying call—both online as appeals to the general public via WeChat and, perhaps more important, offline among picketers and comrades.

From another angle of history regarding the Atlantic system of slavery, however, one should not celebrate Chinese social media on the picket line simply due to the novelty of the phenomenon. Many more extraordinary struggles have happened before. Soon after the transatlantic trade began, there were records of slave resistance, such as the mutiny after the wreck of the British ship *Sea Venture*, which inspired Shakespeare's *The Tempest*.[72] According to Marcus Rediker, "the modern practice called the 'strike'" originates from "the militant action of sailors who 'struck'—took down—the sails of their vessels."[73] Meanwhile,

Rediker wrote about the enslaved at the time: "Amid the brutal imprisonment, terror, and premature death, they managed a creative, life-affirming response: they fashioned new languages, new cultural practices, new bonds, and a nascent community among themselves aboard the [slave] ship."[74]

Most remarkable was the collective forging of a common "African" identity and resistance culture that Rediker considers the equivalence of modern class making. Before capture, the Africans lived in various communities of West Africa speaking different languages, practicing different lifestyles, worshiping different gods. It was during and after the Middle Passage that they realized, in the face of brutal suppression and alienation, the commonalities of their plight and the collective hope of survival through solidarity. Creolization, hybridity, and the fusion of diverse and multilayered cultural elements thus became the rule, between Africans and aboriginal Americans, between gospel music and Christianity, between old tradition, new media technology (for example, the printing press), and ongoing political struggle on the ground.

Breaking loose from the confinement of slavery, the newly liberated also invented new economic and political institutions. As Linebaugh and Rediker point out, "pirates built an autonomous, democratic, multiracial social order at sea."[75] Analyzing the economics of Atlantic pirate organization,[76] Peter Leeson demonstrates that this multi-ethnic workforce of the "motley crew" created their modern division of labor, welfare, and electoral system, which were established and practiced decades before the founding fathers of the United States wrote the principles down—only in principle though, because in practice, African Americans did not enjoy the same political rights as those of European descent well into the modern era. Yet on pirate ships centuries ago, the radically thinking actors of resistance were already eradicating racial discrimination through electoral practices: one man, one vote, regardless of the color of skin.

Social-media practices on Chinese picket lines are, no doubt, still impressive. Compared with the Atlantic history of antislavery struggles, they remain, however, less remarkable in scale and historical impact, at least in this current, initial stage. Or, it is probably more accurate to construe both struggles as components of the same historical process, of protecting human dignity from capitalist exploitation, of building social bonds against slavery. Seen as such, it should be quite meaningful if front-line picketers in China can, so long as time permits, learn a few lessons and tricks of resistance in the Atlantic theater.

•  •  •

The capitalist world-system is approaching its "terminal crisis," as Immanuel Wallerstein contends; he identifies three "secular trends" or "antisystemic movements": increasing cost of labor, rising expense for material input, and growing demand for public services.[77] So far, most studies on social media and political movements have focused on the second and third vectors of change.[78] Yet, what about workers? Is there a new class politics emerging from labor activism online? If so, how do we make sense of it in the context of Appconn and iSlavery?

As argued above, social media on the picket line is characterized by the fusion of media channels, traditions of political culture, and new and old means of solidarity formation. To avoid the constraint of binary thinking, I would structure the following discussion based on Raymond Williams's framework of "the dominant, the residual, and the emergent."[79] This tripartite framework sheds new light on the complex landscape of working-class social media, particularly their historical hybridity, when it comes to collective endeavors of resistance.

By "dominant," Williams means the cultural hegemony of a given society, which may or may not be effective in exercising control, as discussed earlier in the case of Appconn. It nevertheless remains the most commonly seen, heard, and performed category of practices in line with ideologies of the ruling class. In China today, "neoliberalism with Chinese characteristics"[80] has found expressions in not only officialdom and the corporate world but also the daily chores of the workplace, goals of one's personal life, and online behaviors of the ordinary. Under the yoke of manufactured iSlavery, workers may also see themselves as nothing more than individual consumers.

The "residual" includes a culture's past elements, whose "place in the contemporary cultural process is profoundly variable": "A residual cultural element is usually at some distance from the effective dominant culture, but some part of it, some version of it—and especially if the residue is from some major area of the past—will in most cases have had to be incorporated if the dominant culture is to make sense in these areas."[81]

In Chinese contexts, the residual consists of Confucian elements, from filial piety to obedience to authority. Although the Communist Party once tried to uproot Confucianism, since the 1990s Confucian values have been redeployed to prevent unrest. Even without this official revival, Confucian traditions persist in workers' everyday linguistic and social practices, extending online.

Things are more complex when it comes to Maoism, which used to be the cornerstone of Chinese communism but is no longer hegemonic. Although the Party has tried to incorporate Maoist elements, young migrant workers in factory zones often fail to make sense of them. While older workers with personal memories of the previous era have used Maoism, for example, in the rustbelt of China's Northeast, these practices are of a more "residual" nature and have seldom converged with thriving working-class youth cultures emerging from cybercafés and smartphones in the South.

A small number of young workers did discover Maoism by themselves and by using the internet to compare notes, debate and agitate, and build solidarity with strikers and activists across the nation. Wing (pseudonym), a twenty-six-year-old who worked for and blogged from a Foxconn facility in South China, was a seasoned social-media activist. He told me that he became a Maoist in his late teens through self-learning on the internet more than reading books.[82] He was thrown in jail for three months for disseminating leaflets during a large-scale strike in a state-owned enterprise. He learned the hard way that leaflets, and print materials in general, had limited influence yet brought more liability. The internet was, on the other hand, more cost effective. Keenly aware of the pitfalls of online activism and digital divide, he decided to spend more time in real-world class struggle, using blogs, internet forums, Weibo, and WeChat as tools of assistance.

This is not a singular case. Wing has thousands of followers online, and there are other influential worker-bloggers like him. Together they show that Maoism is more than a residual; it can be part of the emergent, too. During what Gramsci calls "a great metaphysical event,"[83] the emergent can even pave the way for proletariat hegemony prevailing over the mainstream ideologies of neoliberalism.

What, then, is the emergent? Again, back to Williams:

> By "emergent" I mean, first, that new meanings and values, new practices, new relationships and kinds of relationship are continually being created. But it is exceptionally difficult to distinguish between those which are really elements of some new phase of the dominant culture (and in this sense "species specific") and those which are substantially alternative or oppositional to it: emergent in the strict sense, rather than merely novel.[84]

For our discussion, it would be reasonable to see iSlavery as "some new phase of the dominant culture," while WGC and social media on the picket line are "substantially alternative or oppositional to it." The emergent is, no doubt, even more a process than an entity when compared with the dominant and the residual. This process is not predetermined to succeed, even to cohere, because a "new class is always a source of emergent cultural practice, but while it is still, as a class, relatively subordinate, this is always likely to be uneven and is certain to be incomplete."[85]

This emergent nature can be seen among the self-taught worker-Maoists these days, who face constant censorship and crackdown. They are caught in the online crossfire between leftists and liberals, between "Maoist-leftists," "liberal leftists," Trotskyists, and anarchists—most of whom are, however, from elitist backgrounds and not workers. Young worker-Maoists are therefore often ridiculed and stigmatized, which makes their online status even more precarious and "emergent."

Meanwhile, one has to realize that Maoism is only part of the emergent, which includes myriad resistance cultures: feminism, eco-socialism, fair trade, and human rights campaigns to eradicate child labor, reduce work injury and occupational disease, or raise awareness about ethnic and religious minorities—to mention just a few. They emerge from concrete struggles, individually and collectively, now converging increasingly via social media into inchoate yet notable political formations of labor resistance against iSlavery.

•  •  •

Like most countries of the Global South, the digital landscape in China is characterized by the predominance of working-class ICTs and by the bulk of the online population being members of the information have-less.[86] The technological reality and demographic features have prepared fertile ground for the emergence of DNA and a new working class in cyberspace.

China has the world's largest internet population: 688 million in December 2015, of which 620 million rely on mobile access.[87] The nationwide penetration is only 50.3 percent, though, given there are more than 1.3 billion Chinese. These are, however, much more than the rich and educated: 80.4 percent of China's online population does not have a college education.[88] 60.1 percent of them earn no more than 3,000 yuan ($483) each month, much lower than the country's average monthly income level of 4,164 yuan ($671) in 2014.[89] It is among these less-privileged sectors of society that one finds the digital equivalence of China's "motley crew."

After years of rapid growth, social media have started to approach saturation in the country. The user population of Weibo, China's largest Twitter-like service, declined to 230.5 million in 2015, 20.3 percent down from 2013. However, Qzone blog service—favored by members of the working class—kept growing to 447.9 million.[90] While those with higher income and education have decreased their activities in Weibo, the have-less groups with lower income and less education have increased their presence.

The diffusion of digital media in China takes place in the seething context of increasing social unrest. From 1993 to 2004, the country's total number of "mass incidents" had jumped from about 10,000 to 74,000, which further increased to more than 180,000 in 2011.[91] Most of these were triggered by land grabs in rural areas, whereas about one-third of them—roughly 60,000 in 2011—were due to labor unrest. Social media is at both the center and the edge of this maelstrom involving workers facing increasing exploitation and state suppression who nevertheless refuse to succumb.

China blocks Twitter, Facebook, and other popular social-media platforms from the West. Although circumvention technologies are commonly used among middle-class netizens, their dissemination is minimal among ordinary picketers. Workers instead utilize domestic social media including (chronologically): QQ, since the turn of century; blogs, online forums, and Internet video sites, since around 2004; and Weibo and WeChat, since 2010.

QQ is the oldest working-class social media. Launched in 1999, this instant-messaging service gained tremendous popularity, first in the export zones of South China, especially among young workers, whose main mode of access was mobile phone. In addition to one-on-one chatting, QQ supports group chatting through its QQ Cluster (*Q qun*) service, which is by far the most preferred tool for information exchange and coordination among strikers regardless of whether the industrial action happens in a factory, a hotel, or among teamsters. Because QQ networks consist mostly of personal friends, the discussions tend to be informal and inaccessible by outsiders.

The year 2004 marked a new beginning for social media on the picket line. In August, three thousand workers in a military-equipment plant in Chongqing occupied their factory to prevent asset privatization. In September, more than ten thousand workers from a textile factory in Xianyang walked out to protest the acquisition of their work unit by a Hong Kong company. In both cases, workers' collective action faced violent suppression and media censorship. However, word spread via QQ and online forums to overseas news portals, breaching the lines of information lockdown.

In December 2004, sixteen thousand workers in Uniden, a Japanese-owned electronics factory in Shenzhen, began a strike, using blogchina. com to record their daily activities, calling for media attention and public support. It was most successful in making international headlines, including in the *New York Times*.[92] Workers were, in these instances, able to use social media for independent public communication prior to China's urban middle class, for whom the moment came only in 2007, the year of Xiamen PX demonstrations.[93]

Due to high labor mobility, limited dormitory space, and affordability issues confronting ordinary Chinese migrants,[94] Uniden workers relied on cybercafé to maintain their blog, which made them vulnerable. Authorities controlled the cybercafé and forced workers to whitewash their blog. But it was too late because by then word had spread via online forums, some more mainstream, others more left leaning. The social media environment of this phase was hence not about one or two services but about "an enlarged media ecology"[95] comprising countless blogs and forums.

Another critical moment came in October 2006, when workers in Ole Wolff, a Danish electronics factory in Shandong, began industrial action, which lasted on and off until 2009. This was the struggle that included Zhang Jun, who was mentioned in earlier discussion of WGC. Here, there was not only a familiar pattern of blog-plus-online-forum interactions but also Zhang Jun's vlog (video blog) titled "Red Ole Wolff Union's Podcast." Besides showing new footage of confrontation, it relayed mass media reports on the strike that workers deemed helpful, which further enlarged the ecology to subsume official and commercial reports.

This new ecology of pro-strike social media, expanding from blogs to forums to videos, is more publically oriented than QQ. It contains more formal content of news releases and open letters, using textual and audiovisual materials, culminating in the 2010 Honda Locks strike, which took place shortly after the Foxconn Suicide Express.[96]

A third phase of working-class social media began with Weibo or micro-blog, then reincarnated through WeChat. By 2009, China already had Fanfou, a Twitter-like service. But the authorities shut down Fanfou in July 2009 following the Urumqi ethnic riot, which was triggered in the first place by mobile-phone images from Xuri Toy Factory, where Han workers attacked Uyghur workers. The next month, August 2009, saw the debut of Weibo, offered by Sina, a major internet portal with deep ties to China's top leadership.

Weibo was upper- and middle-class social media in the first two years, especially given its hierarchical mode of separating ordinary users from influential "big Vs," reproducing class inequalities in the virtual space. But it started to become more working class in 2011, partly due to official crackdown, partly due to China's bottom-heavy demographic structure. In addition to the remarkable expansion of have-less groups online, labor NGOs also started to adopt Weibo. Since 2012, they have been offering Weibo training sessions to workers, including picketers. Although many NGO staff soon acquired impressive Weibo competence, workers often found the new platform less friendly and harder to use because only a few of their fellow workers were on Weibo in 2012. Even if these early adopters sent out posts, they seldom received similar responses as on QQ, which most workers still preferred for communication among themselves.

Things started to change quickly in summer 2012 when local authorities in Guangdong Province began to censor internet forums while clamping down on NGOs.[97] When the affected NGOs tried to use QQ and Tianya (the most important online forum in South China), as they did before, they encountered unprecedented censorship. This happened because both Tianya and Tencent, the company offering QQ, are located within the jurisdiction of Guangdong. Weibo then became the medium of choice because Sina is in Beijing, outside the direct control from Guangdong. Once these NGOs relocated to Weibo, worker-activists followed.

The latest incarnation of Chinese social media, after the downturn in Weibo popularity in 2013, is WeChat, provided also by Tencent. The operation of WeChat is more similar to Facebook, which allows mostly communication among friends. Although users in Mainland China can open "public accounts" to facilitate information flow beyond friendship circles, Tencent has redesigned WeChat to minimize the visibility of public accounts for fear of political risk.

With this review over time, it should be fairly clear that there are multiple types of working-class social media in China and that the technological emergence has gone through at least three phases. These phases, as outlined above, are cumulative instead of successive. To this day, QQ is still around; so are blogs, forums, and videos.[98] Even though WeChat and Weibo have been more popular since 2012, they are but new additions to the same enlarged media ecology of labor activism. It is important to note that all of these tools are subject to government surveillance and corporate censorship—by China's leading internet companies.

· · ·

In their Big Data study conducted in 2011–12, Gary King et al. reveal a surprising pattern: Chinese censors demonstrate quite a bit of tolerance toward sharp critique against the government. What they really try to stamp out is expressions with "collective action potential."[99] Messages are more likely censored if they have the potential to lead to the assembly of people in physical places—for example, on the picket line.

Yet since 2012, workers have kept trying against all odds, making picket-line social-media expressions one of the most prominent subgenres of WGC. How, then, does this digital media practice fit in, even contribute to, the dynamics of labor movement on the ground?

Social media on the picket line is more about workers and their real-world struggles than about the technologies per se. This is the basic pattern emerging from the Uniden strike blog in 2004 to the Ole Wolff vlog in 2008 to the Honda Locks forum discussions in 2010. The actual struggles evade the binary opposition of worker vis-à-vis the establishment, agency vis-à-vis structure, a fundamental paradox in understanding workers' digital-media practices.[100]

Yes, at usual times when individual workers try to attract public attention to their suffering, they have few choices other than relying on mass media and, in so doing, conforming to hegemonic norms of the dominant. But there are also exceptional times of collective action, such as strikes, which occur when new structures—informational, technological, social, and cultural—can and do materialize from bottom-up activism as well as horizontal social networking. This process of the emergent interacts with the dominant as well as the residual, whose combined effects are now catalyzed by social media dynamics.

Following patterns not too different from the Egyptian labor movement observed during the Arab uprisings,[101] the most basic function of Chinese social media during strikes is informational, although workers differ in their informational needs. Older workers, especially in state-owned enterprises, often need to find out about the law and official regulation before they act. They send people to search for legal information or post questions to forums such as Baidu Tieba.

Meanwhile, young workers care less about formal rule. They tend to start collective action immediately and one of the first things they do is to share online. One early example of this subgenre came from Beijing Foxconn, when a worker's mobile-phone video about guards' brutality was first uploaded to QQ.com. It was then broadcast on Beijing TV, following a frame-setting trajectory identified by Yuqiong Zhou and Patricia Moy.[102]

A second and arguably more important function is to mobilize fellow workers and muster public support. Social media persuade, more than just inform, so that workers and citizens change attitudes and behaviors, so that strikers keep high morale while others sign petitions, donate time and resources, and join the collective action. Images—including visual memes—are widely used to achieve persuasive effect, while a small number of worker-bloggers are also good at writing powerful essays of mobilization.

Even without mass media coverage, it is difficult for the authorities to isolate the strikes as local events due to the widespread use of social media. Grassroots labor NGOs, with their nationwide and sometimes international networks, are still indispensable. But increasingly they have become intermediaries for workers in different factories to interact with each other. The Tonggang incident of 2009, for example, involved strikers killing their factory owner, who benefited from assets privatization and laying off workers. News spread online as well as through traditional media from Northeastern China, where Tonggang is located, to the southwestern city of Chengdu, where workers faced similar privatization threats. The Chengdu workers publicized their intention online through both social media and local forums, vowing that they were ready for bloodshed if the authorities attempted to impose privatization by force. The deterrence worked, leading to the abandonment of the old plan for expropriation.

Also in 2009, the year following the Global Financial Crisis, a rare but notable event happened in Jinjiang, Fujian Province, where a strike started in the 361 Shoe Factory. Following the typical pattern of information dissemination and mobilization, workers began to use internet tools, only to discover that the factory enjoyed strong support from state and corporate censors, who deleted most of the workers' posts. To counteract, workers launched an unprecedented offensive by enlisting help from hackers familiar with "search engine optimization."[103] They were able to modify search results so that when someone looked up the company on Google, the results would turn out to be tens of thousands of webpages about the strike, rather than the company. This came at a critical moment one week before the company's planned IPO in New York. The battle of the virtual world ended with the cleansing of strikers' webpages, but such virtual collective activism deserves special attention because they are not only novel tactics: they represent a new emergence, too.

. . .

Since 2014, Chinese workers have deployed social media on their picket lines. QQ, weblogs, online forums, vlogs, Weibo, and WeChat: these digital tools have been added to the toolkit of working-class struggle against iSlavery. The trend has accelerated to emerge all over the country. No economic sector has been left untouched. The result is an enlarged media ecology of resistance, where social media are new instruments for a common goal as old as antislavery itself: collective empowerment.

This is, arguably, not a revolution in itself, but a tactical evolution of the residual and, more crucially, the emergent, within a much longer revolutionary tradition of Chinese workers and of the global working class. Despite persisting issues of internet censorship, digital divide, and communicative capitalism, it qualifies as what Raymond Williams would call an "epochal" transformation because the ecological change only starts in the media system, while extending to systems of politics, economy, and society at large, because this can be seen as marking the end of a dominant cultural system and the beginning of a new epoch.

## Possibilities of Another World

So far I have focused mostly on the endeavors of the enslaved in creating alternative content and carrying out oppositional practices so that Appconn would not have engulfed the entire world commercially, ideologically, and ethically. But what about the general public, the mainstream society, religious support groups, citizen consumers of all complexions, and elite sympathizers? Do they play, structurally speaking, a more important role in the larger project of emancipation?

There is, from my understanding, no consensus among historians who work on antislavery. Traditionally it is common for scholars to attach great, sometimes exclusive, significance to abolitionist initiatives among articulate advocates, influential politicians, and well-educated citizens,[104] with the often-unstated assumption that they are the central force in ending systems of cruel discrimination. This has to do with the researchers' social status, usually closer to abolitionists than to the enslaved.

It was, moreover, a matter of methodological convenience because historical records of resistance were simply harder to come by due to illiteracy among slaves, negligence of suppressors, systematic erasure of collective memory, among other factors that have long colluded to silence the oppressed and render them invisible. The higher class status of abolitionists, on the other hand, translates into additional historical limelight, shining ever more gloriously if they happen to prevail.

However, over the past decades there has been a considerable shift of attention from abolition to resistance with groundbreaking publications such as Herbert Aptheker's *American Negro Slave Revolts*, Eugene Genovese's *Roll, Jordan, Roll*, Henry Reynolds's *The Other Side of the Frontier*, and Peter Linebaugh and Marcus Rediker's *The Many-Headed Hydra*.[105] Attentive readers must have noticed that I am rather influenced by this line of work that salvages stories of the suppressed from oblivion. This decision of mine is, however, neither an attempt to follow a more recent trend nor a sign that consensus has emerged among historians. It is instead a deliberate choice based on the present state of iSlavery.

Back in the Atlantic system, resistance accompanied the enslavement of Africans and African Americans from the early 1500s when mining, plantation, and extractive capitalism in general were still taking shape. Yet abolition of slavery only became influential in public agenda much later, as marked by the milestone Somersett's case of 1772.[106] Not only did resistance predate abolition, the former was also characterized by much looser organization and less coherent class formation among the rebellious in highly divergent forms of runaway, mutiny, maronage, piracy, even witchcraft.[107] This is fairly similar to conditions of resistance against iSlavery nowadays, when acts of defiance are "many-headed" yet often disconnected, where the awareness among consumers is generally low, especially compared to the powerful domination of Appconn.

This does not mean that abolitionism is a less significant endeavor. From the French *Société des amis des Noirs* to the American Anti-Slavery Society, from the British 1807 Slave Trade Act to the Emancipation Proclamation of 1863, from James Field Stanfield (Irish sailor and author) to Thomas Clarkson (Cambridge-educated activist and historian), the contributions made by abolitionists are numerous, heroic, and not to be in any way diminished. In key public debates, they countered proslavery arguments like those from John C. Calhoun.[108] In the decisive moments of the Civil War, they helped strengthen the Union and weaken the Confederacy. Some of their most effective campaigns were carried out through the new media technologies of their time: the printing press.

As mentioned briefly in chapter 2, the press was not only instrumental to the spread of new consumerist lifestyles, it was also fundamental to the rise of an informed citizenry and increasingly organized civil society—for instance, through newspaper coverage on both sides of the Atlantic when major slave insurrections broke out.[109] The abolitionists developed a plethora of antislavery essays, pamphlets, poetry, and novels, including Harriet Beecher Stowe's *Uncle Tom's Cabin*, the second-best-selling book in the United States during the entire nineteenth century, trailing only the Bible.[110]

Meanwhile, as Rediker notes, "probably the most powerful means was visual" in that the abolitionists "produced images of the slave ship that would prove to be among the most effective propaganda any social movement has ever created."[111] The visualization of the slave ship *Brooks* (see figure 3.1) was a great example. Since its first publication in 1788, reprints of the *Brooks* have been widely disseminated from Plymouth to Philadelphia, creating remarkable impact upon public opinion about the slave trade by showing "in gruesome, concrete detail that the slaver was itself a place of barbarity, indeed a huge, complex, technologically sophisticated instrument of torture."[112]

Another iconic image, perhaps even more celebrated at the time, was the image of a kneeling black slave in chains, pleading, "Am I Not a Man and a Brother?" (figure 5.3). It was originally the design for the seal of the Society for Effecting the Abolition of the Slavery Trade in London. Then, from 1787 on, the prominent Quaker abolitionist Josiah Wedgwood mass-produced it as medallions and gave them away generously, which became a huge success among the affluent.[113] As Thomas Clarkson, the first historian of British abolition movement, observed at the time: "Some had them inlaid in gold on the lid of their snuff-boxes. Of the ladies, several wore them in bracelets, and others had them fitted up

FIGURE 5.3 Woodcut image: "Am I Not a Man and a Brother?" Source: Library of Congress (public domain), available at http://www.loc.gov/pictures/item/2008661312.

in an ornamental manner as pins for their hair. At length the taste for wearing them became general, and thus fashion, which usually confines itself to worthless things, was seen for once in the honourable office of promoting the cause of justice and, humanity and freedom."[114]

While music was the most prominent mode of cultural resistance among the enslaved across the Atlantic,[115] it was printed graphics like this, literary works, and, later, countless films that formed a long tradition of abolitionism using modern tools of mediated communication to educate, agitate, and mobilize the public. Revisiting this history yields valuable lessons worth pondering if the dominance of Appconn is to be contested by a broad alliance between the manufacturing and manufactured iSlaves, and concerned citizen consumers.

On the one hand, cultural translation is central for ordinary members of the public to understand the plight of the repressed and the high ethics of emancipation, while inspiring new sociocultural imagination. On the other hand, it is counterproductive to compare efforts of resistance and abolition in an attempt to find out which one is more influential, because the two coexist and play distinct roles among different social groups, while serving each other.

With creative campaign design, even the most privileged circles of society, even global capital itself, can be "short circuited," as Yuezhi Zhao and Rob Duffy argued with regard to China's new working classes.[116] Nick Dyer-Witheford also made the explicit argument that the internet, in addition to becoming new cycles of accumulation, can also serve as the basis of new circuits of struggle.[117] Following this thought, I collaborated with Melissa Gregg and Kate Crawford in proposing "a new labor theory of the iPhone era," which we named "circuits of labor."[118]

This is not the place to explain our model, but its core position is relevant: we need "a holistic framework that helps connect various concepts and traditions in the study of labor and ICTs."[119] This holistic approach necessarily implies more attention to the dynamic flow of labor power and of creative energy, beyond the confinement of the factory or even established models of what Antonio Negri calls "social factory."[120] Can there be, at last, an anti-iSlave documentary that is as successful as *Uncle Tom's Cabin*? A campaign image as "fashionable" as the Wedgwood medallion? An activist smartphone game as popular as Candy Crush?

•  •  •

Abolitionism against iSlavery is, undoubtedly, still in its inception, which makes it premature, even unfair, to compare it with historical precedents centuries ago. There are, however, several outstanding harbingers that deserve underlining, namely, the international "iSlave" campaign against "poisonous Apple," the Fairphone social enterprise, and the Phone Story smartphone game.

The first case of international solidarity against Apple is known under the rubric of "iSlave" and its famous campaign image (figure 5.4). This followed the notorious Foxconn Suicide Express of 2010, which caused an upsurge of abolitionist citizen activism, including the twenty-university joint investigation team that works on Foxconn.[121] A central point of coordination for this team is SACOM, a Hong Kong-based labor NGO, whose past experiences include consumer activism against sweatshop conditions in the clothing and toy factories of South China.[122] But this was the first time in recent years when such a transborder network emerged to connect hundreds of university students and faculty members across Mainland China, Taiwan, and Hong Kong.

In 2011, efforts of this network converged with environmental NGOs such as Friends of Nature (*ziran zhiyou*), who led a major investigation of occupational disease on Apple's production line.[123] Calling the problem "poisonous Apple" (*dupingguo*), the labor groups and environmentalists succeeded in deploying, perhaps inadvertently, a tactic from nineteenth-century abolitionism, using the metaphor of "poison" to emphasize that "the goods were tainted by their associations with cruelty to the producers."[124]

Since summer 2010, I have taken part in the twenty-university team through my writing, multimedia projects, and bringing some of my most gifted students to the factory zones. Amplified by Chinese-language media, including social media, the impact on public opinion was considerable in Chinese societies. But how to take this to a global level so that Apple fans in other parts of the world could also be informed and participate?

This was the beginning of a larger campaign targeting i-consumers worldwide, using the iSlave image as an effective tool (figure 5.4). By 2010, the word "iSlave" was already circulating online, referring, in urbandictionary.com for instance, to "someone who will instinctively purchase any product that is released which is preceded by a small case i, regardless of cost, function or aesthetics."[125] SACOM staff Jenny Chan, Debby Chan, and Yiyi Cheng picked up the idea and transformed it from a label for frenzied Apple consumerists to a descriptor for inhumane working conditions at Foxconn production facilities.

Partnering with European human rights NGOs GoodElectronics and Bread for All, SACOM passed the idea to the Public Eye, a global

FIGURE 5.4   The iSlave image created during the Public Eye campaign to elect the world's worst corporation. First published by Greenpeace Switzerland, available at https://www.flickr.com/photos/greenpeace_switzerland/5354250483.

competition to select the world's worst corporation in terms of its social responsibility performance. The competition is an annual counter-event to the Davos meetings of the World Economic Forum, organized by the Berne Declaration (BD) and Greenpeace Switzerland. The event organizers then worked with Feinheit, a social-media and campaign agency based in Zürich, who used an Adbuster concept to spoof Apple commercials and came up with this outstanding design. The artwork was then released through Greenpeace Switzerland's Flickr account on January 11, 2011, under the Creative Commons license.

The image is in several ways comparable with the design of the Wedgwood medallion (figure 5.3). While the 1780s image of the slave is chained down, wearing shackles on his wrists and ankles, the iSlaves are also depicted as fettered, unable to move around with the characteristic white earphone wires of Apple strangling their throats, like nooses on the death row.

Both the Foxconn workers and the black African slave appear to be obedient, even submissive. The slave has one of his knees down on the ground, looking up, presumably, at his "master." The manufacturing iSlaves, on the other hand, keep working on the assembly line with their heads down, their bodies weighed down by the insatiable global demand for the trendy gadgets as well as Appconn's heavy-handed management.

Despite notable differences among the images—for example, in terms of the gender and race of the typically enslaved—both appeal to the mainstream culture of its time, be it Christianity (hence the scriptural reference to and warning of "man" and "brother") or the Apple Cult (hence the shapes and colors of design—blue, black, and white—mimicking the classic advertisements of iPod).

Fans of sci-fi movies can probably read the message of *The Matrix* from this iSlave image as well because it illustrates the ultimate alienation of human bodies being programed while used as energy sources by an advanced yet antagonistic super-machine. If the African slave can reasonably expect an answer, given the sincerity of his posture and the Christian consciousness of the "master" he was appealing to, the Foxconn workers are completely hopeless to appeal to Appconn, which is, after all, a ruthless system instead of a person.

The iSlave image went viral, inspiring dozens of graphic derivatives using different languages, including Chinese. Some show consumers being chained down by iPhone wires wrapping around their wrists or ankles. Some continue to use the idea of strangling but applying it to unsuspecting consumers, whose necks are yoked. Earlier, a scene from the eighteenth season of *The Simpsons* has three gigantic iPods lashing people into work, making an explicit historical reference to the plantations or the whipping-machines of the past. Now it is referred to as a scene of "iSlaves," too.[126]

The campaign hit the doorsteps of Apple stores, which on February 9, 2012, were surrounded, in some cases blocked, by activists who demanded ethical manufacturing at Foxconn. Before the protests, more than 250,000 signatures had been gathered online to pressure Apple. Civic groups such as change.org were prominent in the collective action.[127]

The campaign theme continues to appear in headlines. In October 2014, Apple's former internet technologies director Don Melton complained publically about nonstop working conditions at the company. British journalists named it "iSlave!"[128] As the iPhone 6 was released in

September 2014, the Hong Kong Apple store was covered with a huge sign—made and held up by SACOM—that read: "iSlave 6: Harsher than Harsher. Still Made in Sweatshops."[129]

It is important to note though that SACOM and its international partners did not call for a boycott of Apple or Foxconn products. Strategically speaking, a boycott may work if the target is a foreigner out there, if the mobilized public has enough purchasing power and can be persuaded to take unified action, things which are nevertheless not likely to happen even among stronger cases of boycotts driven by nationalism.[130] Appconn is, on the other hand, hardly foreign to any IT markets of the world. Components made by Foxconn are so ubiquitous that when MOBS, a civic group in Sacramento, tried to build a computer whose parts are completely "Foxconn-free," it turned out to be mission impossible.[131]

What about boycotting iTunes, Facebook, or Google? Will that be feasible? What side effects will follow that may be detrimental to the movement itself? Herein lies a dilemma for all boycotts: by not consuming the commodities and/or services in question, we reduce our stakes as well as our abilities to sway the company, especially if the company's survival does not depend on our purchase. This is particularly problematic when it comes to social-media platforms, which we may reject, but at our own peril. The digitally networked consumers may have an even slimmer chance to know or to care, while being caught in the endless circuits of manufactured iSlaves.

·  ·  ·

Boycott is, however, only one of many instruments in consumer movement. An innovative move, for example, during the antebellum period before the American Civil War, was the "free produce" stores that first began operation in Baltimore in 1826.[132] Led by "Quaker and free black abolitionists," the goal of the stores and activities around them was to provide an alternative mode of commerce so that consumers could have a choice to "buy for the sake of the slave,"[133] take the blood out of their purchase, and avoid patronizing slave owners, directly or indirectly. This approach partly shifted responsibility from the production processes to ways of ethical consumption and, in so doing, created a new system of "prosumption," an alternative that could self-reproduce.

The Fairphone project is the digital equivalent of an early "free produce" store, which is, in this case, based in Amsterdam. In 2010 it began as a two-person initiative supported by the Waag Society, a Dutch digital media foundation. In 2013 it became an independent social enterprise. Since then, it has built and sold sixty thousand Fairphones, either online through its website or via telecom companies such as KPN.[134] It was also named "Europe's fastest growing start-up of 2015."[135] According to *New York Times*, "Fairphone's aims are to build smartphones using only conflict-free raw materials; to provide fair working conditions during assembly; to design a phone that is robust, long-lived and fixable; to establish a comprehensive recycling system; and to be fully transparent about the entire process, including costs and pricing."[136]

Simple as they may sound, these are formidable goals given the overwhelming complexity of the global smartphone commodity chain, its geopolitics, corruption, and long absence of transparency, as in the case of Foxconn. What Fairphone set out to achieve was nothing short of creating an entire global eco-system of design, supply, assembly, and e-waste processing, while involving and engaging consumers effectively.

How can this be done? First, as Bas van Abel, the founder and CEO of Fairphone said, "don't solve the problem but create a new reality."[137] Rather than trying to educate consumers about problems in Apple or Samsung, or trying to help the corporate giants to fix their contract manufacturers such as Foxconn, they create a new reality by developing and selling the Fairphone, a new competitive product. Van Abel himself is an achieved designer and open-source advocate. As he told *Financial Times*: "We chose to be inside the system to be able to drive change by being part of that system."[138]

When I interviewed Tessa Wernink, Fairphone's communication director, in September 2014, the social enterprise had more than thirty employees, up from a handful people in January 2013. They had a high-profile crowd-funding campaign in May 2013, when $4.3 million was raised from ten thousand customers, who have committed to buy twenty-six thousand Fairphones.[139]

In November 2013 they succeeded in having the first batch of phones made in China, which were delivered to customers around Christmas and generated much press coverage. In so doing, the Fairphone team highlights a central paradox in our relationship with the smartphone.

Again, according to van Abel, a smartphone "is the hyper-symbol of connectivity, but we've lost any connection with the source of how it is made, who made it, where does it come from and the social consequences attached to it during the production process. . . . Every pixel you see, every byte you send, has a whole world of minerals, factories, recycling and distribution behind it."[140]

To put together a "clean" smartphone, untainted by the blood and tears of manufacturing iSlaves, the first challenge is to get key minerals like coltan and tin from the DRC. As discussed earlier, Congolese militia forced miners, including children, to work under horrendous conditions to extract the minerals.[141] But the country also has a serious problem of unemployment, and the mines—many of them not controlled by militia—provide jobs. Fairphone and its partners have to develop a system to trace the minerals in order to know which ones are conflict free. Since 2001, Nokia has taken interests in developing such a system but so far without success.[142] Fairphone admits that it remains impossible to get 100 percent conflict-free minerals for their products, but they are trying their best to make improvements with this new system to get "cleaner" minerals for each new batch of their phones.

Then there is the challenge of labor along the assembly line—in China. To avoid using long-distance migrant workers who have to be separated from their families, Guohong, Fairphone's manufacture partner, hired workers who are originally from Chongqing (where Guohong is located) and nearby.[143]

Unlike Foxconn, which often talks about the minimum wage in press conferences while encouraging overtime work on the shop floor beyond legal caps, Fairphone works with Guohong to provide workers with a "living wage." There is an additional Worker Welfare Fund, established through a contribution of $5 from the average sale price of €257.5 for each handset.[144] This is 1.5 percent of what a consumer pays for a Fairphone, and it does not include wages. It stands in stark contrast with the 1.8 percent of each iPhone or 2 percent of each iPad that goes to all labor cost in China, which include wages, overtime pay, welfare, and above all, Foxconn's corporate profits.[145] The fund is then managed by workers' representatives, who are democratically elected, to decide "how to spend the money on improving work conditions, education and training."[146]

Another measure taken by Fairphone is to avoid "tweaking orders mid-production, which, although common in contract manufacturing, puts pressure on workers."[147] As Fairphone 2, a new model of the smartphone, went to production in Suzhou in November 2015, the team has continued to apply the model of living wage, Worker Welfare Fund, and worker representation.

Fairphone's sustainability goals also focus on the reduction of e-waste, which requires new approaches in design. First, against the trend of "built-in obsolescence,"[148] Fairphone is designed to last. In developing its new Fairphone 2, for example, "the company performed a series of tests to ensure the robustness of the design, including dropping the phone on concrete a number of times on all six [phone] surfaces from a height of six feet."[149]

The device uses a dual SIM card design that allows the phone to place calls, receive messages, or go online using two different mobile networks. If it starts malfunctioning, there is the iFixit app pre-installed in Fairphone that helps customers repair the device. If it is not fixable, there are choices to refurbish or recycle it in socially responsible ways under their "circular economy" model, whose environmental impact had been assessed in terms of climate change, metal depletion, and human toxicity.[150]

When I opened my Fairphone package, which a German friend bought for me (I cannot order it to Hong Kong because it's only sold in Europe), I was surprised that there was no charger in the box. This was intentional because the phone uses mini-USB and can be charged with any mini-USB cord. The decision of not including a new charger may look tiny, but it is environmentally significant by saving the materials in not only making the extra chargers but packaging and shipping them.

Instead of the charger, I found several beautifully designed postcards inviting me to join its online community (https://www.fairphone.com/we-are-fairphone). Once I clicked in, I was greeted "Welcome to the Movement." I saw the hashtag #WeAreFairphone prominently displayed, followed by the latest Twitter updates from Fairphone users, an active community of open-source designers and ethically motivated consumers. Their goal is not to sell a digital product, finished and fetishized. Rather, it is about starting a dialogue that engages developers as well as consumers while nurturing a new participatory culture for a responsible and sustainable smartphone industry. For this reason, Fairphone "acts as a research project into the globalized economy. Their findings are published in extensive blog posts detailing the complex steps of getting a phone from the earth to your hand."[151]

What types of people belong to this Fairphone community? The social enterprise has surveyed its customers, who turn out to be "technologically savvy, social media communicators who are concerned about corporate responsibility." More specifically, "the average Fairphone buyer is about 37 years old. Nearly a third are engineers or technology workers. Many are computer programmers, who tweak and discuss the phone's customized Android operating system and help iron out bugs."[152]

Is it surprising at all that the first customer base of a "fair-trade" and "pure produce" product like the Fairphone largely follows the demographics of the "Net Slaves"?[153] Scholars such as Robert Gehl would probably say no,[154] because these are precisely the people who are familiar with the internal workings of the old system, including its injustice behind the protection of corporate secrecy, and because these are the people who are most motivated to "reverse engineer" the system, open it up, and create a new "design analysis of the system components and their interrelationships within the higher-level discrete system."[155]

What I like the most about my Fairphone is its preinstalled app, EnjoySomePeace. Once I click on it, it shows a bar that allows me to choose anywhere between a few minutes and three hours. This will be the period when the phone remains silent and disconnected from the internet. No SMS or phone calls. This will be the time when I "enjoy some peace" with my "temporal sovereignty."[156] An abolitionist timepiece this is, simple and functional, in the shape of a well-designed app.[157]

• • •

Let me close this chapter with a last case about molding and resisting Appconn: Phone Story, a smartphone game I have used in classroom teaching several times. Produced by Molleindustria, which designs radical games, Phone Story consists of four levels that offer "quality entertainment," or so it claims satirically: (1) children extracting coltan in Congo—gamer needs to keep them working at gunpoint; (2) Foxconn workers jumping off a tall building in China—gamer needs to catch the jumpers; (3) mindless consumerism among iPhone users—gamer needs to shoot crazy consumers with new iPhones; and (4) hazardous e-waste processing in Bangladesh—gamer needs to separate different used parts.

The graphics, music, voiceover, and messages of ridicule delivered through this game are an excellent example of cultural jamming when diverse experiences of iSlavery are brought together from multiple continents and presented in a single app. To get through the four stages, I have to move my finger skillfully around the touchscreen, while listening to monotonous background music and a robotish voice telling me about the dark side, and the internal contradictions, of the smartphone industry. I'm usually too slow to get through level 2. My students have more adept fingers, and they can play through level 4 in a few minutes, just to find the game loops back to level 1, again and again.

Yes, you can play it endlessly. Imagine, what if you have to keep playing this game twelve hours a day, six days a week? "Must be really boring," said one student. "I'd go nuts," said another. Not all of them appreciate the black humor, which is, after all, not funny. But they all found it educational as they learn about the connections between Congo, Bangladesh, China, and their coveted gadgets; between manufacturing and manufactured iSlaves. They have to take part in it, at least in a simulated way, and get a firsthand feeling of how life feels like when they are out of control, "programmed" by some inhumane power. The game is, in this sense, as abolitional as it is educational.

The most shocking learning result for my iPhone-equipped students is that they cannot play it because Apple's App Store banned it.[158] They have to borrow an Android device from their classmate, who can use Google Play (formerly Android Market) to download it. Or they can play it online at phonestory.org, but the gaming experience is not as good. Suddenly, owning an iPhone became a deficiency.

Paulo Pedercini, an Italian designer based in Pittsburgh, is the man behind Molleindustria. When I interviewed him in March 2014, he revealed the beginning of Phone Story. It was not part of a coordinated global campaign. Instead:

> The idea came from Michael Pineschi, a recently graduated student in International Affairs. The conversation happened in the context

of the YesLab (yeslab.org), a creative activism organization put together by media pranksters group the Yes Men. At that point I was already working on a couple of similar concepts so went for it. The design and development was pretty much just me, with music by an artist named Minusbaby. Michael produced the content for the website (phonestory.org).

This sounds like the beginning of a small-scale "motley crew," consisting of a few talented people with very different skills but sharing an ethical concern. According to the Phone Story website, they received institutional sponsorship from the Gwangju Design Biennale (a prestigious contemporary art biennale in Asia) and the AND Festival (AND stands for Abandon Normal Devices, a key British art exhibition for digital media reflections and provocations). The project also collaborates with SACOM and the twenty-university joint investigation team that works on Foxconn.

Initially, Phone Story was made available to as many smartphones as possible, including not only iPhones and Androids but also jailbroken iOS via Apptrackr. (Yes, digital jailbreakers, pirates, and maroons!) According to Pedercini, "We thought it was important to make it available on the very same devices that constituted the subject of the game. Almost like the device itself was speaking to the user. The idea was to make a sort of reminder that you can keep with you, like a way-less-permanent tattoo or a bumper sticker, something that you can carry around and maybe show off as a conversation starter."

Although not as organized as the iSlave campaign or the Fairphone project, the Phone Story game is similar in serving the abolitionist cause through engaging its players, spurring dialogue, and forcing people to reflect. Apparently, these are minor issues to Apple executives, who decided to ban the game from the App Store three hours after its initial launch there on September 13, 2011. The reasons cited are that the game "depict[s] violence or abuse of children"; it "present[s] excessively objectionable or crude content"; allegedly, it also violates Apple's donation rules, which Molleindustria contests.[159]

This is not the only time when Apple censored games for "excessively objectionable" content. Another example is the banning of Sweatshop HD in March 2013.[160] While international media from *La Monde* and

CNN to *New York Times* and *Time* magazine all focus on the act of corporate censorship, Pedercini insists that was a secondary dimension for Phone Story, which was "in part a media intervention." Moreover, "it was about sneaking an ugly gnome inside Apple's walled garden. Because the production of meaning doesn't only happen on the screen, from the interaction between players and software/rules. The context a game inhabits, the community it creates, the platforms and technologies it adopts, all these things are also part of what a game 'says.'"

Fortunately, Google is more tolerant than Apple. Working with SACOM and institutional sponsors, Molleindustria developed its own business model to share profits with grassroots organizations, as depicted in figure 5.5.

As shown in this diagram, when a consumer purchases a copy of Phone Story from Android Market (i.e., Google Play), Molleindustria receives 10 percent of the payment, Google 30 percent. The remaining 60 percent goes to a grassroots organization along with institutional sponsorship. In this case, the selected grassroots organization is SACOM due to its work on Foxconn.[161] The donation made in February 2012 was $6,047, which SACOM redirected to the teenage Foxconn survivor, Tian Yu, whose testimony was presented in chapter 3. As Phone Story's official statement says, "$6,000 won't do that much to an organization but

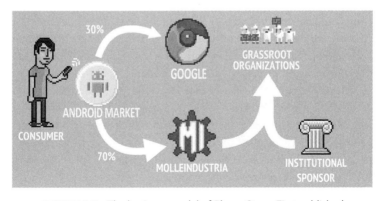

FIGURE 5.5   The business model of Phone Story. First published in http://www.phonestory.org.

they could be significant for an individual who used to earn about $130 a month."[162]

I facilitated the transaction of this donation because Tian Yu is from Hubei, my home province, and I visited her a couple times when I went back; my students made friends with her; she also "starred" in my documentary *Deconstructing Foxconn*.[163]

The suicidal jump permanently disabled Tian Yu, who has to spend most of her time in a wheelchair. But utilizing this donation and other support from the network against iSlavery, Tian Yu and her family started to produce colorful handmade slippers.[164] They used Weibo, China's Twitter-like service, to promote their products, while sending them to fair trade shops as well in mainland China, Hong Kong, Taiwan, and the United States. Soon after her Weibo messages were retweeted by top microbloggers in China, Tian Yu had more than twenty thousand online followers, and her slippers were sold out.

For nearly six months, demand for Tian Yu slippers went strong. Then it subsided, and it was not a sustainable model. However, the experience built Tian Yu's confidence that she could take a job online, which is what she does at the time of this writing. She now works for an e-commerce company in its customer service team. She still has not played Phone Story, but the game has already had a significant impact on her and her family.

## Concluding Remarks

Covering a wide territory of geopolitical change and individual cases, the overall argument of this chapter is that the prevalence of Appconn in the current world system of digital media is far from accidental. Nor is it an unshakable fait accompli. Global capital, geopolitics, Beijing, and local governments in China: all these factors play a significant role in fostering, indeed necessitating, various modes of iSlavery as well as creating internal contradictions and vulnerabilities of the system. Appconn is thus molded in a thick context of power shifts.

All this is being resisted by the iSlaves who not only express their alternative voices through WGC (worker-generated content) but also deploy the latest social media on the picket lines at crucial moments of collective struggle. A new wave of abolitionist movement has emerged using different types of DNA (digitally networked action) strategies to illuminate and exemplify the possibilities of a better world, as seen through the cases of the iSlave campaign, Fairphone, and Phone Story game.

This is, of course, not the first time "the same technology that has taken world capitalism to a new stage of development—corporate globalization—has also provided a significant boost for anti-corporate and anti-globalization movements."[165] Not all of them are successful. Some, like the Mike Daisey show, led to more backfire against the movement than contributing to the common goal of abolition.[166] The point is, there are myriad ways to put the creativity of digital media innovators—ourselves included—to socially productive ends, not only online or in the media world but also in the actual life of the enslaved, their families and communities, which is, after all, another lesson from the history of antislavery.

# 6

# A Temporary Closure

The world is changing, not without its patterns, toward a future of great uncertainties. As I start the last chapter of this small book, the Occupy in Hong Kong has ended for six months. Although failing to change China's decision on Hong Kong's political future, the Occupiers succeeded in mobilizing citizens, forming a considerable resistance—in the streets and in cyberspace—ultimately rejecting Beijing's election plan in the June 18, 2015, vote of the Hong Kong Legislative Council.[1]

On the other side of the planet, on the evening of June 17, 2015, a gunman attacked the Emanuel A.M.E. Church in Charleston, South Carolina, one of the oldest black churches in the United States, killing nine African Americans at their place of worship.[2] In the same issue of the *New York Times* that reported on Hong Kong's legislative vote, a feature story detailed how the Charleston suspect used Facebook to share racist beliefs, for example, by displaying the Confederate battle flag.[3] This was soon followed by a call from South Carolina's governor to remove the flag from the state capitol.[4]

From Hong Kong to South Carolina, a war of symbols continues to unfold in the world writ large. Its life-and-death consequences are not limited to the online sphere. Its political and cultural origins are to be found in both the long history of slavery and the contemporary conditions of enslavement—proliferated, exacerbated, perpetuated, yet also disguised and mitigated by digital media—which this book only begins to reveal.

## Back to the Beginning

This is a manifesto that introduces the notion of iSlavery and, in so doing, pushes readers beyond the comfort zone in rethinking our relationship with digital technologies: how these new media channels are made and managed, how they consume and constitute us, how they have to be fundamentally transformed in order to counter and eradicate twenty-first-century slavery, along the assembly line and in the data mine.

The comparison between the history of slavery and contemporary issues of digital labor is a clear provocation. For too long, the underbellies of the digital industries have been obscured and tucked away; too often, new media is assumed to represent modernity, and modernity assumed to represent freedom; too many of us—myself included—have succumbed to the "technically sweet," as Robert Oppenheimer put it,[5] in ways not too different from the old proletariat of Europe centuries ago being addicted to slave-produced sugar.[6] While providing instant gratification for the consuming individuals, this "sweet tooth," both literally and figuratively speaking, ends up dissolving communities, polarizing societies, and contributing to the long-term disempowerment of the people, be they workers or consumers.

It is my hope that this small book sounds a wakeup call through its voice of constructive dissent. Being contrarian is, however, not my purpose. Nor do I hope to gain any fame, or notoriety, by peddling an excessively offensive moral astonishment. I am fully aware that slavery is a very severe critique. As David Brion Davis wrote, the charge is so serious that "it tended to set slavery off from other species of barbarity and oppression."[7] The result of developing this critique, against not only Appconn, the empire that breeds iSlaves, but also our own servile complacencies, must have shocked some readers. Before embarking on this journey of inquiries, I myself could not have imagined so many horrid parallels between seventeenth-century slavery and the "institutions and practices similar to slavery" in today's digital media industries.

This book is, therefore, nothing more than an invitation—for everyone to reflect on the enslaving tendencies of Appconn and the world system of gadgets; for internet researchers and students of labor to learn from slavery studies in the past and at present; and for historians and legal scholars to investigate things digital when it comes to the deprival, partial or in full, of basic human dignity in the twenty-first century. Programmers, activists, workers of all trades, including employees of Apple and Foxconn—I think you may find one or two useful ideas here, too.

Is the New Economy really weightless, "flat" in its social structure, and emancipatory? So many myths of liberation have been bundled with technological buzzwords, and they are often taken for granted: Web 2.0, social media, smartphone, Big Data, the internet of things. Interrogating Appconn—the alliance between technology giants such as Apple and Foxconn, which acts as the linchpin for a world system of digital gismos—requires de-bundling and dismissing these myths, leading to an understanding of the New Economy closer to reality.

This understanding is informed by our reading of the slavery literature, which covers various domains of the historical, sociological, legal, and activist scholarship dealing with topics from ancient slave regimes and the transatlantic slave trade to contemporary criminal networks of human and organ trafficking. The content is wide ranging, perhaps too eclectic. But it connects previously distinct intellectual traditions through the critical perspectives of slavery studies, while inviting new dialogue, new data gathering, and new analysis.

There are, admittedly, certain constrictions in this framework of slavery, which is, after all, about some of the most fundamental issues of the human condition that resurface in my observations and thoughts about digital media, labor, and capitalism. There is no doubt that my treatment is limited and partial without doing full justice to the awe-inspiring literature of history, law, and critical scholarship on media, culture, and communication. I have only begun to explore the complexities of Appconn and the geopolitics of our digital world.

I have paid less attention, indeed completely ignored, certain dimensions of digital economy and online politics that I remain curious about:

Does the internet create more jobs in the Global South than it destroys? Are new cultures of resistance taking root among young people of the "digital natives" generation? Is net neutrality more important than privacy at times of a major social movement? What's the geopolitical implication of cyberwar for nation-states, nonstate actors, including activists and hacktivists? These are some of the questions that I have not tackled, although more capable scholars are addressing them elsewhere.

Meanwhile, I have only mentioned in passing the legally recognized forms of twenty-first-century slavery: human trafficking, child soldiers, the organ trade, the prison-industrial complex, forced domestic labor. Eradicating these age-old networks and offenses of criminality is more pressing an issue than before at a time when nation-states and international security systems tend to break down frequently against soaring social disparities and environmental crises the world over. The critique of iSlavery extends the endeavors of, rather than diverts them from, the contemporary abolition movement.

What we have gained from this particular lens of slavery is a narrowed conceptual focus that zooms into and sheds light on the darkest corners of digital industries. This is, however, neither a naïve device of dramatization nor an adamant ideological charge. It is instead based on a series of lessons distilled from past scholarship of slavery studies, as summarized toward the end of chapter 2 and at the beginning of chapter 3.

To recap: throughout history, slavery systems have mutated greatly, assuming drastically different forms, even under conditions of modernity. After the end of de jure slavery in most parts of the world since the 1800s, de facto slavery continues to exist, whose essence is to exercise "the powers attaching to the right of ownership" over human beings. The common purpose of these systems is to exploit the labor and/or body of the enslaved through both estranged modes of production and hegemonic consumption cultures.

Modes of slavery work through coercion and/or deception, sociocultural alienation, and politico-economic domination, which is always accompanied by efforts of resistance and/or abolition that constitute a decisive vector in shaping the contours of slavery even to this day. As a result, particular slave systems wax and wane due to the combined effects of domination and resistance, reflecting while shaping geopolitical patterns, sometimes regionally, sometimes across the globe.

Do we see "any or all" of the above characteristics of slavery in our scrutiny of labor conditions in Foxconn and the New World of digital and social media? Evidence discussed so far leaves some room for doubt, but the overall answer is: yes. This is not to say that the plant or the digital ecosystem contains nothing but slavery, which would be a gross overstatement. There are indeed plenty of nonslave components inside Appconn. However, as discussed in chapter 2, the any-or-all approach that we adopt from legal experts sets the bar rather low.

Applying this standard, it is fairly common to see that their corporate policies and acts qualify as de facto "institutions and practices similar to slavery" as in the cases of the student "interns," violent security guards, injured workers, and those with occupational diseases. Although in different moments of iSlavery the specific methods and consequences of exploitation vary, the basic idea of slavery has been effective in helping us understand what is going on, not only with regard to things under normal market conditions but more crucially the abnormalities that have somehow become more often the rule rather than the exception.

With this conceptual framework that links up centuries of human experience, the tragic events of Foxconn Suicide Express, the teenager who sold his kidney for some i-gadgets, the heroic attempts of resistance through worker-generated content and social media on the picket line, the creative digital abolition campaigns through the Fairphone or the Phone Story game—all these suddenly carry an additional weight of historical gravity.

Adding the "i" to slavery is, in this sense, much more than a technological and commercial referent that alludes to the i-devices from Apple, which was the original intention when SACOM and the Public Eye Award teams created the campaign meme "iSlave." The prefix also suggests that regimes of slavery have become more penetrating, embedded more deeply in the individualism of the informational me. Consequently, "i" suffer more from isolation, "social death," or more precisely "natal alienation" which, as Orlando Patterson contends, is the definitive hallmark of enslavement.

Judy Wacjman's penetrating reminder is worth quoting again: "The 'i' word is practically an intoxicant."[8] The sword of intoxication is, however, double-edged. While iSlavery encourages user participation and voluntary servitude at the very heart of our personal experiences, online and off, it also makes Appconn more dependent, indeed more vulnerable, if I withdraw my complacency, and you withdraw yours.

Without the pretense and the allure of the "i," it is, in the end, little more than old-fashioned slavery.

In all, slavery is about the defeat of humanity, a defeat that has been profound and prolonged, even in this era of digital media preeminence. Far from removing slavery from the world while promoting liberties in the expanding spheres of online communication, Appconn has regenerated some of the most brutal, and most deceptive, forces of exploitation. Imposing inequality and breeding voluntary servitude, it has triggered suicidal acts among desperate individuals as well as collective actions of the digitally connected. Again, quoting historian Marcus Rediker:

> I offer this study with the greatest reverence for those who suffered almost unthinkable violence, terror, and death, in the firm belief that we must remember that such horrors have always been, and remain, central to the making of global capitalism.[9]

## Circles of Capitalism

In the preceding chapters, I have examined issues of labor, digital media, and the world economy from a *longue durée* perspective. As Wallerstein writes, "Historical capitalism, like all historical systems, will perish from its successes not from its failures."[10] What, then, are the victorious templates of Appconn and of slavery historically, from where it starts to fall?

A main goal for this comparative thinking is to develop a holistic framework to understand contemporary problems from the vantage point of slavery. This is a deliberate attempt at theory production that provides a way to tie together scattered observations and fragmented arguments, some of which are more tangential than others.

The core models of seventeenth- and twenty-first-century slavery are summarized, at the risk of oversimplification, in the circular models of figures 6.1 and 6.2, while figure 6.3 toward the end of this final chapter presents an alternative model. Linking up continents, peoples, and technologies, these models are all about circuits of capital accumulation, structural domination, and endless struggle. They bring about cultural change, from far-flung communities to everyday practices and mundane social relations, wherever you happen to be.

These schematic models are, of course, nothing more than signposts marking a temporary closure for this small book. They call for rigorous testing and substantiation, while paving the way for a new agenda of digital media research, a renewed interest in slavery studies, and hopefully a new departure for radical thought.

As argued over and again, a productive way to comprehend some of the most perplexing puzzles of digital media today is to revisit seventeenth-century slavery, the transatlantic "triangular" trade system that connected West Africa, the Americas, and Europe into the first capitalist world system in human history. With its origins in the 1500s, the basic structure of this world order took shape in the 1600s when

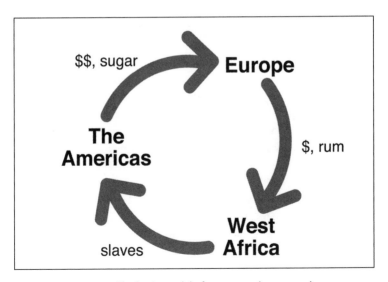

FIGURE 6.1   The basic model of seventeenth-century slavery or the transatlantic triangular trade system.

sizeable forces of resistance also emerged among the "motley crew" of antislavery rebels.

Visualized in figure 6.1, this was a system of intercontinental movements, where labor power was concentrated in feitorias, or "factories"—European forts containing slaves off the coasts of West Africa—as well as planting and manufacture facilities in New World plantations that produced, most importantly, sugar. The making of sugar had side products such as rum, and it was supplemented by other revenue lines of tobacco, coffee, and, at a later stage, cotton. But the basic model persisted and, in retrospect, sugar was "the favored child of capitalism," to borrow from Fernando Ortiz.[11]

Profits from selling slaves went to Europe along with sugar, an addictive commodity that used to be scarce in the Old World, while rum and other goods were traded further with European products such as guns and textiles to West Africa for more slaves. The cycle then continued and expanded from the Caribbean to Latin America to the entire western hemisphere as "the black laborers of the New World were yoked to an implacable treadmill which paced both their toil and that of the new industrial proletariat in the Old."[12]

The most triumphant place in this model was, by several measures, French-controlled San Domingo (renamed Haiti in 1802) given its sugar industry being more productive and better organized than what existed in most other colonies.[13] Yet it was precisely here that the former slaves turned a new page of history through their uprising, expelling slave owners, and establishing a new republic among themselves.

Besides the Haitian revolution, the British Slave Trade Act of 1807 followed the heyday of British transatlantic trade, while Lincoln's Emancipation Proclamation followed not just the Civil War but a remarkable era of expansion for the slave-powered cotton plantations.[14] Although the commodities at stake changed, from sugar to cotton, for example, the same pattern persists as what the Haitian revolution did to the French empire: great moments of slavery's success were followed by its peril.

The rise of Appconn, building on African conflict minerals, the toiling of Chinese migrant workers, and untold amount of "free labor" represents a new phase in the metamorphosis of slavery into the era of digital communication. Figure 6.2 demonstrates the circular movement of gadgets, user-generated content (UGC), research and development (R&D), as well as money.

Apple is the world's most profitable company, whose products have been assembled at Foxconn, by far the world's largest electronics manufacturer. Together they constitute Appconn, the core of a digital media empire, within which Foxconn operates as the functional equivalent of feitorias by concentrating labor power, constraining it using violence and the awful "anti-jumping nets," then exporting it in the condensed form of coveted gadgets.

Gadgets made by Foxconn's manufacturing iSlaves are then sold to manufactured iSlaves who play and labor in cyberspace, another sphere of New World plantations. Revenues from hardware sales as well as the virtual plantations, along with UGC, the new addictive substance, then get transferred back to Apple, who would use these inputs from manufactured iSlaves for R&D-based market expansion, further exploitation, and capital accumulation. Showing clear lineage with the transatlantic

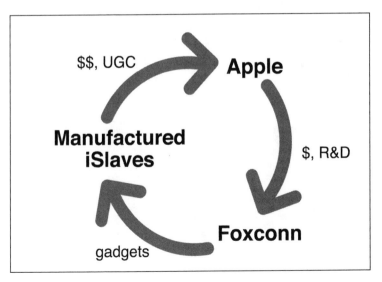

FIGURE 6.2   A model of iSlavery or twenty-first-century slavery dominated by Appconn.

triangular trade system, this circular model of twenty-first-century slavery reveals some of the most fundamental yet hidden dynamics in the digital industries.

The great triumph of this model—the most "technologically sweet" moment, so to speak—is probably UGC exploitation on the backs of manufactured iSlaves. So far the Haitian moment has not come yet, although storms are gathering from open-source movements to Edward Snowden to Chinese hackers assisting factory workers as in their struggle at the Jinjiang shoe plant. Resistance began before and during the Middle Passage, in Chinese factory zones and various realms of online activism. Foxconn used to be a celebrated "success story," too, but since around the 2010 Suicide Express it has become arguably the worst sore spot of Appconn.

Some readers may still wonder: Will the Suicide Express recur? Under what conditions? Seen from this comparative framework, it is reasonable to predict that, without major structural change, continuous self-destruction is neither an ephemeral phenomenon nor a historical coincidence. Tragedies will revisit, especially when there is another major economic crisis (2010 was the year immediately following the 2008–2009 global financial crisis)—that is, if we do not remove this underlying structure of enslavement.

To restate, my critique is, in a more fundamental sense, not about Apple or Foxconn or new cultures of consumerism per se. It is this circular model that haunts us, which we are ultimately after, because it embodies a world system of alienation and exploitation behind the protective façade of corporate secrecy and cultish fandom. The system is still growing, fast growing, with Big Data and cloud computing being its newest frontiers. The capitalist world-economy contained in and sustained through such a model is still expanding, meaning it may still be challenging for most to envision a world of digital media without Appconn. This book, however, encourages everyone to "think different"—turning Apple's advertising slogan on itself.

What does it mean by "think different"? Well, can we imagine a global commodity chain without labor input from children or forced "student interns"? A factory regime in which Foxconn employees enjoy the same respect as those working for Apple, Google, even Fairphone?

A surveillance project only when there is informed consent? A system designed to serve not just corporations, shareholders, or the likes of NSA but the citizenry and public interest? A socially responsible Big Data operation that stops mimicking the patterns of the organ trade, where value moves upward through the social classes whereas those at the bottom of the strata are to be used and abandoned? An internet freed from the domination of commercial enclosures? A World Wide Web of sharing, solidarity, democracy, and collective formation?

## Between the Assembly Line and the Data Mine

The world has not really found its direction after the 2008–2009 global crisis.[15] Many still worship obscene profits in financial markets as the sole purpose of capitalism. This book, on the contrary, tries to shed light on other possibilities, with the ultimate goal of rediscovering and enhancing our humanity. In so doing, it has questioned new and old means to reach the old end—outsourcing and relocating to the developing world, price competition among subcontractors, further centralization and vertical integration along the value chain, and the subsequent disempowerment of both workers and consumers through such global structures as Appconn.

If manufacturing iSlaves at Foxconn and similar production facilities are organized more like gang labor in plantations, then manufactured iSlaves in the shopping malls and online are probably more akin to ordinary crew members onboard a slave ship, who often had to endure high death rates and the insecurity of being abandoned when they fell sick after the Middle Passage.

At most, they can become *familia Caesaris* or the "ultimate slave." They may possess considerable wealth, high social status, and tremendous power, but they are nonetheless no more than an extension of the emperor, who can strip them of their possessions, even kill them, at will. No matter how hard they try, they cannot and will not enjoy "honor" as free citizens of the ruling class.

Big Data operation can, to some degree, also be compared to slave trade, which according to Article 1(2) of the 1926 Slavery Convention "includes all acts involved in the capture, acquisition or disposal of a person with intent to reduce him to slavery." These are all part of the new means created in the cyberworld to help meet the old end of exploitation.

The resulting geopolitics of information thus have more continuity than a break with the past. Digital media diffusion does not decentralize the capitalist world system. Instead, the digital industries have become more concentrated in a few locales of R&D and manufacture, which Appconn prefers. Under the disguise of sharing and collective prosperity, the basic structure remains: the global "race to the bottom," the transnational commodity chain, the suppression of labor rights, and the cultivation of a productive agent without solidarity.

In this digital geopolitics, the role of nation-states has further declined. The prominent role of the local state in fostering Foxconn should, in this sense, be seen as part of the rule, not the exception. It is, however, erroneous to ignore nation-states altogether because, as seen in the Chinese case, Beijing still possesses effective power to restrain Foxconn, sometimes more so than Apple Inc.

Meanwhile, much remains to be seen with China's colossal infrastructure projects, such as One Belt, One Road, and the new Beijing-led AIIB (Asian Infrastructure Investment Bank), which was launched on June 29, 2015, with "sustainable economic development" being its highlighted goal.[16] The peculiar absence of the United States on the AIIB table is a sign that Washington is still grappling with its weakened position in the Asia-Pacific region and Eurasia as a whole.

What will happen if China succeeds in these super-mega-infrastructure projects without antagonizing the United States to the brink of war, which also happens to facilitate Appconn transactions beyond Beijing's geopolitical goals? Can China keep things under control given its internal troubles of unrest? Will the express railway between Beijing and Moscow provide a more efficient conduit to bring European e-waste to Central Asia or China's Muslim northwest? Will the new infrastructure elements become new vulnerabilities of the world-economy when insurgents of regional conflicts start to target them? These are just some of the emerging geopolitical questions one needs to keep wondering about in the context of a persistent theme of great uncertainty in global power shifts, now exacerbated by digital capitalism.[17]

The real question is, Which power shift can transcend the old model of slavery, including its reincarnations in the new millennium? A new geopolitics of information industries where human dignity and sustainable development are prioritized over corporate profit? Today, Congolese miners, Foxconn workers, "playbours"[18] of social media and online games—literally billions around the world remain enslaved through coercion, fraud, and voluntary subjugation, but they lack an acknowledged status—much like the nineteenth-century indentured servants coerced into signing fraudulent labor contracts that left them in legal limbo.[19] Caught in this limbo, they need, first of all, a proper name: *slaves*, regardless of what disguise the exploitative relationship happens to assume.

This is the holistic framework we arrive at: Appconn and its labor issues indeed continue the historical problem of slavery, from the beginning of the capitalist world system to today's digital economy, from its most dehumanizing aspects to the transformative potentials of networked resistance. The theme of iSlavery is, in this sense, a "time machine," a heuristic device deployed to diagnose problems, detecting elements of similarity and continuity across centuries. Although labor conditions in Appconn are not identical to seventeenth-century slavery, conducting this comparative analysis adds greatly to our understanding about the contemporary human condition.

First is our understanding of digital media technology, which can be approached many ways, the most important being the materiality of this digital, yet still industrial, era, especially when one talks about emerging economies like China. Work injuries, the gadgets, e-waste, the discipline of millions of human bodies—these are all facets of the same materiality dimension that have been ignored in conventional conceptions of digital technology as little more than "virtual" formations.

Yet the key resources for digital production are not only material but are also highly concentrated in a few locales. The raw materials for components manufacture, for example, come from very few places. The processing and assembly of the gadgets, on the other hand, require intensive physical labor on the production line.

Labor underlies the materiality of digital technology, especially the production and circulation of gadgets. Transmitters, fiber optic networks, cellular base stations, satellites—these are also material objects requiring precious raw materials as well as the indispensable labor of processing, assembly, and maintenance. All need physical labor input; all have environmental footprints. All require software, cultural content, regulatory systems, and other forms of "invisible labor," including consumption as another mode of "labor-intensive" exploitation, even though it is perceived as more fun.

This is where the two types of iSlaves are introduced, including Foxconn workers on the assembly line as well as manufactured iSlaves in the data mine, where the enslaved wear invisible but omnipresent shackles on their "fifth limb" while their "third skin" is being objectified, codified, and traded, often beyond their control. This is a New Frontier of accumulation. At the very bottom, the internet is just another Atlantic Ocean, and cyberspace another New World. Appconn may have built another circular system of gadgets, bits, and fiber optics, but it is, in the final analysis, a historical throwback.

## The Abolition of iSlavery

Let me conclude with two final lessons from slavery studies. On the one hand, we have been through much worse periods of slavery, and yet humanity and freedom prevailed at the end. On the other hand, as argued convincingly by David Brion Davis and Greg Gradin,[20] endeavors of progress often paradoxically strengthen slavery by making it more resilient and more deceptive, by enlarging the demand for its products and services. Can we build these two insights into a new model for digital labor activism that can both maintain sustainable growth and avoid the dilemma of feeding into another vicious circle of "institutions and practices similar to slavery"?

This manifesto has begun to identify agents of change, of networked resistance, within newly emerging digital cultures as symbolized by worker poetry, picket-line social-media images, the twenty-university joint investigation team, the Fairphone social enterprise, and the Phone Story game. Despite the significance of each of these cases, I have to admit that these are little more than scattered skirmishes against Appconn within the larger context of corporate digital media and increasingly individualized consumption culture. Some of the defiant attempts are more programmatic, while most are post-hoc or one-off acts with little coherence. A typical state of "the emergent" as Raymond Williams would call it.[21]

Nevertheless, the simple fact that such emergent practices and networks exist—against all odds, against the bleak backdrop of neoliberal dominance—is encouraging. The global digital culture is not preordained to be an extension of the capitalist world system. It can and has become a hotbed for progressive social change. If we look carefully and close enough through the comparative lens of slave resistance and abolition, we will see openings for alternative and oppositional developments in grassroots culture, civil society, global markets, even intra-institutional reform in state or transnational governance structures. However, we will not be ready to transform the global digital economy for good unless we know how to work with various existing resources, link them up, create new synergies, and beware of the dilemma pointed out by Davis and Gradin.

To this goal, there can be many formulae of networked resistance and abolition movements, arising from the challenge of Appconn. Figure 6.3

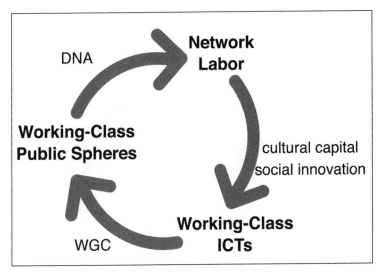

FIGURE 6.3 A model of resistance and abolition movements or an alternative world-system of the digital emergence.

presents one model, a very preliminary sketch indeed, one that should be taken as another provocation, a summary of hypotheses, and an invitation for critique. This is, in a nutshell, an alternative world-system—of gadgets, of the working people, and of democratic communication among those equipped with digital media. The world-system of gadgets may represent another moment of triumph for Appconn, but this triumphant moment is also the beginning of the end because the same electronic device can also be used to serve collective struggle.

The key here is to create new types of social relations because slavery—including manufacturing and manufactured iSlaves—has to exist in a relational context. Enslavement continues not only because there is a slave, over whom a slaveholder exercises "powers attaching to the right of ownership," but more crucially, and structurally speaking, because there is a larger system entailing such inequality.

As discussed earlier, working-class ICTs are not just cybercafé or cheap phones used by low-income workers or other groups of the information have-less. They also provide a new socioeconomic basis and a fertile ground for cultural and political creativity, which has begun to yield notable results responding to the existential needs of working-class populations of the Global South, from Africa to Asia to Latin America. More specifically, in China, which this book is mostly about, there emerges a new alternative "Chinese model" based on the experiences of struggle among the information have-less in the past decade, which draws from the long revolutionary tradition of the Chinese people.

First, Chinese workers use working-class ICTs to produce a variety of WGC (worker-generated content)—first, poetry and blog diaries, but increasingly audiovisual materials. These include Foxconn workers like Xu Lizhi, the worker-poet, or those who edit *Factory Gossip*, the underground worker magazine, as well as labor NGOs, activists, and concerned citizens of the world.

Different strands of WGC converge, regionally and globally, into working-class public spheres, where diverse voices of labor go through a new process of unification and cultural jamming as exemplified in the Phone Story game, in ways long envisioned by Oskar Negt and Alexander Kluge in their critique of the Habermasian bourgeois public sphere.[22]

From working-class ICTs to working-class public spheres, the creation, circulation, and convergence of WGC involve a "motley crew" of very diverse groups of iSlaves and concerned citizens, be they feminist or ethnic, material or immaterial. As Linebaugh and Rediker point out, "The emphasis in modern labor history on the white, male, skilled, waged, nationalist, propertied artisan/citizen or industrial worker has hidden the history of the Atlantic proletariat of the seventeenth, eighteenth, and early nineteenth centuries."[23]

Indeed, contemporary labor struggles, and labor studies as well, need to be freed from the shackles of hegemonic masculinity, ethnocentrism, methodological nationalism, and the biases of class and status within the working people themselves. Only by so doing can we build enough autonomy and reflexivity into this emergent system and prevent it from the pitfalls of paradoxically strengthening slavery again.

The main output of working-class public spheres is DNA—digitally networked action—actions of collective will, connective power, discursively and on the ground; actions that contribute to the rise of network labor that stands on par with network enterprise and network state, and forming dialectical relationship with both, as a third pillar of what Manuel Castells theorizes as the network society.[24] Cultural capital and social innovations are to be generated from network labor for the growth of working-class ICTs to better serve the information have-less through a new cycle of technology-assisted class-formation process among the digital "motley crew."

To caution against nationalistic or ethnocentric myopia, let me emphasize that this model is intended for global application and analysis although its components are drawn from a Chinese test-tube. Without job losses and rising demand around the world, there would not have been such an industrial boom in China; the working conditions in Chinese factories would not have plummeted so astonishingly, either. The fate of manufactured iSlaves, manipulated by corporate giants, knows no national boundary. In the struggle between slavery and antislavery, Chinese workers and the working people of the world have, after all, but one shared lot.

I don't know if this new framework makes sense to you. All I know is that we need to think and act collectively, and this small volume is only a humble start. We must first jettison the "i" in iSlave before ending slavery itself. So long as the "we" is preserved, there is a shield against "natal alienation" and basis for an alternative world-system of digital media.

Limitation of space has made it impossible to engage in more in-depth discussion, although my main purpose is to raise questions and generate hypotheses rather than to provide definitive answers. Much remains to be done as history unfolds, while the working hypothesis at this moment is, allow me to submit, that from the information have-less to network labor, a new process of class formation has already begun.

Despite technological progress, the contemporary world remains haunted by the shadows of slavery, an enduring leitmotif that needs to be teased out from the long history of globalization, extending from four centuries ago to the present. While past forms of slavery are far from extinct, we see, from massive electronics plants to the new frontiers of cyberspace, a return to slave-like working conditions and power relations that have been unprecedented in modern industrial capitalism. Is this what we want—for ourselves, for our children?

Working people of all countries, unite! iSlaves have nothing to lose but our chains. We have a world to win.

# Appendix

## Bellagio-Harvard Guidelines
## on the Legal Parameters of Slavery

We, the Members of the Research Network on the Legal Parameters of Slavery,

*Recognizing* that there has been a lack of legal clarity with regard to the interpretation of the definition of slavery in international law;

*Conscious* that the starting point for understanding that definition is Article 1(1) of the 1926 Slavery Convention which reads: *"Slavery is the status or condition of a person over whom any or all of the powers attaching to the right of ownership are exercised"*;

*Recalling* that this definition is reproduced in substance in Article 7(a) of the 1956 Supplementary Convention on the Abolition of Slavery, the Slave Trade, and Institutions and Practices Similar to Slavery;

*Also noting* that the 1926 definition of slavery is once again reproduced in substance in the definition of enslavement found in Article 7(2)(c) of the 1998 Statute of the International Criminal Court and developed in more detail in the secondary legislation of the Court, in its Elements of Crimes;

*Bearing in mind* the provisions in international human rights law regarding slavery within the 1948 Universal Declaration and 1966 International Covenant on Civil and Political Rights; as well as the provisions regarding slavery in regional human rights conventions of the African, European, and Inter-American systems;

*Considering* the inclusion of slavery as an enumerated type of human exploitation in both the 2000 United Nations Palermo Protocol on Trafficking in Persons and the 2005 Council of Europe Convention on Action against Trafficking in Human Beings;

*Mindful* of the pronouncements and case-law related to slavery of international, regional and domestic courts;

Having met to consider the issue at the 2010 symposium entitled: "The Parameters of Slavery" at the Rockefeller Foundation's Bellagio Conference Centre in Bellagio, Italy; having further deliberated in 2011 at a meeting under the auspices of the Harriet Tubman Institute for Research on the Global Migrations of African Peoples, York University, Canada; and came together once more at a 2011 symposium entitled: "The Legal Parameters of Slavery: Historical to the Contemporary" at Harvard University, under the auspices of the Charles Hamilton Houston Institute for Race and Justice, Harvard Law School; the Harvard Sociology Department; the W. E. B. Du Bois Institute;

*Recommend the following Guidelines related to the legal parameters of slavery*:

## Guideline 1—The Legal Definition

The legal definition of slavery in international law is found at Article 1(1) of the 1926 Slavery Convention, which reads: "Slavery is the status or condition of a person over whom any or all of the powers attaching to the right of ownership are exercised."

## Guideline 2—The Exercise of the Powers Attaching to the Right of Ownership

In cases of slavery, the exercise of "the powers attaching to the right of ownership" should be understood as constituting control over a person in such a way as to significantly deprive that person of his or her individual liberty, with the intent of exploitation through the use, management, profit, transfer or disposal of that person. Usually this exercise will be supported by and obtained through means such as violent force, deception and/or coercion.

## Guideline 3—Possession is Foundational to Slavery

Where there is a right of ownership in respect of a thing, ownership implies a background relation of control. That control is the power attaching to the right of ownership known as possession.

Possession is foundational to an understanding of the legal definition of slavery, even when the State does not support a property right in respect of persons. To determine, in law, a case of slavery, one must look for possession.

While the exact form of possession might vary, in essence it supposes control over a person by another such as a person might control a thing. Such control may be physical, but physical constraints will not always be necessary to the maintenance of effective control over a person. More abstract manifestations of control of a person may be evident in attempts to withhold identity documents; or to otherwise restrict free movement or access to state authorities or legal processes; or equally in attempts to forge a new identity through compelling a new religion, language, place of residence, or forcing marriage.

Fundamentally, where such control operates, it will significantly deprive that person of his or her individual liberty for a period of time which is, for that person, indeterminate.

Cases of slavery are to be distinguished from those where, though there has been control exercised, it does not constitute control tantamount to possession, such as where employers make legitimate decisions about the management of workers.

Possession is foundational in that, not only is it a power attaching to the right of ownership, it also creates the factual conditions for the exercise of any or all of other powers attaching to the right of ownership, such as those set out in *Guideline 4*.

## Guideline 4—Further Examples of Powers Attaching to the Right of Ownership

Where a person controls another such as he or she would control a thing owned, such possession makes possible the exercise of any or all of the powers attaching to the right of ownership.

Correlatively, the exercise of any or all of the powers attaching to the right of ownership may serve to indicate the presence of control of a person tantamount to possession, and so provide evidence of slavery.

The following are further examples of powers attaching to the right of ownership:

a) *Buying, Selling or Transferring a Person*

Buying, selling, or otherwise transferring a person may provide evidence of slavery. Having established control tantamount to possession; the act of buying, selling, or transferring that person will be an act of slavery.

Evidence of slavery may also be found in similar transactions, such as bartering, exchanging, or giving or receiving a person as a gift, where control tantamount to possession has been established.

b) *Using a Person*

Using a person may provide evidence of slavery. Having established control tantamount to possession; the act of using that person will be an act of slavery.

Evidence of such use of a person may include the derived benefit from the services or labour of that person. In such cases, a person might be used by working for little or no pay, utilised for sexual gratification, or used by providing a service.

c) *Managing the Use of a Person*

Managing the use of a person may provide evidence of slavery. Having established control tantamount to possession; the act of managing that person will be an act of slavery.

Evidence of such management of the use of a person may include indirect management such as a brothel owner delegating power to a day manager in a situation of slavery in the context of sex work.

d) *Profiting from the Use of a Person*

Profiting from the use of a person may provide evidence of slavery. Having established control tantamount to possession; the act of profiting from the use of that person will be an act of slavery.

Evidence of profiting from the use of a person may include cases where a person is mortgaged, lent for profit, or used as collateral.

Evidence of profiting from the use of a person may also include making money or deriving any other kind of income or benefit from the use of the person. Such as the use of an agricultural worker in a situation of slavery, where the profit from the picking of a crop is taken or received by another whether in the form of wages or of the harvest.

e) *Transferring a Person to an Heir or Successor*

Transferring a person to an heir or successor may provide evidence of slavery. Having established control over a person tantamount to possession; the act of willing that person to a child or other heir or successor will be an act of slavery.

Evidence of such transferring of a person may include a case of inheritance where a woman, on the death of her husband, is deemed to be inherited by another person.

Evidence of such a transferring of a person may also include the conveying of a status or condition of a person to that of a successive generation, such as from mother to daughter.

f) *Disposal, Mistreatment or Neglect of a Person*

Disposing of a person following his or her exploitation may provide evidence of slavery. Having established control over a person tantamount to possession; the act of disposing of a person will be an act of slavery.

Mistreatment or neglect of a person may provide evidence of slavery. Having established control tantamount to possession, such disregard may lead to the physical or psychological exhaustion of a person, and ultimately to his or her destruction; accordingly the act of bringing about such exhaustion will be an act of slavery.

Evidence of such mistreatment or neglect may include sustained physical and psychological abuse, whether calculated or indiscriminate; or the imposition of physical demands that severely curtail the capacity of the human body to sustain itself or function effectively.

## Guideline 5—Making a Determination as to whether Slavery Exists

The exercise of any or all of the powers attaching to the right of ownership just considered shall provide evidence of slavery, insofar as they demonstrate control over a person tantamount to possession.

Accordingly, in determining whether slavery exists in a given case, it is necessary to examine the particular circumstances, asking whether *"powers attaching to the right of ownership"* are being exercised, so as to demonstrate control of a person tantamount to their possession.

In evaluating the particular circumstances to determine whether slavery exists, reference should be made to the substance and not simply to the form of the relationship in question.

The substance of the relationship should be determined by investigating whether in fact there has been an exercise of one or more of the powers attaching to the right of ownership. This will include a determination as to whether control tantamount to possession is present.

## Guideline 6—Expropriation

Ordinarily exclusion from expropriation or "security of holding" would be deemed a power attaching to the right of ownership. However, as the State generally does not support a property right in persons, a negative obligation against the State generally no longer exists.

However, the State has *at minimum* the positive obligation to bring about the end of either the status or condition of a person over whom any or all of the powers attaching to the right of ownership are exercised.

The State may have further positive obligations with regard to the prohibition against slavery on the basis of domestic law as well as regional or international instruments.

## Guideline 7—Terminology

The term "slavery" has often been utilised to describe circumstances that go beyond the legal definition as established by the 1926 Slavery Convention.

In law, only "slavery" and "institutions and practices similar to slavery," which is often abbreviated to "practices similar to slavery" have standing and are defined in international law via the 1926 Slavery Convention and the 1956 Supplementary Convention.

## Guideline 8—Distinction between Slavery and Forced Labour

The 1926 Slavery Convention recognises that forced labour can develop "into conditions analogous to slavery."

Although forced or compulsory labour is defined by the 1930 Forced Labour Convention as "all work or service which is exacted from any person under the menace of any penalty and for which the said person has not offered himself voluntarily"; forced labour will only amount to slavery when, in substance, there is the exercise of the powers attaching to the right of ownership.

Slavery will not be present in cases of forced labour where the control over a person tantamount to possession is not present.

## Guideline 9—Distinction between Slavery and "Institutions and Practices Similar to Slavery"

Article 1 of the 1956 Supplementary Convention recognises that the "institutions and practices similar to slavery," that is: debt bondage, serfdom, servile marriages, or child exploitation; may be "covered by the definition of slavery contained in article 1 of the Slavery Convention of 1926."

The distinction between these servile statuses as defined by the 1956 Supplementary Convention in the following terms and slavery is that slavery is present where in substance there is the exercise of the powers attaching to the right of ownership.

It should be emphasised that slavery will only be present in cases of such "institutions and practices similar to slavery" where control over a person tantamount to possession is present.

The following are the conventional servitudes set out in the 1956 Supplementary Convention on the Abolition of Slavery, the Slave Trade, and Institutions and Practices Similar to Slavery:

(a) Debt bondage, that is to say, the status or condition arising from a pledge by a debtor of his personal services or of those of a person under his control as security for a debt, if the value of those services as reasonably assessed is not applied towards the liquidation of the debt or the length and nature of those services are not respectively limited and defined;

(b) Serfdom, that is to say, the condition or status of a tenant who is by law, custom or agreement bound to live and labour on land belonging to another person and to render some determinate service to such other person, whether for reward or not, and is not free to change his status;

(c) Any institution or practice whereby:

   (i)   A woman, without the right to refuse, is promised or given in marriage on payment of a consideration in money or in kind to her parents, guardian, family or any other person or group; or

   (ii)  The husband of a woman, his family, or his clan, has the right to transfer her to another person for value received or otherwise; or

   (iii) A woman on the death of her husband is liable to be inherited by another person;

(d) Any institution or practice whereby a child or young person under the age of 18 years is delivered by either or both of his natural parents or by his guardian to another person, whether for reward or not, with a view to the exploitation of the child or young person or of his labour.

## Guideline 10—When Slavery
## and Lesser Servitudes are Present

Accepting that both slavery and lesser servitudes such as forced labour or "institutions and practices similar to slavery" may be found in substance in a particular circumstance; the manner to proceed is by making reference to that substance and not simply to the form, and first ask whether there has been an exercise of the powers attaching to the right of ownership. If so, then the more serious offence of slavery is present.

If not, reference should be made to the legal definition of the lesser servitude which corresponds in substance to the particular circumstance in question.

*Adopted on this day, 3 March 2012, by the Members of the Research Network on the Legal Parameters of Slavery.*

> Jean Allain, Queen's University, Belfast
> Kevin Bales, Free the Slaves
> Annie Bunting, York University
> John Cairns, University of Edinburgh
> William M. Carter Jr., Temple University
> Holly Cullen, University of Western Australia
> Seymour Drescher, University of Pittsburgh
> Stanley Engerman, University of Rochester
> Paul Finkelman, Albany Law School
> Bernard Freamon, Seton Hall University
> Allison Gorsuch, Yale University
> Robin Hickey, Durham University
> Richard Helmholz, University of Chicago
> Antony Honoré, University of Oxford
> Aidan McQuade, Anti-Slavery International
> Orlando Patterson, Harvard University
> James Penner, University College, London
> Joel Quirk, University of Witwatersrand
> Jody Sarich, Free the Slaves
> Rebecca Scott, University of Michigan

# Notes

## Chapter 1. Departure

1. Starting on September 28, 2014, the Umbrella Movement lasted for seventy-nine days, until December 15, 2014, when Hong Kong authorities removed the last barricades. See Elizabeth Barber, "79 Days That Shook Hong Kong," *Time*, December 15, 2014, available at http://ow.ly/OGpOe (accessed January 15, 2015).

2. Lai See and Howard Winn, "World's 'Freest Economy' Accolade Does Hong Kong a Disservice," *South China Morning Post*, January 28, 2014, 1, 10.

3. The original website is occupier.hk/standbyyou. For a comprehensive Chinese-language video introduction of this project, see vimeo.com/109922050.

4. Box Office Mojo, http://www.boxofficemojo.com (accessed January 15, 2015).

5. See http://thecnnfreedomproject.blogs.cnn.com (accessed January 15, 2015).

6. "Blood Money: Pressure Grows for Compensation for the Caribbean Trade," *The Economist*, October 5, 2013, 42.

7. Ta-Nehisi Coates, "The Case for Reparations," *The Atlantic*, June 2014, 54–71.

8. Ross Fitzgerald, ed., *Human Needs and Politics* (Rushcutters Bay, NSW: Pergamon/Australia, 1977).

9. George Fitzhugh. *Cannibals All! or, Slaves without Masters* (Richmond, Va.: Morris, 1857).

10. I coined the term "Appconn," taking inspiration from "Googlezon," a science-fiction Flash movie produced by Robin Sloan and Matt Thompson. See "EPIC 2014," available at http://ow.ly/OSRXJ (accessed November 3, 2014).

11. SACOM, *Workers as Machines: Military Management in Foxconn*, Hong Kong, October 12, 2010. Available at: http://ow.ly/L0ThW (accessed November 3, 2014).

In the first five months, there were fifteen reports of suicides. The rest of the year saw fewer reports of this kind due to Chinese authorities' media censorship of Foxconn suicide stories.

12. Paul Mozur and Lorraine Luk, "Gadget Maker Foxconn Freezes Overall China Hiring," *Wall Street Journal*, February 20, 2013, available at http://ow.ly/MEiLa (accessed May 7, 2015).

13. In-tack Im and Hyung-seob Lee, "Samsung Subcontractor Worker Commits Suicide from Work Stress," *Hankyoreh*, November 2, 2013, available at: http://ow.ly/L0Te9 (accessed November 3, 2014); David Barboza, "Despite a Pledge by Samsung, Child Labor Proves Resilient," *New York Times*, July 10, 2014, available at http://ow.ly/OGoxu (accessed May 7, 2015). See also Li-Gyeong Hong, *Empire of Shame* [documentary film] (South Korea: P.U.R.N. Production, 2013).

14. Boy Lüthje, "The Rise and Fall of 'Wintelism': Manufacturing Strategies and Transnational Production Networks of U.S. Information Electronics Firms in the Pacific Rim," in *Competitiveness of New Industries: Institutional Framework and Learning in Information Technology in Japan, the U.S., and Germany*, edited by Andreas Moerke and Cornelia Storz (London: Routledge, 2007), 180–209; Boy Lüthje, Stefanie Hürtgen, Peter Pawlicki, and Martina Sproll, *From Silicon Valley to Shenzhen: Global Production and Work in the IT Industry* (Lanham, Mass.: Rowman and Littlefield, 2013).

15. R. W. Connell, *Masculinities*, 2nd ed. (Sydney: Allen and Unwin, 2005).

16. Vincent Mosco, *The Digital Sublime: Myth, Power, and Cyberspace* (Cambridge, Mass: MIT Press, 2005).

17. C. L. R. James, *The Black Jacobins: Toussaint L'Ouverture and the San Domingo Revolution* (New York: Dial, 1938).

18. SACOM, *Workers as Machines*; Ngai Pun, Huilin Lu, Yuhua Guo, and Yuan Shen, *Suicide Express behind the Glory of Foxconn* (*Fushikang Huihuang Beihou de Lianhuan Tiao*) (Hong Kong: Commercial Press, 2011). In Chinese.

19. Jean Allain, *The Legal Understanding of Slavery: From the Historical to the Contemporary* (Oxford: Oxford University Press, 2012), loc 7742–868.

20. Ibid., loc 7763.

21. Ibid.

22. Bill Lessard and Steve Baldwin, *Net Slaves: True Tales of Working the Web* (New York: McGraw-Hill, 2000); Steve Baldwin and Bill Lessard, *Net Slaves 2.0* (New York: Allworth, 2003).

23. BBC One, "Panorama: Apple's Broken Promises," December 18, 2014, available at http://ow.ly/L0X6w (accessed March 7, 2015).

24. SACOM, *Workers as Machines*.

25. See, for example, Jenny Chan and Ngai Pun, "Suicide as Protest for the New Generation of Chinese Migrant Workers: Foxconn, Global Capital, and the State," *Japan Focus* 8, no. 37 (September 13, 2010), available at http://apjjf.org/-Jenny-Chan/3408/article.html (accessed February 6, 2016); Ngai Pun, Chris King Chi Chan, and Jenny Chan, "The Role of the State, Labor Policy and Migrant Workers' Struggles in Globalized China," *Global Labor Journal* 1, no. 1 (December 3, 2009): 132–51; Pun et al., *Suicide Express*; Marisol Sandoval, "Foxconned Labor as the Dark Side of the Information Age: Working Conditions at Apple's Contract

Manufacturers in China," *TripleC: Communication, Capitalism and Critique* 11, no. 2 (July 25, 2013): 318–47; Ngai Pun, Jenny Chan, and Mark Selden, *Life and Death behind Apple: Foxconn Workers on the Production Line* (Hong Kong: Zhonghua, 2015). In Chinese.

26. Yuezhi Zhao, "The Life and Times of 'Chimerica': Global Press Discourses on U.S.-China Economic Integration, Financial Crisis, and Power Shifts," *International Journal of Communication* 8 (2014): 419–44.

27. Lance Bennett and Alexandra Segerberg, "The Logic of Connective Action: Digital Media and the Personalization of Contentious Politics," *Information, Communication and Society* 15, no. 5 (June 2012): 739–68.

28. Jack Linchuan Qiu, "Network Labor and Non-Elite Knowledge Workers in China," *Work, Organization, Labor and Globalization* 4, no. 2 (2010): 80–95; Jack Linchuan Qiu, "Network Labor: Beyond the Shadow of Foxconn," in *Studying Mobile Media: Cultural Technologies, Mobile Communication, and the iPhone*, edited by Larissa Hjorth, Jean Burgess, and Ingrid Richardson (London: Routledge, 2012), 173–89.

29. Carolyn Cartier, Manuel Castells, and Jack Linchuan Qiu, "The Information Have-Less: Inequality, Mobility, and Translocal Networks in Chinese Cities," *Studies in Comparative International Development* 40, no. 2 (June 1, 2005): 9–34; Jack Linchuan Qiu, *Working-Class Network Society: Communication Technology and the Information Have-Less in Urban China* (Cambridge, Mass.: MIT Press, 2009).

30. SACOM, *Workers as Machines*; SACOM, *New iPhone, Old Abuses: Have Working Conditions at Foxconn in China Improved?* September 20, 2012, available at http://ow.ly/L0WeA (accessed January 8, 2015).

31. Immanuel Wallerstein, *The Modern World-System* (New York: Academic, 1974). Immanuel Wallerstein, "Globalization or the Age of Transition? A Long-Term View of the Trajectory of the World-System," *International Sociology* 15, no. 2 (2000): 249–65.

32. Samir Amin, "Beyond Liberal Globalization: A Better or Worse World?" *Monthly Review* 58, no. 7 (December 1, 2006): 10, available at http://ow.ly/L0W5F (accessed November 3, 2014).

33. Christian Fuchs, *Digital Labor and Karl Marx* (London: Routledge, 2014), 354.

34. Daya Thussu, ed., *Electronic Empires: Global Media and Resistance* (New York: Oxford University Press, 1998).

35. Tom Standage, *Victorian Internet* (London: Walker, 1998).

36. Dan Schiller, "Poles of Market Growth?" *Global Media and Communication* 1, no. 1 (2005): 79–103.

37. Allain, *Legal Understanding of Slavery*.

38. Sidney Mintz, *Sweetness and Power: The Place of Sugar in Modern History* (New York: Penguin, 1985), 121.

## Chapter 2. Patterns of Slavery

1. Free the Slaves, "Trafficking and Slavery Fact Sheet," January 2015, available at http://ow.ly/Lnz5f (accessed April 9, 2015).

2. Síle Nic Gabhan, "Human Trafficking: A Twenty-First Century Slavery," *The Furrow* 57, no. 10 (2006): 528–37.

3. Fuchs, *Digital Labor and Karl Marx*, 177.

4. Ibid., 155–56.

5. Ibid., 174.

6. Free the Slaves, "Pioneering New Frontiers in the Fight against Slavery: 2013 Annual Report" (Washington, D.C., 2014), available at http://ow.ly/LnAwW (accessed April 9, 2015), 12.

7. Ibid., 8.

8. Tim Steinweg and Esther de Haan, *Capacitating Electronics: The Corrosive Effects of Platinum and Palladium Mining on Labour Rights and Communities* (SOMO—Center for Research on Multinational Corporations, 2007), available at http://ow.ly/LnBhM (accessed April 9, 2015).

9. Free the Slaves, "Pioneering New Frontiers," 8.

10. Fuchs, *Digital Labor and Karl Marx*, 172–73.

11. George Monbiot, "My Search for a Smartphone That Is Not Soaked in Blood," *The Guardian*, March 11, 2013, available at http://ow.ly/OxfRt (accessed June 19, 2015).

12. BBC, "Apple 'Deeply Offended' by BBC Investigation," December 19, 2014, available at http://www.bbc.com/news/technology-30548468 (accessed June 19, 2015). For the original documentary program, see http://www.bbc.co.uk/programmes/b04vs348 (accessed June 19, 2015).

13. Fuchs, *Digital Labor and Karl Marx*, 194.

14. David Brion Davis, *Slavery and Human Progress* (Oxford: Oxford University Press, 1984), 81.

15. Claude Meillassoux, ed., *L'esclavage en Afrique précoloniale* (Paris: Maspéro 1975), 20. Translated in Davis, *Slavery and Human Progress*, 9.

16. Orlando Patterson, *Slavery and Social Death: A Comparative Study* (Cambridge, Mass.: Harvard University Press, 1982), 5.

17. Davis, *Slavery and Human Progress*, 14.

18. Orlando Patterson, "Trafficking, Gender, and Slavery: Past and Present," in Allain, *Legal Understanding of Slavery*, 325.

19. Robin Blackburn, *The Making of New World Slavery: From the Baroque to the Modern, 1492–1800* (London: Verso, 1997), 3.

20. Patterson, *Slavery and Social Death*, 5.

21. Jenny Chan and Ngai Pun, "Suicide as Protest for the New Generation of Chinese Migrant Workers: Foxconn, Global Capital, and the State," *Asia-Pacific Journal: Japan Focus* 8, no. 37 (2010), available http://japanfocus.org/-jenny-chan/3408; For earlier accounts of *dagongmei* see Ngai Pun, "Becoming *Dagongmei* (Working Girls): The Politics of Identity and Difference in Reform China," *China Journal*, no. 42 (July 1999), 1–18; Ngai Pun, *Made in China: Women Factory Workers in a Global Workplace* (Durham, N.C.: Duke University Press, 2005); Hairong Yan, *New Masters, New Servants: Migration, Development, and Women Workers in China* (Durham, N.C.: Duke University Press, 2008).

22. Carolyn Cartier, *Globalizing South China* (Malden, Mass.: Wiley, 2001), 176.

23. Jack Linchuan Qiu, *Working-Class Network Society: Communication Technology and the Information Have-Less in Urban China* (Cambridge, Mass.: MIT Press, 2009), 113–16.

24. Pun et al., *Suicide Express*; Pun Ngai and Jenny Chan "Global Capital, the State and Chinese Workers: The Foxconn Experience," *Modern China* 38, no. 4 (2012), 383–410. For an earlier account of electronics factory in the 1990s, see Ching Kwan Lee, *Gender and South China Miracle: Two Worlds of Factory Women* (Berkeley: University of California Press, 1998).

25. Raewyn Connell, *Confronting Inequality: Gender, Knowledge and Global Change* (Cambridge: Polity, 2011), loc 2289.

26. Herbert Aptheker, *American Negro Slave Revolts* (New York: Columbia University Press, 1943).

27. See for example Seymour Drescher, *Abolition: A History of Slavery and Antislavery* (Cambridge: Cambridge University Press, 2009).

28. Peter Linebaugh and Marcus Rediker, *The Many-Headed Hydra: Sailors, Slaves, Commoners, and the Hidden History of the Revolutionary Atlantic* (Boston, Mass.: Beacon, 2013).

29. Ibid., 8–35; 327–54.

30. Blackburn, *Making of New World Slavery*, 393, with reference to Johannes Postman, *The Dutch in the Atlantic Slave Trade* (Cambridge: Cambridge University Press, 1990), 166.

31. Marcus Rediker, *The Slave Ship: A Human History* (New York: Viking Penguin, 2007).

32. David Richardson, "Shipboard Revolts, African Authority, and the Atlantic Slave Trade," *William and Mary Quarterly* 58, no. 1 (2001), 69–92.

33. C. L. R. James, *The Black Jacobins: Toussaint L'Ouverture and the San Domingo Revolution* (New York: Dial, 1938).

34. See the Ibis Trilogy by Amitav Ghosh: *Sea of Poppies* (New York: Picador, 2008), *River of Smoke* (New York: Farrar, Straus and Giroux, 2011), and *Fire of Flood* (New York: Farrar, Straus and Giroux, 2015).

35. Walter Scheidel, "Human Mobility in Roman Italy, II: The Slave Population," *Journal of Roman Studies* 95 (2005): 64–79.

36. Rudolph T. Ware III, "Slavery in Islamic Africa, 1400–1800," in *The Cambridge World History of Slavery, Volume 3*, edited by David Eltis and Stanley L. Engerman (Cambridge: Cambridge University Press, 2011), 53–54. Note these estimates from ancient and medieval times are usually subject to methodological challenge.

37. Immanuel Wallerstein, *The Modern World System, Volume 3* (Berkeley: University of California Press, 2011), 143.

38. Ibid.

39. Eduardo Galeano, *Open Veins of Latin America: Five Centuries of the Pillage of a Continent* (New York: Monthly Review, 1971); Peter John Bakewell, *Miners of the Red Mountain: Indian Labor in Potosí, 1545–1650* (Albuquerque: University of New Mexico Press, 1984).

40. Robert J. Samuelson, "China's Wrong Turn on Trade," *Newsweek*, May 13, 2007, available at http://ow.ly/LrLWZ (accessed April 10, 2015).

41. Pepe Escobar, *The Empire of Chaos: The Roving Eye Collection* (Ann Arbor, Mich.: Nimble, 2014), loc 9251.

42. Zhao, "Life and Death of 'Chimerica.'"

43. "Time Series Data of International Investment Position of China, Quarterly," State Administration of Foreign Exchange, the People's Republic of China, available at http://ow.ly/LrLRE (accessed April 10, 2012).

44. Blackburn, *Making of New World Slavery*, 584.

45. Stanley Engerman, "Some Considerations Relating to Property Rights in Man," *Journal of Economic History* 33 (1973): 43–65.

46. Ghaith Abdul-Ahad, "We Need Slaves to Build Monuments," *The Guardian*, October 7, 2008, available at http://ow.ly/LteRm (accessed April 11, 2015).

47. Fernando Ortiz, *Cuban Counterpoint* (New York: Knopf), 267.

48. Mintz, *Sweetness and Power*, 32.

49. Blackburn, *Making of New World Slavery*, 235.

50. Ralph Davis, *The Rise of the Atlantic Economies* (Ithaca, N.Y.: Cornell University Press, 1973), 251.

51. Donald C. Coleman, *The Economy of England, 1450–1750* (London: Oxford University Press, 1977), 118.

52. Blackburn, *Making of New World Slavery*, 377.

53. Arthur L. Stinchcombe, *Sugar Island Slavery in the Age of Enlightenment: The Political Economy of the Caribbean World* (Princeton, N.J.: Princeton University Press, 1995).

54. Mintz, *Sweetness and Power*, 47.

55. Cited in Carl Bridenbaugh and Roberta Bridenbaugh, *No Peace beyond the Line: The English in the Caribbean, 1624–1690* (New York: Oxford University Press, 1972), 301.

56. Pun et al., *Suicide Express*; Pun et al., *Life and Death*.

57. Pun et al., *Suicide Express*, 197.

58. Eric Hobsbawm, "The Crisis of the Seventeenth Century," in *Crisis in Europe: 1560–1660*, edited by Trevor Aston (London: Routledge/Kegan Paul, 1965), 46.

59. Mintz, *Sweetness and Power*, 194.

60. Patterson, *Slavery and Social Death*, loc 209.

61. Jacob M. Price. "What Did Merchants Do? Reflections on British Overseas Trade, 1660–1790," *Journal of Economic History* 49, no. 2 (1989): 267–84.

62. Mintz, *Sweetness and Power*, 122–23.

63. Ibid., 194.

64. Ibid., 201–2.

65. Patterson, *Slavery and Social Death*.

66. Elizabeth Eisenstein, *The Printing Revolution in Early Modern Europe*, 2nd ed. (Cambridge: Cambridge University Press), 33.

67. Blackburn, *Making of New World Slavery*, 581.

68. Patterson, *Slavery and Social Death*, chap. 11.

69. Ibid., loc 7053.

70. Ibid., loc 7020.

71. Ibid., loc 7788.

72. Daniel Pipes, "From Mawla to Mamluk: The Origins of Islamic Military Slavery," PhD diss., Harvard University, Cambridge, Mass., 1978.

73. Karl Marx and Friedrich Engels, *The Communist Manifesto* (New York: Penguin, 1998), 58.

74. Karl Heinz Roth and Marcel van der Linden, eds., *Beyond Marx: Theorising the Global Labour Relations of the Twenty-First Century* (Leiden, Neth.: Brill, 2014).

75. Ibid., 472.

76. Blackburn, *Making of New World Slavery*, 4.

77. Ibid., 590.

78. Ibid.

79. Davis, *Slavery and Human Progress*, 14.

80. Orlando Patterson, *Freedom: Freedom in the Making of Western Culture* (London: Tauris, 1991), 402.

81. Ibid.

82. Ibid.

83. William Clarence-Smith and David Eltis, "White Servitude," in Eltis and Engerman, *Cambridge World History of Slavery*, 3:132.

84. See, for example, Kevin Bales, *Disposable People: New Slavery in the Global Economy*, rev. ed. (Berkeley: University of California Press, 2012).

85. The list of participating countries is available at https://treaties.un.org/Pages/ViewDetails.aspx?src=TREATY&mtdsg_no=XVIII-2&chapter=18&lang=en (accessed February 12, 2016).

86. Allain, *Legal Understanding of Slavery*, 199–200.

87. Robin Hickey, "Seeking to Understand the Definition of Slavery," in Allain, *Legal Understanding of Slavery*, 221.

88. Davis, *Slavery and Human Progress*, 315.

89. Chief Justice Gleeson, *The Queen v. Tang* (High Court of Australia, 2008).

90. Allain, *Legal Understanding of Slavery*.

91. Matteo Fiori, "The Foča 'Rape Camps': A Dark Page Read Through the ICTY's Jurisprudence," *Hague Justice Journal* 2, no. 3 (2007): 9–27, available at http://ow.ly/LPqJV (accessed April 20, 2015).

92. Holly Curren, "Contemporary International Legal Norms on Slavery Problems of Judicial Interpretation and Application," in Allain, *Legal Understanding of Slavery*, 304.

93. Kunara, Dragoljub (The Hague Justice Portal), available at http://ow.ly/LPrcw (accessed April 20, 2015).

94. Allain, *Legal Understanding of Slavery*, 199–200.

95. Ibid., 375–80.

96. Ibid., 378.

97. Allain, *Legal Understanding of Slavery*.

98. Bernard Freamon, "Definitions and Conceptions of Slave Ownership in Islamic Law," in Allain, *Legal Understanding of Slavery*, 60.

99. Gleeson, *The Queen v. Tang*, 39, paragraph 20.

100. Allison Mileo Gorsuch, "To Indent Oneself: Ownership, Contracts, and Consent in Antebellum Illinois," in Allain, *Legal Understanding of Slavery*, 136.

101. Ibid., 151.

102. Rebecca J. Scott, "Under Color of Law: *Siliadin v. France* and the Dynamics of Enslavement in Historical Perspective," in Allain, *Legal Understanding of Slavery*, 164. See also Curren, "Contemporary International Legal Norms," 304. For *The Queen v. Tang* see High Court of Australia, available at http://ow.ly/LUVxK (accessed April 21, 2015).

103. Guideline 3 also specifies: "Cases of slavery are to be distinguished from those where, though there has been control exercised, it does not constitute control tantamount to possession, such as where employers make legitimate decisions about the management of workers." Guideline 8 further states: "Forced labour will only amount to slavery when, in substance, there is the exercise of the powers attaching to the right of ownership." It is likely that many of Foxconn's managerial activities fall in this realm of "legitimate decisions." But this does exclude the possibility that, in other instances, Foxconn management may escalate its control efforts into conditions "tantamount to possession."

104. Cullen, "Contemporary International Legal Norms," 319.

105. Ibid., 318.

106. Hickey, "Seeking to Understand the Definition," 235. Here, Hickey maintains that immunities are as important an indicator for slavery as the other "powers attaching to ownership."

107. Scott, "Under Color of Law," 155.

108. See http://fightslaverynow.org; and http://slaverytoday.org/tag/organ-trafficking (accessed April 20, 2015).

109. United Nations Global Initiative to Fight Human Trafficking, *Human Trafficking for the Removal of Organs and Body Parts* (Austria Center: Vienna Forum to Fight Human Trafficking Background Paper, February12–15, 2008), 3, available at http://files.meetup.com/1337582/OrganRemoval.pdf (accessed April 20, 215).

110. Kevin Bales, "Slavery in Its Contemporary Manifestations," in Allain, *Legal Understanding of Slavery*, 289.

111. Ibid.

112. Bales, *Disposable People*.

113. Bales, "Slavery in Its Contemporary Manifestations," 289.

114. Ibid.

115. Orlando Patterson, "Rejoinder: Professor Orlando Patterson's Response to Professor Kevin Bales," in Allain, *Legal Understanding of Slavery*, 373. See also Patterson, "Trafficking, Gender and Slavery," 322–59.

116. Patterson, "Trafficking, Gender, and Slavery," 323.

117. Allain, *Legal Understanding of Slavery*, 6.

118. Ibid., 3.

119. Scott, "Under Color of Law," 162.

120. Allain, *Legal Understanding of Slavery*, 6.

121. Joel Quirk, "Defining Slavery in All Its Forms: Historical Inquiry as Contemporary Instruction," in Allain, *Legal Understanding of Slavery*, 278.

122. Gorsuch, "To Indent Oneself," 151.

123. Patterson, "Trafficking, Gender, and Slavery"; Patterson, "Rejoinder"; Bales, "Professor Kevin Bales's Response to Professor Orlando Patterson," in Allain, *Legal Understanding of Slavery*, 360–72.

## Chapter 3. Manufacturing iSlaves

1. Fuchs, *Digital Labor and Karl Marx*, 155–56, 172–73; Free the Slaves, "Pioneering New Frontiers"; Jim Edwards, "Apple's iPhone Suppliers Use Children to Dig in Lethally Dangerous Mud Pits for Tin Ore, the BBC Alleges," *Business Insider*, December 18, 2014, available at http://ow.ly/MzA4G (accessed May 6, 2015).

2. Mingtian Xu, *Guo Tai-ming and Foxconn* (Beijing, China CITIC, 2007), 18, 23. In Chinese.

3. Ibid., 29–30.

4. In Chinese: "niyao tade qian, tayao nide ming" (personal interview with retired IT manufacturing engineer, Taipei, May 30, 2010).

5. Yawei Lin and Hongwen Lin, "Nine Generals of Hon Hai Extinguishing Six Kingdoms," *PChome*, March 14, 2005, available at http://ow.ly/MzEjx (accessed May 6, 2015). In Chinese.

6. Clare Jim, "Apple Is Snubbing Foxconn after iPhone 5 Production Problems," Reuters, May 13, 2013, available at http://ow.ly/MzOYG (accessed May 6, 2015).

7. Shuyi Zhang, Dianwen Zhang, and Zhifang Lu, *Legend of Three Hundred Billion: Foxconn's Guo Tai-ming* (Beijing: Machinery Industry, 2002), 9. In Chinese.

8. Ibid., 8–9.

9. Nick Webster, "Welcome to iPod City: The 'Robot' Workers on 15-hour Days." *The Mail on Sunday*, June 14, 2006, available at http://ow.ly/MzEF6 (accessed May 6, 2015).

10. Jason Dean, "The Forbidden City of Terry Guo," *Wall Street Journal*, August 11, 2007; Dan Liu and Wei Wang, "*First Financial Daily* and Foxconn Jointly Rescind Law Suit," XinhuaNet, available at http://ow.ly/MzRyB (accessed May 6, 2015). In Chinese. Foxconn is widely known, especially in Chinese-language media world, for its tough dealing with journalists. Since its early days in Taiwan, the company has used lawsuits to silence reporters in Taiwan, although it seldom does so against English-language media overseas.

11. "Taiwan's Richest Man Choosing Wife, Messy Relationships among Five Parties," *Sing Tao Daily*, March 20, 2007. In Chinese.

12. Belinda Goldsmith, "Who is the Mystery iPhone Girl?" Reuters, August 28, 2008. The iPhone Girl frenzy was captured by a *Wired* article that reads: "Way to go, iPhone Girl! We still have no idea what your name is or how old you are, but you've won a place in Gadget Lab's hearts. If you ever read this: Would you mind saving photos of yourself on Apple's next revolutionary device?" Brian Chen, *Wired*, August 2008, available at http://ow.ly/O3h2G (accessed May 6, 2015).

13. Ting-I Tsai, "Employee's Suicide Puts Hon Hai, Apple in Spotlight," *Wall Street Journal*, July 23, 2009.

14. Li Xiong, "Foxconn Statement: Sun Danyong Suicide Reflects Shortcomings in Internal Management," Sina Technology, available at http://ow.ly/MzZBH (accessed May 6, 2015). In Chinese.

15. Jiabin Du, "Foxconn Failed in Both E-Commerce and Material Stores," *Global Entrepreneurs*, June 2, 2013, available at http://ow.ly/O3hVQ (accessed May 8, 2015). In Chinese.

16. If the time frame is extended from June 2010 to November 2011, there would be nine additional cases of employee suicides, which were reported in Chinese media despite Beijing's censorship order against such reporting. The total number of victims onboard the "Foxconn suicide express" would be twenty-four in twenty-two months.

|    | Name | Age | Location | Time |
|----|------|-----|----------|------|
| 16 | LIU (given name unknown) | 18 | Foshan | July 20, 2010 |
| 17 | LIU, Ming | 23 | Kunshan | August 4, 2010 |
| 18 | HE (given name unknown) | 22 | Guanlan | November 5, 2010 |
| 19 | WANG, Ling | 25 | Longhua | January 7, 2011 |
| 20 | HOU (given name unknown) | 20 | Chengdu | May 26, 2011 |
| 21 | CAI (given name unknown) | 21 | Longhua | July 18, 2011 |
| 22 | LI, Baoqiang | 18 | Guanlan | October 15, 2011 |
| 23 | LI, Rongying | 21 | Taiyuan | November 23, 2011 |
| 24 | XIE, Yanshe | 21 | Longhua | November 26, 2011 |

17. Richard Jones, "Something Rotten at Apple's Core? Shocking Toll of Suicides at iPad Factory in China Revealed," *Daily Mail*, May 29, 2010, available at http://ow.ly/MA3TR (accessed May 6, 2015).

18. Jenny Chan, "iSlave," *New Internationalist*, Issue 441 (April 1, 2011), available at http://ow.ly/MA5Cr (accessed May 6, 2015).

19. Charles Isherwood, "Speaking Less than Truth to Power," *New York Times*, March 18, 2012).

20. Netease Tech Channel, "The Twenty-Universities Joint Team Investigation Report on Foxconn," October 9, 2010, available at http://ow.ly/O3j1u (accessed May 6, 2015) (in Chinese); Caixin Net, "Universities Investigation Report Shows Foxconn Abusing Student Workers," May 21, 2011, available at http://ow.ly/O3joS (accessed May 6, 2015) (in Chinese); Sina Technology, "Foxconn: Have You Changed?" April 1, 2012, available at http://ow.ly/O3jz5 (accessed May 6, 2015) (in Chinese); iLabour, "Investigation Report on Labor Union in Foxconn," September 16, 2013, available at http://ow.ly/O3k9l (accessed May 6, 2015) (in Chinese); iLabour, "2015 Investigation Report on Salary, Work Hours, and Current Management of Foxconn," April 25, 2015, available at http://ow.ly/O3kiX (accessed May 6, 2015) (in Chinese).

21. Michael Kan, "Foxconn CEO Blames Past Worker Suicides on Breakups, Family Disputes," June 25, 2014, available at http://ow.ly/O1bHm (accessed May 7, 2015).

22. Rhiannon Willams, "Apple Goes to War with the BBC," *The Telegraph*, December 19, 2014, available at http://ow.ly/O3ldY (accessed May 7, 2015).

23. Eva Dou, "Apple Shifts Supply Chain Away from Foxconn to Pegatron," May 29, 2013, available at http://ow.ly/O3lkb (accessed May 7, 2015).

24. Ishaan Tharoor, "The Haunting Poetry of a Chinese Factory Worker Who Committed Suicide," *Washington Post*, November 12, 2014, available at http://ow.ly/MDaWh (accessed May 7, 2015).

25. Emily Rauhala, "The Poet Who Died for Your Phone," *Time*, June 5, 2015, available at http://time.com/chinapoet (accessed June 9, 2015).

26. BBC, "Apple's Broken Promises," December 18, 2014, available at http://www.bbc.co.uk/programmes/b04vs348 (accessed May 7, 2015).

27. Tencent Commentaries, "The Myth of Voluntary Overtime at Foxconn," February 5, 2015, available at http://ow.ly/O3lOE (accessed May 7, 2015). In Chinese.

28. Abigail Phillips, "Twenty Things You Don't Know about the Man Who Makes Your iPhone," *Manufacturing Global*, January 15, 2015, available at http://ow.ly/Mdje4 (accessed April 28, 2015).

29. Slavoj Zizek, *First as Tragedy, Then as Farce* (London: Verso, 2009), 6.

30. Michael Burawoy, *The Politics of Production: Factory Regimes under Capitalism and Socialism* (London: Verso, 1985).

31. Shen, Yuan (2010). "The Face of Chinese Nongmingong," paper presented at the workshop "Network Society of China." September 2010, Barcelona: Open University of Catalonia.

32. See entry in OxfordDictionaries.com at http://ow.ly/OaVfs (accessed June 11, 2015).

33. *Amistad*, directed by Stephen Spielberg (Los Angeles: DreamWorks, 1997).

34. Pun et al., *Suicide Express*.

35. Michel Foucault, *Discipline and Punish: The Birth of the Prison* (New York: Pantheon, 1977).

36. Chan and Pun, "Suicide as Protest."

37. Mozur and Luk, "Gadget Maker Foxconn," *Wall Street Journal*, February 20, 2013. By the end of 2016, there were 1,301,300 personnel on active duty in the U.S. armed forces. See United States Department of Defense, "Department of Defense Releases Fiscal Year 2017 President's Budget Proposal," available at http://ow.ly/ZKkhn (accessed February 19, 2016).

38. Hang Zeng, *The Global Travel of an iPhone* (Nanjing: Phoenix, 2011), 58. In Chinese.

39. Dianwen Zhang, *Tiger and Fox: Terry Guo's Global Competition Strategies* (Taipei: Tianxia Publication, 2008), 81. In Chinese.

40. Interview with local police officer, Shenzhen, December 18, 2013.

41. Pun et al., *Suicide Express*, 60.

42. Ibid., 71.

43. Rediker, *Slave Ship*, loc 4080.

44. Pun, Chan, and Selden, *Life and Death behind Apple*, 75.

45. Guideline 3—Possession Is Foundational to Slavery, the 2012 Bellagio-Harvard Guidelines, in Allain, *Legal Understanding of Slavery*, 376.

46. Personal interview, July 9, 2013.

47. Today's News Network, "Former Foxconn Employee Reveals That Foxconn Guards Are Like Mafia," available at http://ow.ly/OTtDj (accessed May 7, 2015). In Chinese.

48. Li Li, "Ma Xiangqian's Relatives Suspect He Was 'Suicided,' Apple Issues First Response," Apolo News, May 27, 2010, available at http://ow.ly/MEoOY (accessed May 7, 2015). In Chinese.

49. Lengbin Gu and Peiyao Pan, "Life and Death Evidence for Foxconn Tragedies," *Asia Weekly*, July 25, 2010, 29–31. In Chinese.

50. "Families of Foxconn Victims Reveal *Jinyiwei* Torture" *Next Magazine*, June 3, 2010, 50–56. In Chinese.

51. Fieldtrips to Shenzhen, March 12 and 20, 2011.

52. See more discussions about these "teachers" in Pun et al., *Suicide Express*, 32–35; Pun, Chan, and Selden, *Life and Death behind Apple*, 86–91.

53. Pun et al., *Suicide Express*, 102–3.

54. Probably because of this special issue, the magazine was shut down in May 2013.

55. *Factory Gossip*, April 2013, issue 7 (Foxconn Special Issue), 42.

56. Ibid., 7.

57. Pun et al., *Suicide Express*, 73.

58. Rui Zhai, "Basic Information at Foxconn Longhua," June 19, 2013, available at http://ow.ly/OGA8X (accessed May 7, 2015).

59. Personal interview, November 27, 2011.

60. Guideline 2—The Exercise of the Powers Attaching to the Right of Ownership, the 2012 Bellagio-Harvard Guidelines, in Allain, *Legal Understanding of Slavery*, 376.

61. Ibid.

62. Pun, Chan, and Selden, *Life and Death behind Apple*, 85; See also Earl Brown and Kyle DeCant, "Exploiting Chinese Interns as Unprotected Industrial Labor," *Asian Pacific Law and Policy* 15, no. 2 (2014): 149–95; Jenny Chan, Ngai Pun, and Mark Seldon, "Interns or Students: China's Student Labor Regime," *Asian Studies* 1, no. 1 (March 2015): 1–31;

63. Foxconn Technology Group, "Foxconn Is Committed to a Safe and Positive Working Environment," October 11, 2010, available at http://ow.ly/MEHqo (accessed May 8, 2015). In comparison, Disney's College Program has only recruited fifty thousand interns over the past three decades. See Ross Perlin, *Intern Nation* (London: Verso, 2012), 6. For more discussion on Foxconn interns see Pun, Chan, and Selden, *Life and Death behind Apple*, 85.

64. See Article 4 of the 2010 Education Law of the People's Republic of China; Pun et al., *Suicide Express*, 9.

65. Mark Bendeich, "Foxconn Says Underage Workers Used in China Plant," Reuters, October 17, 2012, available at http://ow.ly/MD9uB (accessed May 7, 2015).

66. See Pun et al., *Suicide Express*, 18–38, for more findings about Foxconn's illegal treatment of student interns.

67. Personal interview, April 17, 2012.

68. Kevin Voigt, "Foxconn Denies Forced Chinese Student Labor on iPhone 5 Lines," CNN, September 11, 2012, available at http://ow.ly/MFZl7 (accessed May 8, 2015).

69. Sarah Mishkin, "Foxconn Admits Student Intern Labor Violations at China Plant," *Financial Times*, October 10, 2013, available at http://ow.ly/MFW1H (accessed May 8, 2015).

70. Brown and DeCant, "Exploiting Chinese Interns," 183–84.

71. Ibid., 22.

72. Guideline 5—Making a Determination as to Whether Slavery Exists, the 2012 Bellagio-Harvard Guidelines, in Allain, *Legal Understanding of Slavery*, 378.

73. Guideline 4—Further Examples of Powers Attaching to the Right of Ownership, the 2012 Bellagio-Harvard Guidelines, in Allain, *Legal Understanding of Slavery*, 377.

74. Rutvica Andrijasevic and Devi Sacchetto, "China May Be Far Away but Foxconn Is on Our Doorstep," *Open Democracy*, June 5, 2013, available at http://ow.ly/OGE0n (accessed June 14, 2015).

75. Cuijun Zu, "Firing and Hiring Tens of Thousands of Employees at Will?" *China Computer Daily*, March 25, 2009, available at http://ow.ly/OhJhQ (accessed June 14, 2015). In Chinese.

76. Ibid.

77. Pun et al., *Suicide Express*, 167.

78. Rediker, *Slave Ship*, loc 2472–545.

79. Ibid., loc 5316.

80. William Wilberforce, "On the Horrors of the Slave Trade," in *The Parliamentary History of England, from the Norman Conquest in 1066 to the Year 1803*, edited by William Cobbett (London: Hansard, 1806–1820), 28 (years 1789–1791), col. 45.

81. Qiang Li and Juan Zhang, "Foxconn Workers: Lowest Salary 340 Yuan per Month, 700-Plus People Sharing One Room." Neteast Commercial Channel, June 17, 2006, available: http://ow.ly/MG8m1 (accessed May 8, 2015). In Chinese.

82. Ibid.

83. Rediker, *Slave Ship*, loc 4628.

84. iPod City, *Daily Mail*.

85. Patterson, *Slavery and Social Death*.

86. Ngai Pun and Jenny Chan, "The Spatial Politics of Labor in China: Life, Labor, and a New Generation of Migrant Workers." *South Atlantic Quarterly* 112, no. 1 (January 1, 2013): 179–90.

87. Pun et al., *Suicide Express*, 113–14.

88. Olaudah Equiano, *The Interesting Narrative of the Life of Olaudah Equiano; or, Gustavus Vassa, the African, Written by Himself* (London, 1789), reprinted in Vincent Carretta, ed., *The Interesting Narrative and Other Writings* (New York: Penguin, 1995).

89. Ibid., loc 5472.

90. DreamWorks and HBO, *Amistad*, film, directed by Stephen Spielberg (1997, Los Angeles); Jeremy Krikler, "The *Zong* and the Lord Chief Justice," *History Workshop Journal* 64, no. 1 (2007): 29–47; Rediker, *Slave Ship*, loc 4092–101.

91. Marcus Rediker, *The Amistad Revolution: An Atlantic Odyssey of Slavery and Freedom* (New York: Penguin, 2012), 58.

92. Guideline 4—Further Examples of Powers Attaching to the Right of Ownership, the 2012 Bellagio-Harvard Guidelines, in Allain, *Legal Understanding of Slavery*, 377.

93. Tan EE Lyn, "Family of Brain-Damaged Worker Takes Foxconn to Court in China," Reuters, October 30, 2012, available at http://ow.ly/OTwIT (accessed June 16, 2015).

94. Yong Li and Wenfeng Wen, "26-Year-Old Foxconn Engineer after Surgical Removal of His Left Brain," *Jingbao*, September 28, 2012, available at http://ow.ly/OGXQt (accessed June 16, 2015); Tan EE Lyn, "Worker's Injury Casts Harsh New Light on Foxconn and China," Reuters, October 10, 2012, available at http://ow.ly/On7j7 (accessed June 16, 2015).

95. Personal interview, November 22, 2014.

96. Tingting Shen, "After Work Injury, Foxconn Said: Not My Worker," *Yangcheng Evening News*, December 19, 2013, available at http://ow.ly/OGZxS (accessed June 16, 2015).

97. Shikai Xu, "Protesting Foxconn Causing Workers to Have Cancer," *Civil Media*, June 24, 2015, available at http://ow.ly/OUBsE (accessed June 29, 2015). In Chinese.

98. See http://whopaysfilm.org (accessed June 16, 2015). This documentary records several of the high-profile Foxconn victims, including Zhang Tingzhen and Tian Yu.

99. Yuezhi Zhao, "China Media Colloquium: An Introductory and Overview Essay," *International Journal of Communication* 4 (2010): 11.

100. Allain, *Legal Understanding of Slavery*, loc 7777.

101. Rediker, *Slave Ship*, loc 4887.

102. Ibid., loc 4975.

103. Ibid., loc 5189.

104. Ibid., loc 1251.

105. Olaudah Equiano, *The Life of Olaudah Equiano* (Mineola, N.Y.: Dover, 1999), 34.

106. "Foxconn Shenzhen Workers, Same Pay for Less Work," China News Agency, August 20, 2010. In Chinese.

107. See the beginning of my short documentary film: Jack Linchuan Qiu, *Deconstructing Foxconn*, SACOM, December 2010, available at https://vimeo.com/17558439.

108. China News Agency, "Except Apologies, There're Still Apologies." May 27, 2010. In Chinese.

109. Chaowen Li, "Foxconn Starts to Demolish Protection Nets Installed Less than Two Months Ago," *Daily Economic News*, August 18, 2010, 13.

110. Michael Kan, "Foxconn CEO Blames Past Worker Suicides on Breakups, Family Disputes," *PC World*, June 26, 2014, available at http://ow.ly/OH0Ib (accessed May 8, 2015).

111. Pun, Chan, and Selden, *Life and Death behind Apple*.

112. Yang Yan, "Will High Compensation Unwittingly Encourage Employee Suicides?" *Prosecution Daily*, May 28, 2010, 4. In Chinese.

113. Peter Ha, "Foxconn Suicides: Eh, They Are 'Below Average,' Says Apple CEO," *Time*, June 1, 2010, available at http://ow.ly/OMrpg (accessed June 25, 2015).

114. "Methods Used in Completed Suicides in Hong Kong, 1999–2013," Hong Kong Jockey Club Center for Suicide Research and Prevention, University of Hong Kong, available at http://ow.ly/OMs4i (accessed June 25, 2015).

115. "Back from the Edge: A Dramatic Decline in Suicides," *The Economist*, June 28, 2014, available: http://ow.ly/OMsph (accessed June 25, 2015).

116. Ibid.

117. "Crunching the Suicide Statistics at Foxconn," *China Economic Review*, May 28, 2010, available at http://ow.ly/MGC8G (accessed May 8, 2015).

118. Pun, Chan, and Selden, *Life and Death behind Apple*.

119. "Memo on Suicides in Huawei," Sohu.com, available at http://tv.sohu.com/s2008/huawei (accessed June 25, 2015). In Chinese.

120. June Yang, "Samsung Electronics Workers Commit Suicide, Policy Say," Bloomberg, January 13, 2011, available at http://ow.ly/OMtzY (accessed June 25, 2015).

121. John Lichfield, "Telecoms Giant Hit by 'Suicide Epidemic,'" *The Independent*, March 21, 2014, 27.

122. "Ex-France Telecom CEO Probed over 35 Suicides," France 24, July 6, 2012, available at http://ow.ly/OMtIF (accessed May 9, 2015).

123. "France Telecom Suicide Case Ends," from *Factiva*, "French Collection," January 7, 2015.

124. Sarah Waters, "A Capitalism That Kills," *French Politics, Culture and Society*, 32, no.3 (2014): 121–41.

125. Jack D. Douglas, "The Sociological Analysis of the Social Meanings of Suicide," in *The Sociology of Suicide*, edited by Anthony Giddens (London: Cass, 1971), 135.

126. Shiyu Liu, "Foxconn Publicizes Employee Last Words," *Apolo News*, June 9, 2010, available at http://ow.ly/MMhDg (accessed June 25, 2015). In Chinese.

127. Lei Zhang, "Foxconn Suicide Survivor Tian Yu," *Southern People*, November 11, 2011, available at http://ow.ly/OAfKa (accessed on June 20, 2015). In Chinese.

128. See https://vimeo.com/17558439.

129. Qiao Tu, "*Fly to Ascend [Feisheng]*," 2014. In Chinese.

130. Pun, Chan, and Selden, *Life and Death behind Apple*, 12.

131. Allain, *Legal Understanding of Slavery*, loc 7777.

132. Pun, Chan, and Selden, *Life and Death behind Apple*, 18.

133. Patterson, *Slavery and Social Death*, loc 33.

134. Barbara Solow, *Slavery and the Rise of the Atlantic System* (New York: Cambridge University Press, 1993), 20.

135. Joel Mokyr, *The Gifts of Athena: Historical Origins of the Knowledge Economy* (Princeton, N.J.: Princeton University Press, 2002), 297.

136. Maxwell and Miller, *Greening the Media*.

137. *Factory Gossip*, 5 (author's translation).

138. Emile Durkheim, *On Suicide*, translated by Robin Buss (New York: Penguin, 2006).

139. Quoted in Pun, Chan, and Selden, *Life and Death behind Apple*, 16 (author's translation). Original weblink: http://ow.ly/OMx2e. The blog was deleted on May 30, 2010.

## Chapter 4. Manufactured iSlaves

1. A Gan, "Youngster Selling Kidney: Fatal Luxury Consumes Youth and Life," *Family Life Guide*, no. 9 (2011): 50–51. In Chinese.

2. Wei Zeng and Cuihua He, "The Case of Seventeen-Year-Old Selling Kidney: Seven Convicted in Chenzhou, Hunan," China News Agency, November 29, 2012. In Chinese.

3. Qiu, *Working-Class Network Society*.

4. Zeng and He, "Case of Seventeen-Year-Old."

5. Scott Carney, *The Red Market: On the Trail of the World's Organ Brokers, Bone Thieves, Blood Farmers, and Child Traffickers* (New York: Morrow, 2011), loc 188.

6. Dudu Yu and Jianfeng Guo, "Selling Daughter Online for Several Thousand Dollars," *Xinmin Evening News*, October 18, 2013. In Chinese.

7. Xiaolong Chen, "Ridiculous Advertisement: When Selling Kidneys Becomes a Habit," *Shenzhen Evening News*, December 28, 2012.

8. Étienne de La Boétie and Murray N. Rothbard, *The Politics of Obedience: The Discourse of Voluntary Servitude*, trans. Harry Kurz (Auburn, Ala.: Ludwig von Mises Institute, 2011), 53.

9. Hannah Beech and Chengcheng Jiang, "The Cult of Apple in China," *Time*, July 2, 2012, 30–35.

10. Henry Jenkins, *Textual Poachers: Television Fans and Participatory Culture* (New York: Routledge, 1992), 12. See also Henry Jenkins, *Convergence Culture* (New York: New York University Press, 2008).

11. Mark Andrejevic, "Social Network Exploitation," in *A Networked Self*, edited by Zizi Papacharissi (New York: Routledge, 2008), 82–101.

12. Fuchs, *Digital Labor and Karl Marx*, loc 2975.

13. Tiziana Terranova, "Free Labor: Producing Culture for the Digital Economy," *Social Text* 18, no. 2 (2000): 37.

14. Walter Benjamin, "The Work of Art in the Age of Mechanical Reproduction," in *Illuminations* (New York: Schocken, 1969), 217–51.

15. Michael Burawoy, *Manufacturing Consent: Changes in the Labor Process under Monopoly Capitalism* (Chicago: University of Chicago Press, 1979); Edward Herman and Noam Chomsky, *Manufacturing Consent: The Political Economy of Mass Media* (New York: Pantheon, 1988).

16. Richard Florida, *The Rise of the Creative Class* (New York: Basic, 2002).

17. Ibid.

18. See Phone Story demo video at http://ow.ly/O0uAf (accessed June 8, 2015).

19. Free the Slaves, "Pioneering New Frontiers"; Edwards, "Apple's iPhone Suppliers."

20. Mintz, *Sweetness and Power*, 121–23, 201–2.

21. Anthony Smith, *Geopolitics of Information* (Oxford: Oxford University Press, 1980).

22. Vijay Prashad, The Poorer Nations: A Possible History of the Global South (London: Verso, 2012), 10–11; see also Yuezhi Zhao, "The BRICS Formation in Reshaping Global Communication: Possibilities and Challenges," in *Mapping BRICS Media*, edited by Kaarle Nordenstreng and Daya Kishan Thussu (London: Routledge, 2015).

23. Dan Schiller, *Digital Depression: Information Technology and Economic Crisis (Urbana: University of Illinois Press, 2014)*; Paula Chakravartty and Yuezhi Zhao, eds.,

*Global Communications: Toward a Transcultural Political Economy* (Lanham, Mass.: Rowman and Littlefield, 2008).

24. Jiyong Hou, "Microsoft Reincarnated?" *Twenty-First-Century Economic Report*, June 20, 2012. In Chinese.

25. Barry Wellman and Lee Rainie, "If Romeo and Juliet Had Mobile Phones," *Mobile Media and Communication* 1, no. 1 (2013): 167.

26. Jack Linchuan Qiu, "The Wireless Leash: Mobile Messaging Service as a Means of Control," *International Journal of Communication* 1, no. 1 (2007): 74–91.

27. Judy Wajcman, *Pressed for Time: The Acceleration of Life in Digital Capitalism* (Chicago: University of Chicago Press, 2014).

28. Dallas Smythe, "On the Audience Commodity and Its Work," in *Dependency Road: Communications, Capitalism, Consciousness, and Canada* (Norwood, N.J.: Ablex, 1981), 22–51. See also Christian Fuchs, "Dallas Smythe Today: The Audience Commodity, the Digital Labor Debate, Marxist Political Economy and Critical Theory," *TripleC: Communication, Capitalism, Critique* 10, no. 2 (2012): 692–740.

29. David Harvey, *A Brief History of Neoliberalism* (Oxford: Oxford University Press, 2005), 13.

30. Antonio Negri, *Red Notes: Working-Class Autonomy and the Crisis: Italian Marxist Texts of the Theory and Practice of a Class Movement: 1964–79* (London: CSE, 1979), 34. See also Raewyn Connell, *Confronting Equality: Gender, Knowledge and Global Change* (Cambridge: Polity), loc 2288.

31. Michael Hardt and Antonio Negri, *Empire* (Cambridge, Mass.: Harvard University Press, 2001); Michael Hardt and Antonio Negri, *Multitude* (New York: Penguin, 2005).

32. Patterson, *Slavery and Social Death*.

33. Ibid., chapter 11.

34. Maurizio Lazzarato, "Immaterial Labor," in *Radical Thought in Italy*, edited by Paolo Virno and Michael Hardt (Minneapolis: University of Minnesota Press, 1996), 133.

35. Ibid., 136.

36. Lessard and Baldwin, *Net Slaves*.

37. Beech and Jiang, "The Cult of Apple in China," 30.

38. Jay J. Wang, "Consumer Nationalism and Corporate Reputation Management in the Global Era," *Corporate Communication* 10, no. 3 (2005): 223–39.

39. Leopoldina Fortunati, "Immaterial Labor and Its Machinization," *Ephemera: Theory and Politics in Organization* 7, no.1 (2007): 145, available at http://ow.ly/O0yrb (accessed June 3, 2015).

40. Ibid., 153.

41. Ibid., 154.

42. Jack Linchuan Qiu, Melissa Gregg, and Kate Crawford, "Circuits of Labor," *TripleC: Communication, Capitalism, Critique* 12, no. 2 (2014): 564–81.

43. Leopoldina Fortunati, "Real People, Artificial Bodies," in *Mediating the Human Body: Technology, Communication and Fashion*, edited by Leopoldina Fortunati, James E. Katz and Raimonda Riccini (Mahwah, N.J.: Erlbaum, 2003), 61–73.

44. Fortunati, "Immaterial Labor and Its Machinization," 154.

45. "Cooks: China Accounts for More than 20% of Apple's Global Sales," Finance Net, May 18, 2015, available at http://ow.ly/O0AeH (accessed June 8, 2015).

46. Beech and Jiang, "Cult of Apple in China."

47. Andrew Trotman, "Apple Sells More iPhones in China than US for First Time," *The Telegraph*, April 27, 2015, available at http://ow.ly/O0AQN (accessed June 8, 2015).

48. Beech and Jiang, "Cult of Apple in China."

49. Trebor Scholz, ed., *Digital Labor: The Internet as Playground and Factory* (New York: Routledge, 2012).

50. Julian Kücklich, "Precarious Playbour: Modders and the Digital Games Industry" *Fibreculture Journal* 5 (2005), available at http://ow.ly/O0CbV (accessed June 8, 2015).

51. La Boétie, *Politics of Obedience*, 63.

52. Elizabeth Abbott, *Sugar: A Bittersweet History* (New York: Overlook, 2010), loc 383.

53. Mintz, *Sweetness and Power*.

54. David Eltis, "Precolonial Western Africa and the Atlantic Economy," in *Slavery and the Rise of the Atlantic System*, edited by Barbara Solow (Cambridge: Cambridge University Press, 1991), 97–119.

55. Leif Svalesen, *The Slave Ship Fredensborg*, translated by Pat Shaw and Selena Winsnes (Bloomington: Indiana University Press, 2000), 168.

56. Rediker, *Slave Ship*, loc 5991.

57. Bales, "Slavery in Its Contemporary Manifestations," 289.

58. Andrew Ross, "In Search of the Lost Paycheck," in *Digital Labor: The Internet as Playground and Factory*, edited by Trebor Scholz (New York: Routledge, 2013), 16.

59. Nancy Holmstrom, "Exploitation," in *Exploitation: Key Concepts in Critical Theory*, edited by Kai Nielsen and Robert Ware (Amherst, N.Y.: Prometheus, 1997), 79.

60. Fuchs, *Digital Labor and Karl Marx*, 263.

61. Ibid.

62. Ethan Zuckerman, "The Internet's Original Sin." *The Atlantic*, August 14, 2014, available at http://ow.ly/O0EeA (accessed June 8, 2015).

63. Mark Andrejevic, "Exploitation in the Data Mine," in *Internet and Surveillance: The Challenge of Web 2.0 and Social Media*, edited by Christian Fuchs, Kees Boersma, Anders Albrechtslund and Marisol Sandoval (London: Routledge, 2012), 71–88.

64. Ibid., 74.

65. Ibid., 82.

66. Ian Ayres, *Super Crunchers: How Anything Can Be Predicted* (London: Murray, 2007), 33, 44.

67. Blackburn, *Making of New World Slavery*, 581.

68. Jason Mander, "Daily Time Spent on Social Networks Rises to 1.72 Hours," Global Web Index, January 26, 2015, available at http://ow.ly/NU8TZ (accessed June 5, 2015).

69. See http://newsroom.fb.com/company-info (accessed February 19, 2016).

70. Dallas Smythe, "Communications: Blindspot of Western Marxism," *Canadian Journal of Political and Social Theory* 1, no. 3 (1977): 1–27; Dallas Smythe, "Critique of the Consciousness Industry," *Journal of Communication* 27, no. 1 (1977): 198–202.

71. Sut Jhally and Bill Livant, "Watching as Working: The Valorization of Audience Consciousness," *Journal of Communication* 36, no. 3 (1986): 124–43.

72. Andrejevic, "Exploitation in the Data Mine."

73. Wajcman, *Pressed for Time*.

74. Ibid., 183.

75. Ibid., 173. See also Ben Agger, "iTime: Labor and Life in a Smartphone Era," *Time and Society* 20, no. 1 (2011): 124.

76. Wajcman, *Pressed for Time*, 5.

77. Ibid., 1–2.

78. Ibid., 2–3.

79. See http://ow.ly/O17Ez (accessed June 8, 2015).

80. Wajcman, *Pressed for Time*, 171.

81. Ibid., 169.

82. Ibid., 164.

83. Ibid., 11.

84. Douglas Rushkoff, *Program or Be Programmed* (New York: OR Books, 2010).

85. Jelle van Wijhe, "Tech5: Fairphone Named Europe's Fastest-Growing Startup of 2015," April 25, 2015, available at http://ow.ly/O18Mj (accessed June 8, 2015).

86. Sidney Mintz, "The Power of Sweetness and the Sweetness of Power," 8th Duijker Lecture (Deventer, Neth.: Van Loghum Slaterus, 1988), 14.

87. David Harvey, *Seventeen Contradictions and the End of Capitalism* (Oxford: Oxford University Press, 2015), 95.

88. Burawoy, *Manufacturing Consent*; Herman and Chomsky, *Manufacturing Consent*.

89. Jacob Silverman, *Terms of Service: Social Media and the Price of Constant Connection* (New York: HarperCollins, 2015), ix.

90. Vincent Mosco, *To the Cloud: Big Data in a Turbulent World* (New York: Routledge, 2014).

91. Wajcman, *Pressed for Time*, 178

92. David Hesmondhalgh, "User-Generated Content, Free Labor and the Cultural Industries," *Ephemera* 10 (2010): 267–84. Here, Hesmondhalgh contends that Terranova failed to appreciate the autonomy free labor enjoy, even though they are unpaid.

## Chapter 5. Molding and Resisting Appconn

1. Samir Amin, "Beyond Liberal Globalization: A Better or Worse World?" *Monthly Review*, December 1, 2006, available at http://ow.ly/OjyKq (accessed June 15, 2015).

2. Immanuel Wallerstein, *Geopolitics and Geoculture: Essays on the Changing World System* (Cambridge: Cambridge University Press, 1991), 166.

3. Lisa Nakamura, "Don't Hate the Player, Hate the Game," in Scholtz, *Digital Labor*, 187–204.

4. William Phillips, "The Old World Background of Slavery in the Americas," in Solow, *Slavery and the Rise of the Atlantic System*, 43–61. Note in particular that before the European colonization of the New World, sugar plantations in the Canary and Madeiras Islands used a combination of free labor and slaves, including black Africans as well as slaves from other places (pp. 49–51).

5. Eugene Genovese, *Roll, Jordan, Roll: The World the Slaves Made* (New York, Vintage, 1976).

6. Jack Linchuan Qiu, "China and the Internet: Technologies of Freedom in a Statist Information Society," in *The Network Society: A Global Perspective*, edited by Manuel Castells (London: Elgar, 2004), 99–124.

7. International Labor Organization, "Wages in Asia and the Pacific: Dynamic but Uneven Progress" (December 2014), available at http://ow.ly/O9MMI (accessed on June 10, 2015). China's average monthly wages have gone through double-digit growth every year since 2010 to reach $613 in 2013, significantly higher than Thailand ($391), India ($215), Vietnam ($197), Indonesia ($183), Cambodia ($121), Pakistan ($119), and Nepal ($73).

8. Lüthje, "Rise and Fall of 'Wintelism'"; Lüthje, *From Silicon Valley to Shenzhen*.

9. Schiller, "Poles of Market Growth."

10. Philip Stephens, "Now China Starts to Make the Rules," *Financial Times*, May 29, 2015, 7. See also Jane Cai and Laura Zhou, "China-Led AIIB Reflects Mainland's Rising Power," *South China Morning Post*, March 25, 2015.

11. Yuezhi Zhao, *Communication in China: Political Economy, Power, and Conflict* (Lanham, MD: Rowman and Littlefield, 2008); Yuezhi Zhao, "China's Pursuits of Indigenous Innovation in Information Technology Developments: Hopes, Follies and Uncertainties," *Chinese Journal of Communication* 3, no. 3 (September 2010): 266–89; Yu Hong, *Labor, Class Formation, and China's Informationized Policy of Economic Development* (Lanham, Md.: Lexington, 2011); Yu Hong, *Networking the Nation: Communication and Economic Restructuring in China* (Champaign, IL: University of Illinois Press, forthcoming).

12. Mike Bird, "China Just Overtook the US as the World's Largest Economy," *Business Insider*, October 8, 2014, available at http://ow.ly/O9UCd (accessed June 11, 2015).

13. Howard French, *China's Second Continent: How a Million Migrants Are Building a New Empire in Africa* (New York: Knopf, 2014).

14. "Japan Outspends China on African Projects," *South China Morning Post*, March 25, 2015.

15. Yuezhi Zhao, "The BRICS Formation in Reshaping Global Communication: Possibilities and Challenges," in *Mapping BRICS Media*, edited by Kaarle Nordenstreng and Daya Kishan Thussu (London: Routledge, 2015), loc 2012.

16. Ibid., loc 2323.

17. Miguel Korzeniewicz, "Commodity Chains and Marketing Strategies, Nike and the Global Athletic Footwear Industry," in *Commodity Chains and Global Capitalism*, edited by Gary Gereffi and Miguel Korzeniewics (Santa Barbara, Calif.: Greenwood, 1994), 247–66,

18. Desmond Bell and David McNeill, "Multimedia and the Crisis Economy in Japan," *Media Culture and Society* 21, no. 6 (1999): 759–85.

19. Folker Frobel, Jurgen Heinrichs, and Otto Kreye, *The New International Division of Labor: Structural Unemployment in Industrialized Countries and Industrialization in Developing Countries* (Cambridge: Cambridge University Press, 1981), 15.

20. See also Jenny Chan, Ngai Pun, and Mark Selden, "The Politics of Global Production, Apple, Foxconn and China's New Working Class," *Technology, Work and Employment* 28, no. 2 (2013): 100–115.

21. Robin Blackburn, *The Making of New World Slavery* (London: Verso, 1997), 3.

22. Dianwen Zhang, *Tiger and Fox*, 254–57.

23. "Shenzhen Seeks Big Development to Preempt Crises, Hong Kong Has to Act in Response," *Hong Kong Commercial Daily*, June 11, 2001. In Chinese.

24. Pun et al., *Suicide Express*, 5.

25. Vaclav Smil, *Made in the USA: The Rise and Retreat of American Manufacturing* (Cambridge, Mass.: MIT Press, 2013), 22. Measured in 2010 dollars, China's manufacturing sector was worth $1.923 trillion, whereas for the United States it was $1.856 trillion, although measured by 2005 dollars the United States was still ahead.

26. Mou Hu, "Vice Mayor Investigates Series of Nine Suicides at Foxconn," *People's Daily*, May 21, 2010, available at http://ow.ly/Oa4VA (accessed June 11, 2015). In Chinese.

27. Xinhua Net, "Shenzhen Government Reports on Reasons of Suicides and Preventive Measures," May 26, 2010, available at http://ow.ly/Oa575 (accessed June 11, 2015). In Chinese.

28. Cong Li, "ACFTU Officials: Worker Rights Have Not Improved at Foxconn," *China Entrepreneurs*, November 4, 2010, available at http://ow.ly/Oa5Ce (accessed June 11, 2015). In Chinese.

29. "Terry Guo: Preliminary Conclusion Indicates No Connection between Employee Suicides and Management," China News Network, May 26, 2010, available at http://ow.ly/Oa5RW (accessed June 11, 2015). In Chinese.

30. Kecheng Li, "Terry Guo Claims Foxconn Passing Investigation and Planning to Hand Dormitories to Government Supervision," *Eastern Morning Post*, June 9, 2010, available at http://ow.ly/Oa6wd (accessed June 11, 2015). In Chinese.

31. Yuezhi Zhao, *Communication in China*, 313.

32. Jinghua Daily, "Foxconn Responded to ACFTU's Accusation, Calling It Hasty," February 4, 2015, available at http://ow.ly/Oa7yU (accessed June 11, 2015). In Chinese.

33. Pun, Chan, and Selden, *Life and Death behind Apple*.

34. Smil, *Made in the USA*, 176.

35. Xiong Huang, "Wage Deduction Agreed On through Negotiation in Dongguan," *Southern Workers' Daily*, April 27, 2009, 4. In Chinese.

36. Zu, "Firing and Hiring."

37. Pun et al., *Suicide Express*, 198.

38. Harvey, *Seventeen Contradictions*, 95.

39. Netease Technology Report, "Foxconn Shenzhen Longhua Campus: Inside the Forbidden City of Terry Guo," September 30, 2009, available: http://ow.ly/OhAYZ (accessed June 12, 2015). In Chinese.

40. Luo Wensheng, "Chengdu and Chongqing Fighting to Host Foxconn," December 9, 2010, available at http://ow.ly/OhBd1 (accessed June 12, 2015), in Chinese; Li Baoping, "Tale of Two Cities: Chengdu and Chongqing," *Chinese Economy and Informatization*, December 22, 2010, available: http://ow.ly/OhCvq (accessed June 12, 2015), in Chinese.

41. Huaxia Jingwei Net, "New City-Making Movement against the Backdrop of Crises," May 21, 2009, available at http://ow.ly/OhBWc (accessed June 12, 2015). In Chinese.

42. Jing Qin, "Qingkangtang Township Helps with Foxconn Recruitment," September 2, 2013, available at http://ow.ly/OhCsb (accessed June 12, 2015). In Chinese.

43. Philip Elmer-DeWitt, "Inside the Apple iPad Factory," *Fortune*, May 21, 2011, available at http://ow.ly/Ojqwx (accessed June 15, 2015); Jenny Chan, Ngai Pun and Mark Selden, "Apple's iPad City: Subcontracting Exploitation to China," in *Handbook of the International Political Economy of Production*, edited by Kees van der Pijl (Cheltenham, U.K.: Elgar, 2015), 76–97.

44. Dexter Roberts, Henry Meyer, and Dorothee Tschampa, "The Silk Railroad of China-Europe Trade," *Bloomberg*, December 20, 2012, available at http://ow.ly/OhSvm (accessed June 12, 2015); Kathrin Hille, "China's Computer Makers March Inland," *Financial Times*, May 23, 2011, available at http://goo.gl/XsnqEB (accessed June 12, 2015).

45. *Factory Gossip*, 48.

46. Allain, *Legal Understanding of Slavery*, 378.

47. For an extended and more historicized discussion on WGC, especially video content, see Jack Linchuan Qiu, "Locating Worker-Generated Content in the World's Factory," in *The Routledge Companion to Labor and Media*, edited by Richard Maxwell (London: Routledge, 2015), 303–14.

48. C. L. R. James, *Black Jacobins*.

49. Sky Canaves and James Areddy, "Murder Bares Worker Anger over China Industrial Reform," *Wall Street Journal*, July 31, 2009, available at http://ow.ly/OF7hJ (accessed June 23, 2015).

50. Genovese, *Roll, Jordan, Roll*.

51. Patterson, *Slavery and Social Death*, loc 7788.

52. Linebaugh and Rediker, *Many-Headed Hydra*, loc 5666–722.

53. Qiu, *Working-Class Network Society*.

54. Marion Walton, "Pavement Internet: Mobile Media Economies and Ecologies in South Africa," in *The Routledge Companion to Mobile Media*, edited by Gerald Goggin and Larissa Hjorth (London: Routledge, 2014), 450–61.

55. Fang Lan, "Wave of Strikes in Dalian Involved 73 Enterprises since May," *Caing.com* September 19, 2010, available at http://ow.ly/OF87t (accessed June 23, 2015). In Chinese.

56. David Barboza and Keith Bradsher, "In China, Labor Movement Enabled by Technology," *New York Times*, June 16, 2010.

57. Fengchang Wang, "Wuhan Foxconn Employees Threatened to Jump from Building on Wednesday," Reuters Chinese service, April 28, 2012, available at http://ow.ly/OjVVH (accessed June 15, 2015).

58. Stuart Hall, "The Problem of Ideology: Marxism without Guarantees," in *Critical Dialogues in Culture Studies* edited by David Morley and Chen Kuang-Hsing (London: Routledge, 1996), 28–44.

59. Howard Becker, *Tricks of the Trade* (Chicago: University of Chicago Press, 1998), 234–40.

60. Wanning Sun, "Amateur Photography as Self-Ethnography: China's Rural Migrant Workers and the Question of Digital-Political Literacy," *Media International Australia*, no. 145 (2012), 135–44.

61. Jodi Dean, "Communicative Capitalism: Circulation and the Foreclosure of Politics," *Cultural Politics* 1, no. 1 (2005): 51–74; Jodi Dean, *Blog Theory: Feedback and Capture in the Circuits of Drive* (Cambridge: Polity, 2010).

62. Wehua Liao, "The Debacle to Shut Down Tongxin Experimental School," *Law Network (fazhi wang)*, October 25, 2012, available at http://ow.ly/On5Mz (accessed June 16, 2015). In Chinese. In July 2012 local authorities tried to shut the school down. Teachers, parents, and a local NGO, Beijing Workers' Home, started to use Weibo to call for support, which was relayed widely by NGOs, workers, activists, and concerned citizens nationwide. The local government eventually backed down, and the school remains open. Most vibrant formats of this WGC campaign include Beijing residents carrying water into the school (because the authorities briefly stopped water supply) and sharing pictures of the activity; Chinese netizens from all over the country posting images of themselves holding up a supportive sign; and an MTV program about the school's history, which includes photos of group activities and needy children from migrant-worker families. This campaign mobilized considerable support online and, more important, in its working-class residential community, which came together to defend the school—and they won.

63. Lyn, "Worker's Injury Casts Harsh New Light."

64. This occurred in July 2012 when the labor NGO members were violently removed from their office. The process was captured in a seven-minute video showing hired guards and thugs attacking the NGO staff, throwing the office furniture and stationery into the street. The video (see http://ow.ly/On90r accessed June 16, 2015) caused an uproar in Chinese cyberspace, when netizens also shared images of themselves upholding signs condemning violence using a popular format of pictorial WGC. Although the video met its goal of exposing to the world what happened, it was unsuccessful in preventing the eviction or reversing the decision of local authorities.

65. Gary King, Jennifer Pan, and Margaret Roberts, "How Censorship in China Allows Government Criticism but Silences Collective Expression," *American Political Science Review* 107, no. 2 (2013): 326–43.

66. "Pneumoconiosis Activist Zhang Haichao Gets Life-Saving Double-Lung Transplant," China Labor Bulletin, July 15, 2013, available at http://ow.ly/OnggG (accessed June 16, 2015).

67. "Workers Fight to Save Their Union Activists: The Case of Ole Wolff (Yantai) Electronics Ltd," China Labour News Translations, October 2008, available at http://ow.ly/OFa3U (accessed June 23, 2015).

68. Tanja Dreher, "Speaking Up or Being Heard? Community Media Interventions and the Politics of Listening," *Media, Culture and Society* 32, no. 1 (2010): 85–103.

69. This section includes excerpts and revised text from Jack Linchuan Qiu, "Social Media on the Picket Line," *Media, Culture and Society* (forthcoming 2016).

70. Teresa Cheng, "48,000 Chinese Strikers Say, Adidas, Nike, Timberland: You Fix It!" *LaborNotes*, April 23, 2014, available at http://ow.ly/Oq4cU (accessed June 17, 2015).

71. Dan Levin, "Plying Social Media, Chinese Workers Grow Bolder in Exerting Clout," *New York Times,* May 2, 2014, available at http://ow.ly/Oq5cw (accessed June 17, 2015).

72. Linebaugh and Rediker, *Many-Headed Hydra,* 8–15.

73. Rediker, *Slave Ship,* loc 4443.

74. Ibid., loc 194.

75. Linebaugh and Rediker, *Many-Headed Hydra*, 328.

76. Leeson, *Invisible Hook.*

77. Immanuel Wallerstein, "Globalization or the Age of Transition?" *International Sociology* 15, no. 2 (2000): 258–63.

78. Jenny Pickerill, *Cyberprotest: Environmental Activism Online* (Manchester: Manchester University Press, 2010); Paolo Gerbaudo, *Tweets and the Streets: Social Media and Contemporary Activism* (London: Pluto, 2012); Manuel Castells, *Networks of Outrage and Hope: Social Movement in the Internet Age* (Malden, Mass.: Polity, 2013).

79. Raymond Williams, *Marxism and Literature* (Oxford: Oxford University Press, 1977), 121–27.

80. David Harvey, *A Brief History of Neo-Liberalism* (Oxford: Oxford University Press, 2005), 120.

81. Williams, *Marxism and Literature*, 122–23.

82. Personal interview, March 16, 2013.

83. Antonio Gramesci, *Selections from the Prison Notebooks* (New York: International, 1971), 357.

84. Williams, *Marxism and Literature*, 123.

85. Ibid., 124.

86. Qiu, *Working-Class Network Society.*

87. China Network Information Center (CNNIC), The 37th *Statistical Report on Internet Development in China*, January 2016, available at http://ow.ly/ZKuy2 (accessed February 16, 2016). In Chinese.

88. Ibid.

89. Wang Youling, "National Bureau of Statistics: Last Year Average Wages among Employees Nationwide Was 49969 Yuan," *XinhuaNet*, May 28, 2015, available at http://ow.ly/OozRv (accessed June 16, 2015). In Chinese.

90. CNNIC, 37th *Statistical Report*, 2016.

91. Xin Ying, "Collective Contentious Action in China," *Twenty-First Century* [*Ershiyi shiji*], no. 134 (December 2012): 17–25. In Chinese.

92. Howard French, "Workers Demand Union and Wal-Mart Supplier in China," *New York Times* (December 16, 2004).

93. Baohua Zhou, "Media Consumption, Public Participation and Political Efficacy in Public Crisis: Empirical Study of the Xiamen PX Incident," *Open Times (Kaifang Shidai)*, no. 5 (2011): 123–40. In Chinese.

94. Qiu, *Working-Class Network Society*, 21–50, 97–101.

95. Jack Linchuan Qiu, "Mobile Civil Society in Asia: A Comparative Study of People Power II and the Nosamo Movement," *Javnost: The Public* 15, no. 5 (2008): 56.

96. Jianhua Wang, "Internet Mobilization and Collective Contention among Workers in Sub-Contract Factories," *Open Times (Kaifang shidai)*, no. 11 (2011): 113–28. In Chinese.

97. Fiona Tam, "Guangdong Shuts Down at Least Seven Labor NGOs," *South China Morning Post*, July 27, 2012, available at http://ow.ly/Oqu12 (accessed June 17, 2015).

98. Lingling Liu and Qian Peng, "No Happiness at Changsha Pepsi Cola," *Sanxiang Metropolitan Daily*, November 16, 2011, available at http://ow.ly/OFcEg (accessed June 23, 2015). In Chinese.

99. King, Pan, and Roberts, "How Censorship in China Allows," 327.

100. Wanning Sun, "Desperately Seeking My Wages: Justice, Media Logic, and the Politics of Voice in Urban China," *Media, Culture & Society* 34, no. 7 (2012): 864–79.

101. Anne Alexander and Mostafa Bassiouny, *Bread, Freedom, Social Justice* (London: Zed, 2014).

102. Yuqiong Zhou and Patricia Moy, "Parsing Framing Processes: The Interplay between Online Public Opinion and Media Coverage," *Journal of Communication* 57, no. 1 (2007): 79–98.

103. Shiqiu, "Brief Summary of Internet Activities by Chinese Workers in 2009," Maoist Hammer Forum, January 19, 2010, available at http://ow.ly/Oqz5u (accessed June 17, 2015). In Chinese.

104. William Law Mathieson, *British Slavery and Its Abolition, 1823–1838* (London: Longmans, Green, 1926); Arthur Zilversmit, *The First Emancipation: The Abolition of Slavery in the North* (Chicago: University of Chicago Press, 1967); David Eltis and James Walvin, *The Abolition of the Atlantic Slave Trade: Origins and Effects in Europe, Africa, and the Americas* (Madison: University of Wisconsin Press, 1981); Drescher, *Abolition: A History of Slavery and Antislavery*.

105. Herbert Aptheker, *American Negro Slave Revolts*; Eugene Genovese, *Roll, Jordan, Roll*; Henry Reynolds, *The Other Side of the Frontier* (Kensington: University of New South Wales Press, 1981); Linebaugh and Rediker, *Many-Headed Hydra*.

106. George van Cleve, "Somerset's Case and Its Antecedents in Imperial Perspective," *Law and History Review* 24, no. 03 (2006): 601–46.

107. Linebaugh and Rediker, *Many-Headed Hydra*.

108. John C. Calhoun, "Slavery a Positive Good," February 6, 1837, available at http://ow.ly/OyKwA (accessed on June 19, 2015); Hermann von Holst, *John C. Calhoun* (Honolulu: University Press of the Pacific, 2001, reprint from the 1883 edition).

109. Rediker, *Slave Ship*, loc 5153.

110. Gail K. Smith, "The Sentimental Novel: The Example of Harriet Beecher Stowe," in *The Cambridge Companion to Nineteenth-Century American Women's Writing*, edited by Dale Bauer and Philip Gould (Cambridge: Cambridge University Press, 2001), 221.

111. Rediker, *Slave Ship*, loc 5295.

112. Ibid., loc 5315.

113. British Museum, "Anti-slavery Medallion, by Josiah Wedgwood," available at http://ow.ly/OvOTu (accessed June 19, 2015).

114. Thomas Clarkson, *The History of the Rise, Progress, and Accomplishment of the Abolition of the African Slave-Trade by the British Parliament* (London: Parker, 1839), 417.

115. Linebaugh and Rediker, *Many-Headed Hydra*, 334.

116. Yuezhi Zhao and Rob Duffy. "Short-Circuited? The Communication of Labor Struggles in China," in *Knowledge Workers in the Information Society*, edited by Catherine McKercher and Vincent Mosco (Lanham, Md.: Lexington, 2007), 229–47.

117. Nick Dyer-Witheford, *Cyber-Marx: Cycles and Circuits of Struggle in High-Technology Capitalism* (Champaign: University of Illinois Press, 1999).

118. Jack Linchuan Qiu, Melissa Gregg, and Kate Crawford, "Circuits of Labor: A Labor Theory of the iPhone Era," *TripleC: Communication, Capitalism, Critique* 12, no. 2 (2014): 486–563.

119. Ibid., 577.

120. Antonio Negri, *Social Factory* (New York: Autonomedia, 1983).

121. Netease Tech Channel, "MTHK Joint Universities Investigation Report on Foxconn"; Caixin Net, "Universities Investigation Report Shows Foxconn Abusing Student Workers"; Sina Technology, "Foxconn: Have You Changed?"; iLabour, "Investigation Report on Labor Union in Foxconn"; iLabour, "2015 Investigation Report on Salary, Work Hours, and Current Management of Foxconn."

122. See http://sacom.hk/about-us/ (accessed June 19, 2015).

123. Friends of Nature, IPE, Green Beagle, *The Other Side of Apple*, January 20, 2011, available at http://ow.ly/Ow3Mf (accessed June 19, 2015).

124. Lawrence B. Glickman, *Buying Power: A History of Consumer Activism in America* (Chicago: University of Chicago Press, 2009), loc 6159.

125. See http://www.urbandictionary.com/define.php?term=iSlave (accessed December 16, 2015).

126. Tim Newman, "iSlaves," May 4, 2009, available at http://ow.ly/OwdbO (accessed June 19, 2015).

127. Christina Bonnington, "Protestors Crash Apple Stores, Demand Apple 'Manufacture Different,'" *Wired*, February 9, 2012, available at http://ow.ly/OFflM (accessed June 19, 2015).

128. Sarah Dean, "iSlave! Former Apple Managers Dish the Dirt Claiming Employees Are Expected to Be on Call 24 Hours a Day," *Mail Online*, October 2, 2014, available at http://ow.ly/OwhX3 (accessed on June 19, 2015).

129. Jennifer Ngo and Chris Lau, "Queues, Anger, Cash-Ins . . . It's Another iPhone Launch," *South China Morning Post*, September 20, 2014.

130. Wang, "Consumer Nationalism."

131. "Dreamwork China: The Workers of Foxconn," MOBS, February 2012, available at http://ow.ly/Owrwm (accessed June 19, 2015).

132. Glickman, *Buying Power*, loc 1497.

133. Ibid., loc 1463, 1559.

134. Nathan Eddy, "Fairphone 2: A Repairable, Recyclable Android Smartphone," *InformationWeek*, June 17, 2015, available at http://ow.ly/Oxrnr (accessed June 19, 2015).

135. van Wijhe, "Tech5."

136. Christopher Schuetze, "Building 'Conflict-Free' Smartphones," *New York Times*, June 2, 2014, available at http://ow.ly/Oxoso (accessed June 19, 2015).

137. Bas van Abel, "Generation Y Challenges!—Max Havelaar Lecture," October 29, 2014, Erasmus University Rotterdam.

138. Sarah Mishkin, "The Last Word: Designers Hear the Call For Making a Fair-Trade Smartphone," *Financial Times*, May 10, 2013.

139. Shaun Pett, "Turning a Protest into a Product," *Globe and Mail*, February 15, 2014.

140. Schuetze, "Building 'Conflict-Free' Smartphones."

141. Free the Slaves, "Pioneering New Frontiers."

142. Monbiot, "My Search for a Smartphone."

143. Sean Ansett, "Made with Care: Social Assessment Report," Fairphone.com, December 10, 2013, available at http://ow.ly/OyYRY (accessed June 19, 2015).

144. Pett, "Turning a Protest into a Product."

145. Kenneth Kraemer, Greg Linden, and Jason Dedrick, "Capturing Value in Global Networks: Apple's iPad and iPhone," July 2011, available at http://ow.ly/Oxnes (accessed June 19, 2015).

146. Schuetze, "Building 'Conflict-Free' Smartphones."

147. Mishkin, "Last Word."

148. Wajcman, *Pressed for Time*, 171.

149. Nathan Eddy, "Fairphone 2: A Repairable, Recyclable Android Smartphone," *InformationWeek*, June 17, 2015, available: at http://ow.ly/Oxrnr (accessed June 19, 2015).

150. Merve Guvendik, "Examining the Fairphone's Environmental Impact," Fairphone, January 22, 2015, available at http://ow.ly/Oz03n (accessed June 19, 2015).

151. Pett, "Turning a Protest into a Product."

152. Schuetze, "Building 'Conflict-Free' Smartphones."

153. Lessard and Baldwin, *Net Slaves*.

154. Robert Gehl, *Reverse Engineering Social Media: Software, Culture, and Political Economy in New Media Capitalism* (Philadelphia: Temple University Press, 2014).

155. Kathryn Ingle, *Reverse Engineering* (New York: McGraw-Hill, 1994), 9.

156. Ibid., 164.

157. This app can be downloaded to all Android devices even if it's not a Fairphone. Go to http://ow.ly/OzwOc or search "Peace of Mind+" in Google Play.

158. Stuart Dredge, "Apple Bans Satirical iPhone Game Phone Story from Its App Store," *The Guardian*, September 14, 2011, available at http://ow.ly/OA9M2 (accessed June 20, 2015).

159. See http://www.phonestory.org/banned.html for Molleindustria's statement on the App Store ban.

160. Mark Brown, "Sweatshop HD Is the Latest Victim in Apple's War on Serious Games," *Pocket Gamer*, March 21, 2013, available at http://ow.ly/OAbts (accessed June 20, 2015).

161. Phone Story, "Phone Story Revenues Donated to Former Foxconn Worker Who Attempted Suicide," February 2012, available at http://www.phonestory.org/donation.html (accessed June 20, 2015).

162. Ibid.

163. See https://vimeo.com/17558439.

164. Zhang, "Foxconn Suicide Survivor Tian Yu."

165. Maria Martinez-Torres, "Civil Society, the Internet, and the Zapatistas," *Peace Review* 13, no. 3 (2001): 347–55.

166. Isherwood, "Speaking Less than Truth to Power."

## Chapter 6. A Temporary Closure

1. Michael Forsythe and Alan Wong, "Hong Kong Lawmakers Reject Beijing Election Plan," *New York Times*, June 19, 2015.

2. Sarah Pulliam Bailey, "The Charleston Shooting Is the Largest Mass Shooting in a House of Worship Since 1991," *Washington Post*, June 18, 2015, available at http://ow.ly/OIkVK (accessed June 24, 2015).

3. Frances Robles, Jason Horowitz, and Shaila Dewan, "Flying the Flags of White Power," *New York Times*, June 19, 2015.

4. Frances Robles, Richard Fausset, and Michael Barraro, "Governor Joins the Call to Take Down Rebel Flag," *New York Times*, June 23, 2015.

5. Robert Oppenheimer, "When You See Something That Is Technically Sweet," in *In the Matter of J. Robert Oppenheimer: The Security Clearance Hearing*, edited by Richard Polenberg (Ithaca, N.Y.: Cornell University Press, 2002), 41.

6. Mintz, *Sweetness and Power.,,*

7. David Brion Davis, *The Problem of Slavery in the Age of Revolution 1770–1823* (Oxford: Oxford University Press, 1999), 564.

8. Wacjman, *Pressed for Time*, 178.

9. Rediker, *Slave Ship*, loc 285.

10. Immanuel Wallerstein, *Geopolitics and Geoculture: Essays on the Changing World System* (Cambridge: Cambridge University Press, 1991), 15.

11. Ortiz, *Cuban Counterpoint*, 267.

12. Blackburn, *Making of New World Slavery*, 582.

13. Stinchcombe, *Sugar Island Slavery*; James, *Black Jacobins*.

14. Greg Gradin, *The Empire of Necessity: Slavery, Freedom, and Deception in the New World* (New York: Metropolitan, 2014).

15. Schiller, *Digital Depression*.

16. Jane Perlez, "China and 56 Partners, but Not U.S., Inaugurate New Asian Bank," *New York Times*, June 30, 2015.

17. Zhao, "Communication, Crisis, and Global Power Shifts."

18. Kücklich, "Precarious Playbour."

19. Gorsuch, "To Indent Oneself," 150.

20. Davis, *Slavery and Human Progress*; Gradin, *Empire of Necessity*.

21. Williams, *Marxism and Literature*, 123.

22. Oskar Negt and Alexander Kluge, *Public Sphere and Experience: Toward an Analysis of the Bourgeois and Proletarian Public Sphere* (Minneapolis: University of Minnesota Press, 1993).

23. Linebaugh and Rediker, *Many-Headed Hydra*, loc 5718.

24. Manuel Castells, *The Rise of the Network Society* (Malden, Mass.: Blackwell, 1996).

# Index

JACK LINCHUAN QIU is a professor at the School of Journalism and Communication at the Chinese University of Hong Kong. He is the author of *Working-Class Network Society: Communication Technology and the Information Have-Less in Urban China.*

## THE GEOPOLITICS OF INFORMATION

The University of Illinois Press
is a founding member of the
Association of American University Presses.

---

Composed in 9.75/13 Chaparral Pro
with Avenir LT Std display
by Kirsten Dennison
at the University of Illinois Press
Cover design by Faceout Studio, Derek Thornton
Manufactured by Sheridan Books, Inc.

University of Illinois Press
1325 South Oak Street
Champaign, IL 61820-6903
www.press.uillinois.edu